Computers and the History of Art

Edited by

Anthony Hamber, Jean Miles and William Vaughan

MANSELL

LONDON AND NEW YORK

First published 1989 by
Mansell Publishing Limited, *A Cassell Imprint*
Artillery House, Artillery Row, London SW1P 1RT, England
125 East 23rd Street, Suite 300, New York 10010, U.S.A.

British Library Cataloguing in Publication Data

Computers and the history of art.
1. Visual arts. Historiology. Applications of computer systems
I. Vaughan, William, *1943-* II. Hamber, Anthony
III. Miles, Jean
702'.8'5

ISBN 0-7201-1980-4

Library of Congress Cataloging-in-Publication Data

Computers and the history of art / edited by Anthony Hamber, Jean Miles and Vaughan William.
p. cm.
Includes index.
ISBN 0-7201-1980-4 : $58.00
1. Art—Historiography—Data processing. 2. Cataloging of art—Data processing. I. Hamber, Anthony. II. Miles, Jean. III. William Vaughan.
N380.C66 1989
702'.85—dc20 89-35093
CIP

Printed and bound in Great Britain by
Biddles Ltd, Guildford and King's Lynn

Contents

Foreword

The decision to hold the third CHArt conference in November 1987 at the Victoria & Albert Museum, London, was, on the face of it, a brave and somewhat incongruous gesture. The largest museum of the decorative arts in the world, with over five million objects in its care, has no more advanced technology to assist in collections management or art historical research than a vast number of 5 × 3 inch catalogue cards, ledgers and knowledgeable expert curators! Incongruous maybe, inappropriate never, for over the last three years, the V & A, as the Museum is affectionately known, has been engaged in a period of intensive learning and experimentation.

Starting with the appointment of a computer consultant on a short-term contract, the staff of the Museum began to consider ways in which computer technology could assist in making information easier to access, control and disseminate. Following a period of consultation and analysis, word processing facilities were introduced, using SAMNA software and IBM Personal Computers. The intention was to provide a machine in each of the Museum's departments, to enable staff to familiarize themselves with the potential of the equipment and to gain hands-on experience.

This embryonic stage of development was a novel experience for me when I joined the Museum in May 1985 as Keeper of the National Art Library (a department of the V & A). I came to the Museum from a university where networking around the campus was already common, where the use of fibre optics in communication was well-advanced, where the university library had been computerized since 1972 and where pioneering on-line databases had been created in toxicology and the bio-medical sciences.

However, starting from the lowest possible baseline, an impressive beginning is being made in all areas of the Museum. The Conservation Department are recording the progress of an object through the specific phases of its treatment and building up case history; the Far Eastern Department are developing a system for cataloguing Japanese prints; the Department of Designs, Prints and Drawings have catalogued the vast Searight Collection on Middle Eastern topography acquired in 1984, and provided a computer index to the material in it; while the National Art Library have already input over 3,000 records onto COM format and are finalizing an Operational Requirement for a fully integrated system to go out to tender in 1988–89. The Museum accounts are being transferred to an in-house micro-based system. A great deal has been achieved in a short period and from many points of view it is perhaps an advantage that the Museum has been slow in recognizing the importance of computing to its operation.

While simple familiarization processes have been developing at the V & A, in other museums, galleries and libraries progress is far more advanced and the opportunity to learn from systems developed in similar relevant contexts is an important bonus for the V & A. There are exciting lessons to be learned from such projects as the Aga Khan Program for Islamic Architecture run jointly with MIT and Harvard University; the AVIADOR Project at the Avery Library, Columbia University, which is building on the RLIN (Research Libraries Information Network) system to catalogue architectural drawings and record them on laser disc — already over 13,000 items have been captured. In the library field, important primary tools for art historical research are well-advanced, for example the SCIPIO database for auction house sale catalogues, which deals with both current and retrospective material. Beginning in 1985, using software known as PARIS, the Canadian museums and galleries have been creating a national locations register with exemplary thoroughness and efficiency. Theoretical explanation has not been neglected: the Comité International d'Histoire de l'Art (CIHA) recently published a report by Deidre Stam and François Hautpoul on the factors affecting authority work in art historical systems, concluding that, so far, leadership has been lacking to pursue the concept of the Thesaurus Artis Universalis and that CIHA might well be the right body to encourage and organize the flexible standards necessary to genuine progress.

Other pioneering art historical ventures into computing have been developed in San Francisco. AGEN (Art COM Electronic Network) is a non-profit making organization of artists united in the exploration of experimental art forms. It runs an electronic bulletin board and interactive projects, as well as several off-shoots like NET DRAMA, an on-line telecommunications theatre project conceived by a group of women artists.

It is clear from the range of activities which I have briefly mentioned, that art historical research is burgeoning with a wide variety of experiments and applications to both information access and retrieval and creative innovation. CHArt members are pioneers in the use of computers in art history in the United Kingdom. There is a long way to go to catch up with the scientists, but that is not necessarily a drawback for, in the period of gestation and contemplation which has largely characterized art history and the new technology so far, it has become abundantly clear that format standards and authority files are the key to producing and exchanging compatible data.

Elizabeth A. L. Esteve-Coll
Director
Victoria & Albert Museum, London

Introduction

CHArt — the Computers and Art History Group — was established in October 1985. It came into being because of a need felt by a number of individuals involved in art and its history — academics, museum curators, archivists, visual resources managers and others — for an organization that would promote understanding and discussion of the potential and problems that were opening up for the subject as a result of the impact of computers. There had, of course, been many examples of the application of information technology to the recording and cataloguing of works of art by that time. These had, on the whole, been large scale projects, and their very size suggested that computerization was essentially an institutional matter. Paradoxically, their existence tended to reduce the possibilities as they were perceived by individuals. They seemed to imply that there was no serious place in this field for the single or small-group researcher, and to rule out areas of speculative exploration and discussion. On the other hand it was clear, from the example of innovative small scale projects in related subjects — notably archeology and history — that such a role was possible. Indeed, it seemed to be a highly important one, if the subject was to maintain an active dialogue with the new technology. From the very beginning, therefore, CHArt set out to have the character of a 'user group'. It intended — both through the production of a regular newsletter and the holding of annual conferences — to show that it was perfectly feasible to use modern computer technology to carry out individual research projects, and to emphasize that there was a general need for art historians to become more familiar with the possibilities and problems created by computerization.

This is a period in which computers are radically changing the way people work and live. Rather as in the early days of the automobile, this requires adjustments. The day will eventually come when the computer will cause no more problems to the individual than the car does today. But for the moment it would seem that there is a place for organizations devoted specifically to their use and their capabilities. This means not only general applications but also highly specific ones. The history of art, like every other subject, is facing a whole range of problems, some of which are of a general nature and others which address specific issues within the discipline. Many of these issues have already emerged but there are certainly as least as many to come. Some people may see this development in a negative light as the application of crude mechanical processes to a subject in which subjectivity and perceptiveness play such a central role. But the point surely is that computerization is providing an opportunity for a review of the practices of the discipline. The very need to describe things in terms of logical structures can be exhilarating and will often point to contradictory preconceptions that have previously remained undetected. Only when art historians have become familiar with the kinds of opportunities offered by computerization will it be possible for sensible and informed decisions to be made about where the new technology may be usefully applied.

The papers in this volume give an idea of the issues raised during the short course of CHArt's history. They are mostly taken from the CHArt conferences, of which some have been published in the *Newsletter*. They range from detailed descriptions of actual projects in progress to predictions and debates about possibilities. Some of them are aimed at the beginner. These come, by and large, from the 'Getting Started' section of the CHArt conferences. For it has been felt important to keep the introductory role of CHArt in view while at the same time encouraging advanced development. The topics covered by the papers also reflect the variety of issues. There are papers on aspects that are of importance to all arts subjects, notably word processing and databasing. But there are also papers on areas of special concern to those dealing with works of art, such as pictorial analysis, museums and curatorial problems, and conservation. Consideration is given to techniques employed in other disciplines that deal with the recording and visual analysis of physical objects, such as archeology, geography, medicine and crystallography. It emerges from these analogies that there are special issues relating to imagery within the field of the history of art. There is important work being done now in the use of automated forms of visual analysis. These areas will undoubtedly expand as the techniques of Artificial Intelligence become more sophisticated. An equally crucial area is that of the referencing and storing of works of art. Historians of art have lagged far behind others in turning to new electronic imaging technologies such as the videodisc for the storing and retrieval of images. Amongst these papers are examples of two such projects that are now being used in university teaching programmes. There is also a thorough exploration of the exciting potential to be offered by using high resolution digitization techniques for storing reproductions of pictures. The use of three dimensional images for the reconstruction of sculptures and buildings is also discussed. There are interesting lines of enquiry here which might link up with the work being carried out by artists using computers.

At the moment the use of computers by academic art historians (as opposed to those, for example, working in museums and art galleries) is largely restricted to simple databasing and word processing. This situation is likely to change dramatically over the next few years. There are several reasons for this. First, a new generation of computer literate students will enter higher education, bringing with them more sophisticated demands in this area. Second, the developments in computer hardware and software technologies continue unabated and are now becoming both readily available to and affordable by individual scholars. Third — despite the cutbacks in government spending on higher education and the arts evident both in this country and in many others — there are signs that increased funding is likely to be available for computer applications in the humanities. Some might see this last factor as a mixed blessing. Undoubtedly it is; and those who are likely to be the recipients of such an ambivalent gift would be well advised to equip themselves with a little foreknowledge before it arrives. That way they may be able to profit from its more advantageous parts.

For all these reasons, therefore, it seems that the need for organizations like CHArt will grow rather than diminish in the immediate future. The field is an exciting and expanding one. These papers will, it is hoped, give some idea both of what is being done, and what there is still left to do.

Part I
OVERVIEW

1
Computers in the History of Art

Lutz Heusinger

Computers and the history of art is a topic that is not confined to the use of computers in institutes of art history. We must first examine the use of computers within those areas which have an effect upon the history of art — the military, industry, police, administration and banking — where decisions are made concerning the future of art and the history of art.

Among the few people who are sensible and at the same time have some understanding of computers, such as computer scientist Joseph Weizenbaum of MIT, it has long been an uncontested fact that the breakdown of one military computer can lead any day to the annihilation of whole peoples. The probability of this happening is 100 times greater than the likelihood that computers — used by art historians — can contribute anything substantial to the enrichment of culture.

Less dangerous, but much more pervading than military computers, are computers in industry and in banking, in administration and in executive power. They constitute the force behind the magical power of electronic data processing. A great number of computers are standing around without ever having produced anything but expense and annoyance; the profitability/benefit ratio of art-historical computer projects might be absurd in the extreme, nevertheless, we have allowed ourselves to become converts — in many cases we no longer ask about the usefulness of computers.

Applications of computers in the history of art

1. To collect data.
2. To retrieve data.
3. To examine issues.
4. To reconstruct, simulate and produce objects.
5. To administrate and organize people and objects.
6. To communicate and produce things of beauty.

1. Data collection

This happens essentially in four separate ways; three mechanical and one human.

a. The good old photogrammetry of the 1950s has received a tremendous impetus thanks to improved cameras and subsequent digital photo processing, not only particularly in the military sphere, but also in the field of cultural studies. It makes possible the production of scale drawings to determine the structure, form, size and position of objects, that is, the investigation by mechanical means of the physical data about them.[1]

b. A variant of optical data investigation nowadays makes use of a videocamera and aims at recording fragments of pottery from prehistoric times and antiquity. Here, the computer has the function of storing data and, if circumstances are favourable, of reconstructing the shape of the vessel.[2]

c. A new addition is the convenient possibility of storing two-dimensional objects[3] and photographs as digitalized pictures in a personal computer with the help of a small, inexpensive scanner although this should not be attempted with too many pictures on account of the modest storage capacity of PCs.

With a much more sophisticated machine and a scanner capable of the highest possible resolution available, one can experiment on computing the original colours of missing parts of pictures. Italian and Dutch restorers working together with IBM have tried to make this process the basis of their restoration work.[4]

Less problematic than this procedure is the way the computer is used in the Sistine chapel. Here, the restoration work carried out on the ceiling every day is recorded on the screen in reproductions of Michelangelo's 'giornate' or daily production (Fig. 5).

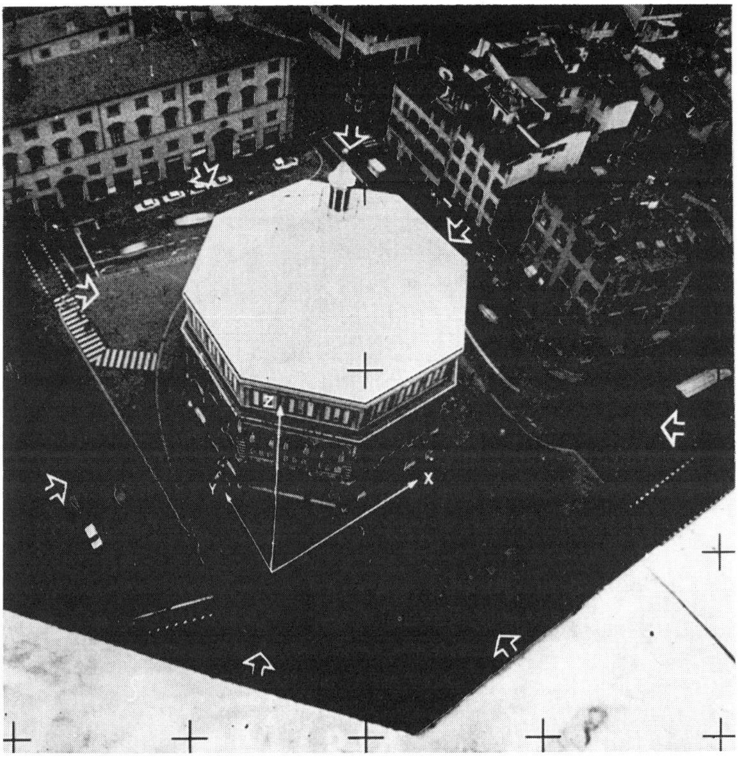

Figure 1. The Baptistry of S. Giovanni, Florence. Arrangement of photograph for co-ordinate adjustment. The camera used was a Rolleiflex SLX with diffraction grating.

d. The human method of collecting data on artists, works of art, patrons, iconoclasts, etc., has remained as it always was: mostly fascinating and stimulating, sometimes wearisome or even enough to drive one to despair. It should in principle not be affected by the medium in which the proceeds of collection are stored. It is sufficient therefore to address our attention to it later in another context.

2. Data retrieval

Like white elephants, the retrieval of data is supposed to exist — and is as rare. There are noteworthy projects in our subject where for years

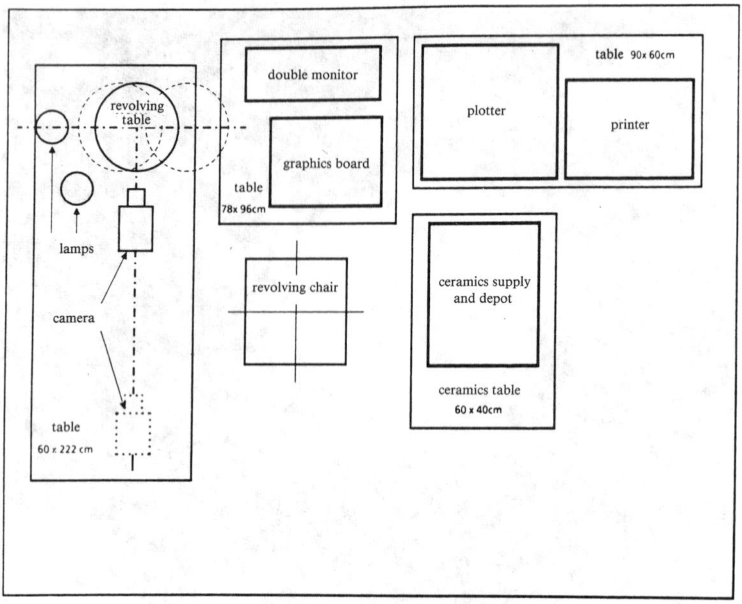

Figure 2a. Groundplan of the ARCOS workstation.

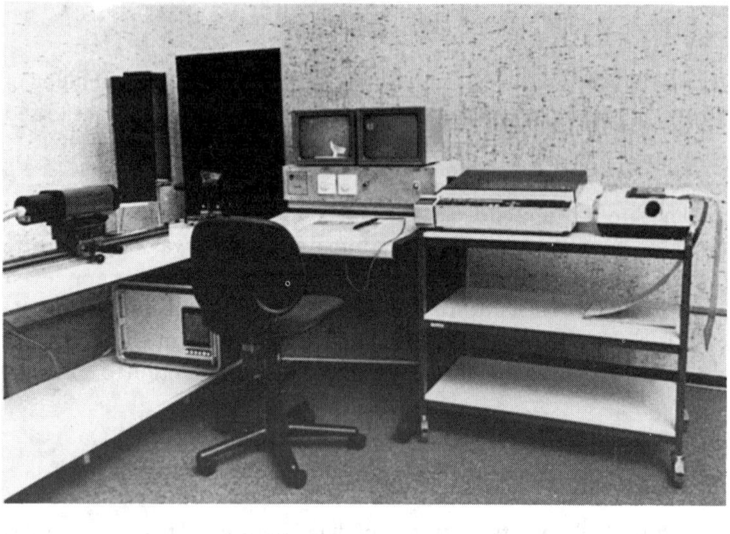

Figure 2b. View of ARCOS workstation.

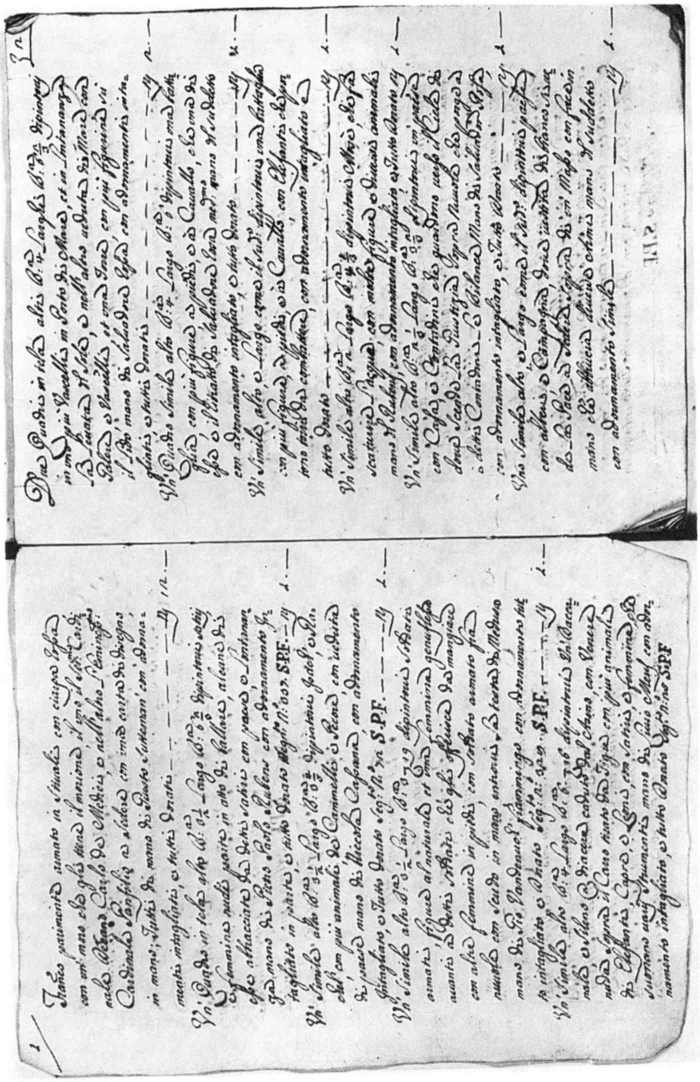

Figure 3. Inventory of the Medici collection, Florence, 1721–3.[3]

```
obj 00033326                                                midas
D-Befehl ===>                                    scroll ===  page
                (1. Ebene)                                1.Blk  0
Objekt-Nr.      300  00033326
MAI-Nr.         830  MAI,04351,B,11
Kuenstler       505  Chappel, R (?)
  Funktion      553  Maler
E-Land          215  Frankreich?
Datierung       140  1877
Obj-Titel       310  "Dione" von Hamburg, Bark von 1877
Farbmater.      350  Tempera
HoehexBreite    370  38 x 53
Gattung         330  Malerei
U-Gattung       331  Tafel-Malerei
Sache           336  Bild
Standort        260  Bremerhaven
Verw-Art        270  (öffentliche) Sammlung
Verwalter       272  Deutsches Schiffahrtsmuseum
prim. Icon.     400  46 C 21 4 &
                     46 C 24 (BARK) (+63) :
                     61 G (DIONE)
lok. Bezug      406  61 E (HAMBURG)
```

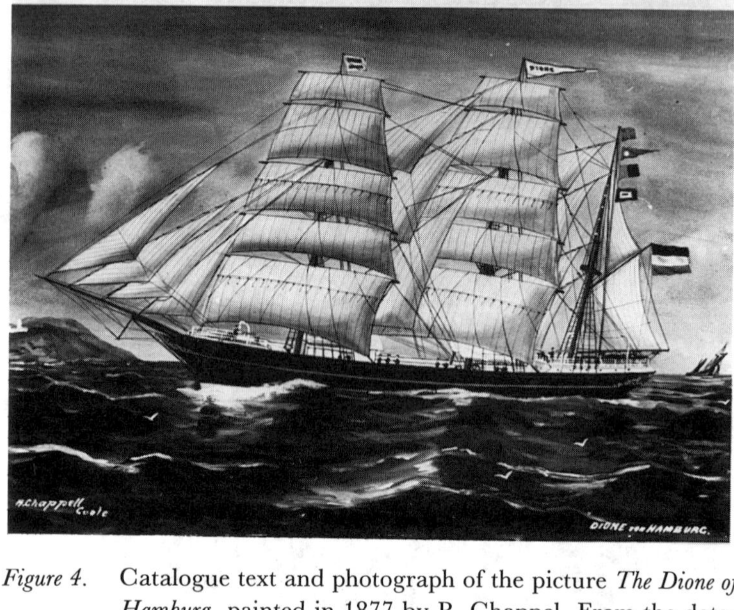

Figure 4. Catalogue text and photograph of the picture *The Dione of Hamburg*, painted in 1877 by R. Chappel. From the databank of the Bildarchiv Foto Marburg.

data has been flowing assiduously into the latest generation of computers; data for which no retrieval system is as yet available. There are projects with whose inventory of data one is thoroughly familiar by virtue of incessantly repeated demonstrations, so that further inquiry is unneccessary. Finally, databanks of literature — for example the

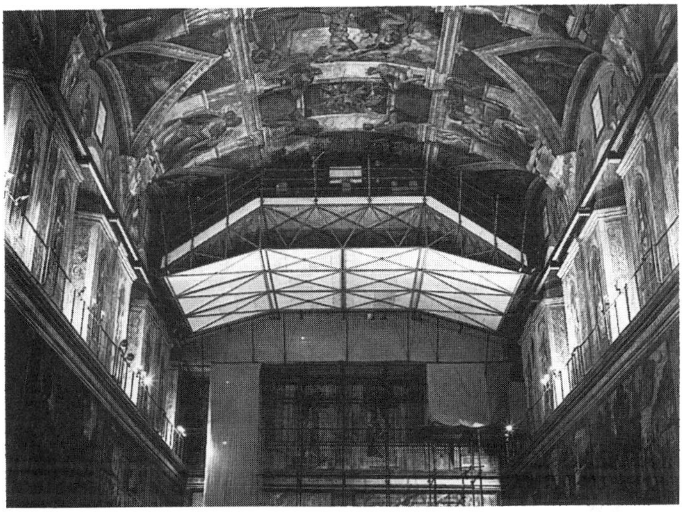

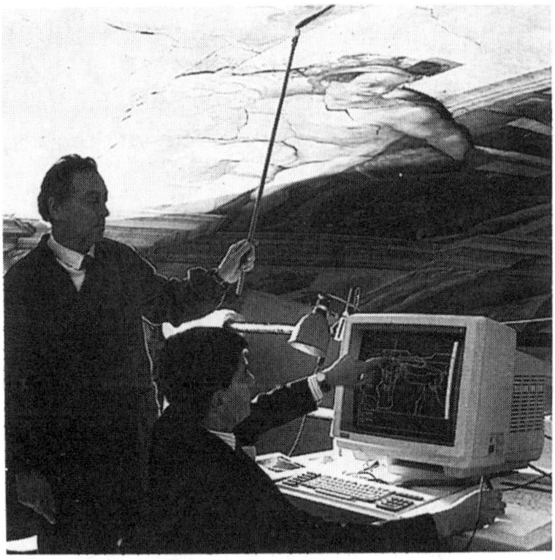

Figure 5. Restoration of Michelangelo's Sistine Chapel ceiling in the Vatican, Rome. View showing use of computer for monitoring progress.

Répertoire d'Art et d'Archéologie and the *Répertoire International de la Littérature d'Art* — are on hand; identical in up to 45 per cent of their contents. One might prefer in the long run to use the printed versions of both bibliographies. The transference of human knowledge from manuscript into printed books is not complete. How then should the transference of knowledge from printed books into the computer now have reached proportions worth mentioning?

3. Examination of issues

Still very much in its infancy is the use of computers for the examination of art-historical issues. At the conference on Automatic Processing of Art History Data and Documents in Pisa in 1984, Russell A. Kirsch reported on research in the field of optical picture analysis using computers.[5] Not long ago the most significant art-theoretical justification of this kind of investigation was presented by Werner Müller, a chemist in Ludwigshafen.[6] He postulates a grammar of forms, as found in medieval books of patterns for tracery or as suggested by Frank Lloyd Wright for architectural drawings.

As far as figures are concerned, Müller calls to mind the codified choreographic notation of figures developed by Beauchamps, the ballet master of Louis XIV. While this notation only lays down movements on a basal surface (Fig. 6), H. Frank has proposed a notation of bodily movement in space.[7] Once programmed with such a notation or grammar, a computer should — according to Müller and others — be able to analyse pictures, just as texts can be analysed with the help of linguistic grammar.

With regard to pattern-recognition, the West German police are making great efforts in trying to extend the success of fingerprint identification to the heads of citizens, but are obviously still having problems at present. In cultural history pattern-recognition methods have only met with success, to date at least, in the case of prehistoric ceramics; that is, with vessels whose profiles are comparatively simple.

4. Reconstruction, simulation and production of objects

Having been fed with data of a fragment of a vessel that still exhibits at least a small piece of the upper or lower rim via a videocamera, a computer can, with the help of an appropriate program, draw a reconstruction of the vessel (Fig. 7), as may be demonstrated by an example from the ARCOS project of the Fraunhofer Institute in Karlsruhe.[8]

In 1984 Christof Thoenes had a computer copy of Paolo Uccello's famous sketch of a chalice (Fig. 8) made up of a network of straight lines (Fig. 8b) in order to illustrate how easy it would have been for the

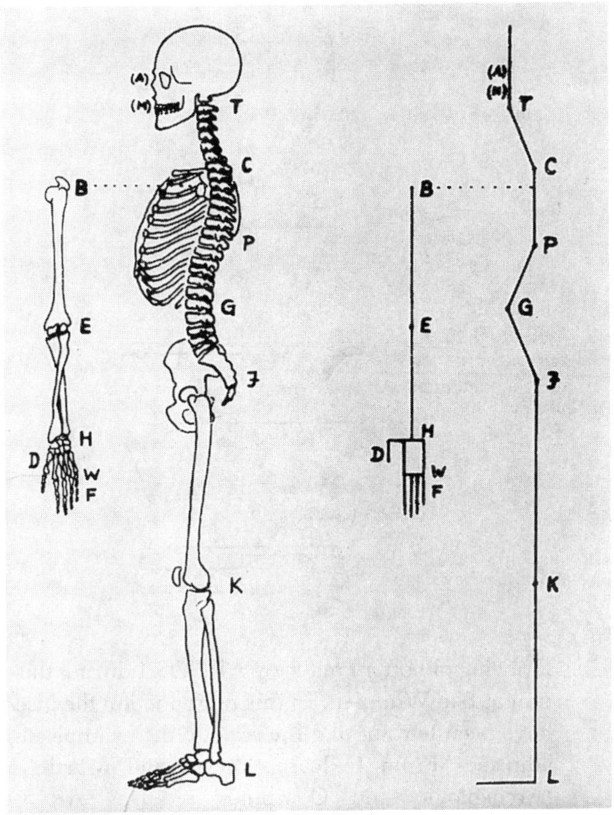

Figure 6. Adaptation of choreographic notation for description of bodily movement in space. From H. Frank, Grundlagenprobleme der Informationsaethetik und erste Andwendung auf die mime pure'. (Disseration, Stuttgart, 1959.)

artist had he used a computer.[9] In 1987, G. Mazzola, D. Krömker and G.R. Hofmann carried out a graphic simulation and a geometric analysis of Raphael's *School of Athens* (Fig. 9).[10] Writing on the subject Werner Müller says

> Here the complex composition of figures and interior architecture awakens the desire to investigate the spatial relations in the work with the methods of modern computer reconstruction, so as to trace 'hidden' symmetries by varying the perspective.

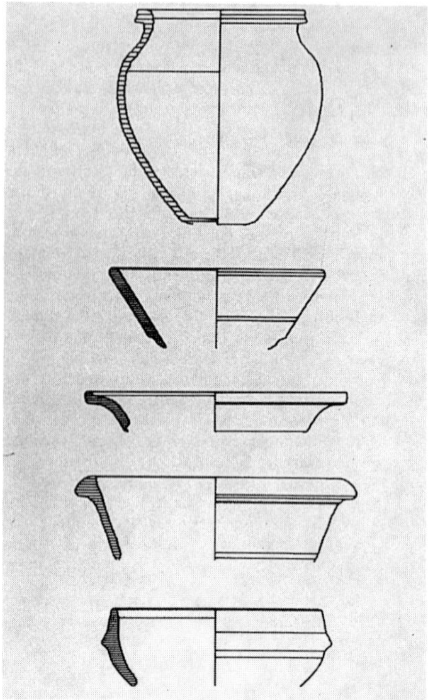

Figure 7. Drawing of pottery made by ARCOS 1 during the excavation at Bad Wimpfen. In this reproduction the inscriptions have been left out and the scale of the examples has been adjusted. From U. Kampffmeyer and Martin Pietsch, 'Archäologie und Computer — Das ARCOS zur Keramikerfassung auf der Ausgrabung in der römischen Stadt von Bad Wimpfen in Tal', *Denkmalpflege in Baden-Würtemberg* 14 (July–September 1985), 178–82.

> Opinions about the value of such a procedure will be very divided and depend on whether one considers it a meaningful venture to look for structures in a work of art that are not immediately accessible to human perception.[11]

Whereas here Müller still has doubts, in the wake of the art historian Hans Sedlmayr, he is convinced that it is possible, indeed necessary, for verifying scientific interpretation, to construct new works of art on the basis of structural principles considered determinant in traditional

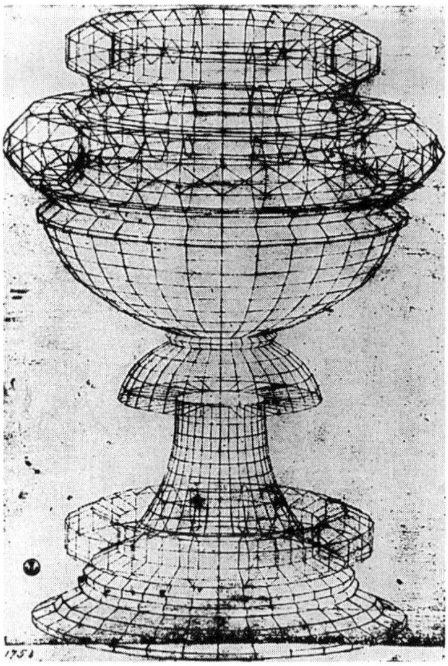

Figure 8a. Uccello's chalice.

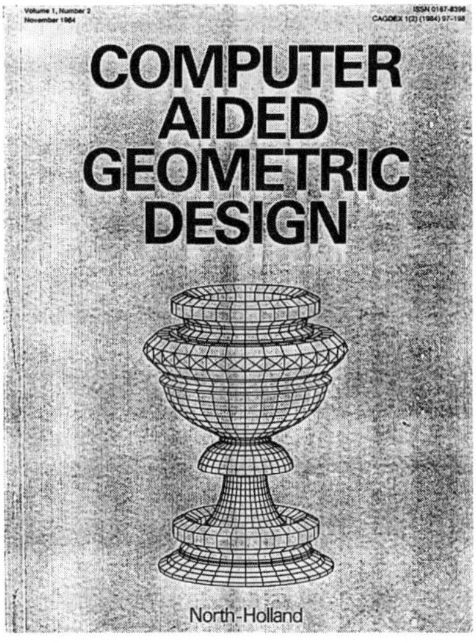

Figure 8b. Computer generated reconstructions of chalice designed by Paolo Uccello from Christof Thoenes 'Uccello's chalice', *Computer Aided Geometric Design* 1, (1984), 97–9.

Figure 9. Geometric analysis of Raphael's *School of Athens*. From G. Mazzola, D. Krömker and G. R. Hofmann, *Rasterbilder — Bildraster, Anwendung der Graphischen Datenverarbeitung zur geometrischen Analyse eines Meisterwerks der Renaissance: Raffael's 'Schule von Athen'*, Berlin-Heidelberg, 1987.

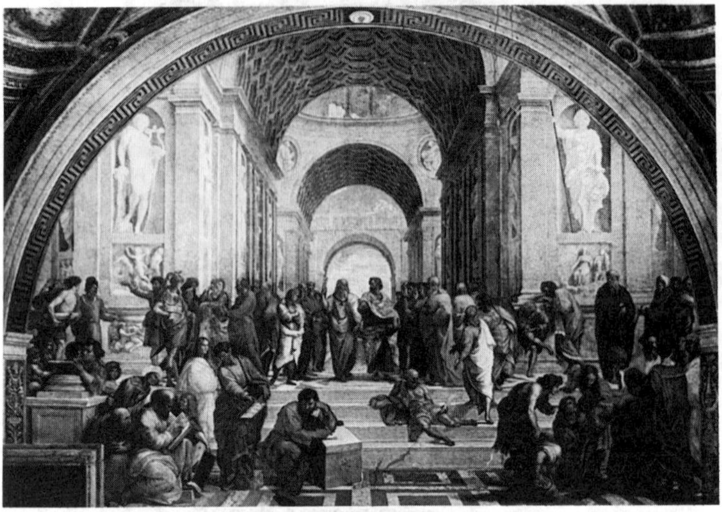

Figure 9a. Raphael, *School of Athens*, Fresco, Stanza della Segnatura, Vatican

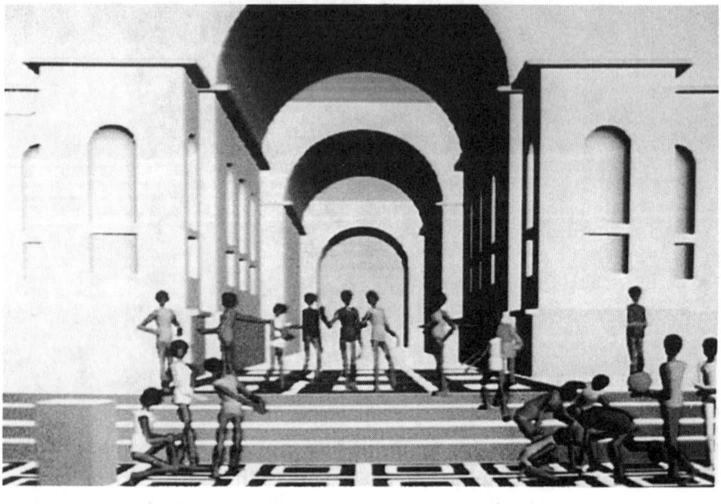

Figure 9b. View of the models in the perspective of the fresco.

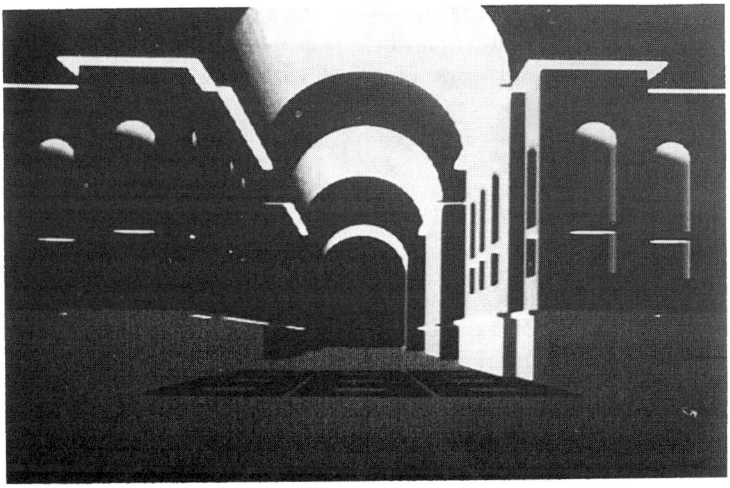

Figure 9c. Original perspective with changed lighting.

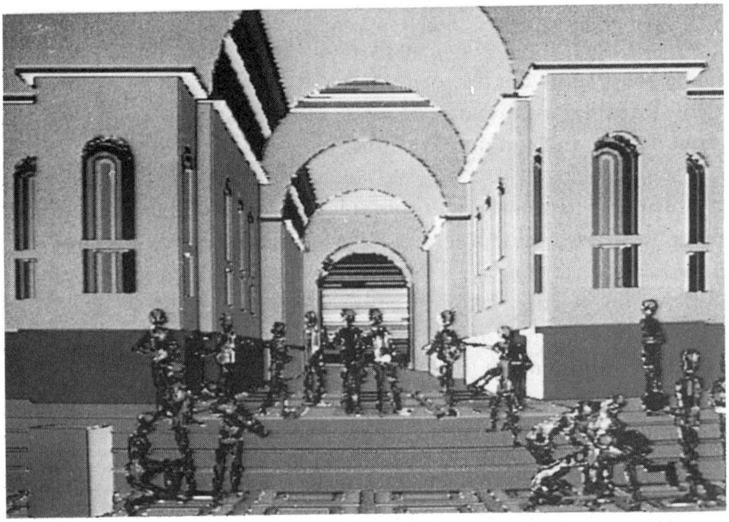

Figure 9d. Original perspective in 'false colour technique'.

works of art. Müller holds the view that art scholarship would be well advised to adjust to a situation whereby dissatisfaction with the visible object and control over works of art will very soon be the prerogative not only of the artist but of the art historian too. This assessment should at any rate liven up the discussion.

5. Administration and organization of people and objects

Computers in the history of art aims at improving the administration and organization of people and objects. Far more interesting, however, is the application of the computer for communication and production.

6. Communication and production

Electronically stored data can be sent around the world in a matter of seconds or, dispensing with this for convenience sake, simply to make it possible for others to read one's own data and copy it for themselves from a distance whenever they like. If up to now this option has not really been made use of, it has been for three reasons:

a. What is possible in theory often does not function faultlessly in practice.
b. So far there are not very many data inventories to read.
c. People are unwilling to open their data to others since our branch of learning is organized according to principles of private enterprise and can only be transmitted via marketable products.

With an end to promoting communication the Hamburg Kunsthalle deliberately used computers within an encompassing exhibition entitled 'Art Network'.[12] The attractively priced catalogue of the exhibition offered the visitor the chance to comment upon each exhibit freely or with recourse to the suggested associative concepts and to input these comments in the form of simple key words. The computer replied by showing digitalized reproductions of the exhibits for which the same linking concepts had already been keyed in. Thus, a very complex network of concepts gradually built up in the computer, which Michael Hübl reviewed after the exhibition closed.[13]

For the project 'Art Network' the new possibilities of cooperation between many that the computer creates have been made use of in a

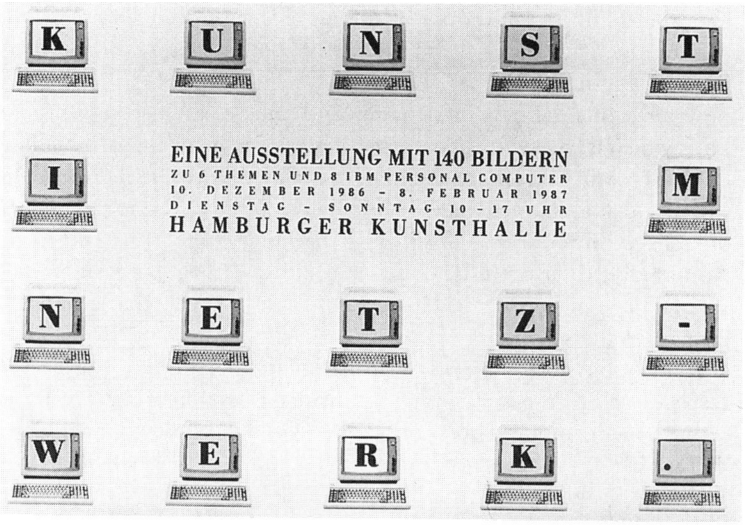

Figure 10. *Kunst im Netzwerk* exhibition catalogue cover.

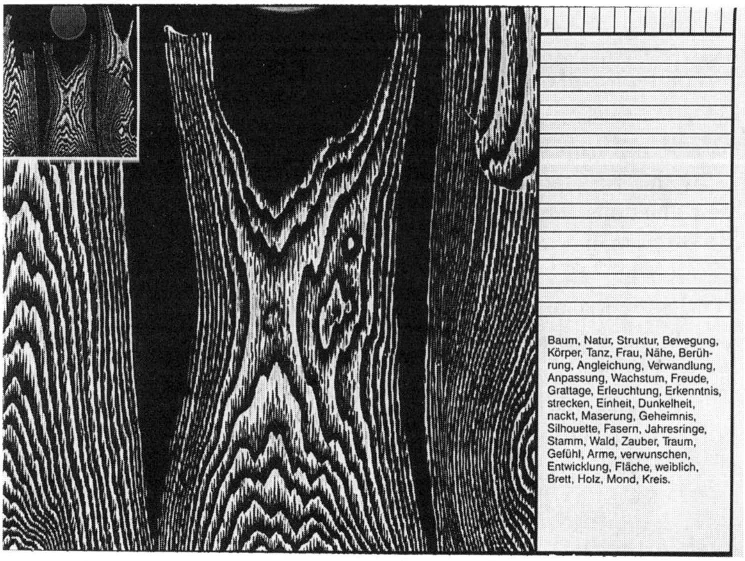

Figure 11.

logical fashion. 'Art Network' is therefore an excellent example of the communicative as well as the productive power that a computer can develop in our field.

Against this the new information system of the Musée d'Orsay in Paris which is based on optical discs may be technically more ingenious but it is certainly not more inspired, reducing the user, as it does, to the role of a simple recipient. Incidentally, I have yet to see better digitalized reproduction of paintings than that in the Musée d'Orsay. Admittedly, each reproduction also requires 4 megabytes of storage space and — in spite of local wide-band cable — seventeen seconds for display on the screen.

It is not possible to report as positively on the Hamburg project in respect of other products which art historians are creating or want to create using computers, because they are mainly conventional objects that should be produced in a more rational way. This applies to articles and monographs, bibliographies and dictionaries alike.

Videodiscs, however, with which art historians are experimenting more and more, are a subject in themselves. A videodisc of the National Gallery in Washington, D.C., with 54,000 pictures has been combined with a didactically conceived textual databank for school teaching purposes and transferred into a 'Visual Art Index System' which was demonstrated during the International Conference on Databases in the Humanities and Social Sciences, at Auburn University in Montgomery, Alabama, 1987. At the same conference a videodisc was presented for university teaching. It ranged chronologically from antiquity to the present and geographically from Northern Europe to Japan.

In the Federal Republic of Germany a videodisc with 25,000 reproductions of masterpieces of western painting has been produced. Attempts to market it have failed because nobody can afford the cost of reproducing 25,000 colour slides. Likewise, the videodiscs of the Galeria Spada in Rome, the Bibliothèque Geneviève in Paris, the Dutch Royal Library in The Hague, or the Service Informatique of Paris are not for sale. How many art-historical books one could have printed and given away as presents with the money spent on these discs does not concern us here.

Unfortunately, products with machine-readable data on floppy discs or CD ROM hardly play a role at all. To be sure, it does occasionally happen that institutes on friendly terms exchange data tapes, but the offer of a disc at a price of £5 with an extendable databank containing the basic data and addresses of all those artists who have ever taken part in a *Dokumenta* exhibition, for example, is still an exception.

Problems of using computers in the history of art

Although computers have been used for over twenty-five years in the field of art history, not many end-products have been successfully accomplished. Reasons for this failure are the technical, institutional, individual and systematic problems of using computers in this subject area.

1. Technical problems

The technical problems are easy to explain. They lie in the insufficient capacity of available hardware and software. To date no databank or retrieval system is known to this author that can cope with the complexity of art-historical data. The old systems like STAIRS or BASIS were two-level systems at most. The new relational databases like ORACLE or SYBASE or dB III PLUS will indeed someday be usable by art historians. At present however they do not allow input of art-historical data on a serious scientific level, as far as is known.

Equally useless for our requirements are the existing methods for the digital storing and transmission of reproductions. The information that art historians have imparted visually up to now, will still be difficult to express in words a hundred years hence. The possibility of storing pictures in a computer in a satisfactory quality and great quantity must always remain a desideratum.

Another technical deficiency is the complicated operation of many computers and programs, which is all the more irksome the shorter-lived the combination of hardware and software is. Anybody who has reconciled himself to the shortcomings of his apparatus and acquired a working knowledge of it can become a professional dropout when his new apparatus, while not giving him increased performance, turns out to need quite different handling.

As art historians are unable to influence the development of computer technology, there is only one way to resolve technical problems. We must learn to differentiate between what someone else can do with a computer and what we ourselves can accomplish. Thus, it is certainly of no help to us if the Pentagon can take satellite photos of individual stones on the pinnacles of Westminster Abbey when we cannot obtain permission to take photographs of its interior.

Moreover, we must, in spite of the optimism of the computer industry, again ask ourselves objectively whether what we want in individual cases is altogether practicable with the computers we can afford. Unfortunately, in all too many cases the answer will be negative even in the present day.

2. Institutional and individual problems

The same situation prevails in our art-historical institutes. As a rule we have neither data processing (DP) staff nor even the funds to attend DP courses. Only in very rare cases is there a chance of obtaining exactly the right amount of money for a concrete task at the right moment. More often an absurd sum of money is made available at an unsuitable time with the injunction to buy immediately.

If this state of affairs is further enriched by having one person purchase a computer so that another can produce some splendid result, the institute in question is generally equipped with a topic of conversation for years to come. How such a catastrophe can be forestalled, I do not know. In case of doubt I would prefer to return the money rather than enter into a never ending conflict without at least a chance of winning.

A further difficulty which causes many art-historical projects to fail resides in the often unclear objectives of the people involved. Sometimes it is a case of wanting to modernize an institute or win outside sponsors via computers, sometimes of wanting at long last to catalogue in full a large collection of material or improve controls and streamline the administration. Usually, one wants a bit of everything. If the preparatory work is proportionally vague, the consequences are fatal, at least as far as the most frequent application of computers in art history up to now is concerned, that is, the cataloguing of works of art.

If this routine task is to be mastered using a computer, a few plain but crucial questions must first be asked. Is it simply going to be a matter in future of understanding the daily inventory of new accessions with a computer and subsequently producing a few cards for various card indexes, or is the goal the compilation of a new catalogue in book form? Is a survey catalogue of the entire inventory, or a more thorough scholarly catalogue of part of it, to be produced?

In other words: are many works of art to be covered superficially or fewer in depth? Is the data to be used in primary printed form or on-line? Is the work to be carried out by a specialist or by auxiliary personnel? Is the required data already on hand or does it first have to be culled? What is the deadline for which target?

3. Systematic problems

Once these questions have been answered, it becomes possible to attack the systematic problems and to define the necessary preparatory work. Let us now take the standard case in which a printed inventory and a databank — both roughly of the standard of an average museum catalogue — are to be prepared in a single operation. After joint discussion what could we advise here? Probably, not to pursue both tasks at the same time, but first to produce the printed catalogue with good indexes with the help of a powerful formatter such as Document Composition Facility, since this is comparatively easy and can be effected quickly.

Furthermore, we would very likely recommend that the second stage, namely the compilation of a databank, be prepared throughly and that answers for the following problems, among others, held in readiness:

- how to catalogue works of art comprising several parts, comprising several parts, comprising several parts, comprising several parts, etc.
- how to catalogue works of art in which other works of art are depicted, in which other works of art are depicted, in which other works of art are depicted, etc.
- how to catalogue works of art commissioned jointly by many, executed jointly by many, written about by many art historians, photographers by many photographers, etc.
- how to catalogue works of art about which one knows nothing.
- how to catalogue works of art about which everything is known, including their provenance.
- how to make a rational index of verbal dating of every kind.
- how to take into account all other conceivable art-historical matter in a homogeneous yet scientific way.

As a final piece of advice, it is only possible to effectively build up a databank on works of art if — by whatever means and wherever — auxiliary files can be obtained, for example, biographic, historico-geographic and iconographic files. For reasons of economy files of this sort are indispensable.

Without an artist index documenting that, for example, Donatello is a Florentine Renaissance sculptor, this information has to be repeated in every catalogue entry treating a work by Donatello, so as to ensure that the computer can locate the works when they are requested under the reference 'Florentine Renaissance'.

In order to enable the computer to identify Donatello's *Judith* as a quattrocento (fifteenth-century) representation of an Old Testament theme, the following would be needed:

1. A file in which the concepts Renaissaince and quattrocento are linked with one another via numerical values.
2. A file in which Florence is defined as a part of Tuscany.
3. A file in which the representation of Judith with the head of Holofernes is classified as the treatment of a theme from the Book of Judith in the Old Testament.

The cataloguing of works of art by computer thus only becomes fruitful through the incorporation of other machine-readable data — just as, conversely, the input of biographic data on artists is only worth while when it can be linked with data on the works of artists.

Here, we touch upon the essential problem of the use of computers in the history of art. Using computers only makes sense if we call into question the principles organizing our discipline at present: the principles of private ownership in scholarship, of all-out competition and of the system of remuneration. Using computers makes possible:

- the reading by any one person of another person's file free of charge.
- an almost inconceivable extension and intensification of the availability of works of art to any one person.
- the reproduction and distribution of knowledge and findings without cost.

It is the task of everyone who introduces computers into art history to ensure that the possibilities they provide are actually put into practice.

Notes and references

1. Wilfried Wester-Ebbinghaus, 'Zur Verfahrensentwicklung in der Nahbereichsphotogrammetrie', Dissertation Bonn, 1981, p. 39, illus. no. 18. (Veröffentlichung des Instituts für Photogrammetrie der Universität Bonn).
2. Ulrich Kampffmeyer, 'ARCOS: Eine Textuntersuchung auf der Saalburg' in *Saalburg-Jahrbuch* 40–41 (1984/85), pp. 121–33, illus nos 1 and 2.
3. 'Sommo Pontefice Innocenzio XIII. Gran Duca Cosimo III. felicemente regnante; *Inventario di Quadri* che si ritrovano negli appartamenti del Gran Palazzo de'Pitti di S.A.R. alcuni de quali sono dell'Eredità del Ser.mo Pri.pe Cardinale Leopoldo e per distinzione degli altri, non solo si noteranno qui col proprio numero, come anco per maggior chiarezza con la presente cifra S.C.L. Altri sono dell'Eredità del Ser.mo Gran Pri.pe Ferdinando ambi di Gloriosa memoria, e questi si noteranno qui col proprio numero e con la presente cifra S.P.F. Altri sono di proprietà de Ser.mo Gran Duca Cosimo Terzo Felicemente Regnante, e questi si noteranno col numero, e saranno segnati senza Cifra'.

   This inventory is in the Archivio di Stato di Firenze in the Guardaroba Medicea, 1304 ter.

   The date can be deduced from the evidence given in the first lines of the text. This indicates that the inventory must have been prepared during the Pontificate of Pope Innocent XIII (which began on 8 May 1721) and prior to the death of Grand Duke Cosimo III (which took place on 31 October 1723).

   The inventory is restricted to paintings that were at that time in the Pitti Palace. These paintings come from the collections of Cardinal Leopoldo, the Crown Prince Ferdinando and the Grand Duke Cosimo. Leopoldo and Ferdinando were already dead at the time that the inventory was prepared. The pictures from their estates were marked respectively with the initials S.C.L. and S.P.F.
4. 'Kunst — Als Information verschlüsselt', *IBM-Nachrichten* 285 (October 1986), 8–9; Alexander Eliot, 'Was wird davon übrig bleiben?' *ART* 11 (1987), 28–44, illus. no. 44.
5. Russell A. Kirsch, 'Making art historical sources visible to computers — pictures as primary sources for computer-based art history data', in *Automatic Processing of Art History Data and Documents*, Papers II, 41, Pisa, 1984.
6. Werner Müller, *Kunstwerk, Kunstgeschichte und Computer*, München, 1987.
7. H. Frank, 'Grundlagenprobleme der Informationsasthetik und erste Anwendung auf die mime pure', Dissertation, Stuttgart, 1959.
8. Ulrich Kampffmeyer and Martin Pietsch, 'Archäologie und Computer — Das ARCOS zur Keramikerfassung auf der Ausgrabung in der

römischen Stadt von Bad Wimpfen im Tal', *Denkmalpflege in Baden-Württemberg*, 14 (July–September 1985), 178–82.

9. Christof Thoenes, 'Uccello's chalice', *Computer Aided Geometric Design* 1 (1984), 97–9.
10. G. Mazzola, D. Krömker, and G.R. Hofmann, *Rasterbilder — Bildraster, Anwendung der Graphischen Datenverarbeitung zur geometrischen Analyse eines Meisterwerks der Renaissance: Raffaels 'Schule von Athen'*, Berlin-Heidelberg, 1987, illus. 1 and 2; 22 and 23.
11. See note 6 above, page 114.
12. Achim Lipp, *Kunst in Netzwerk*, Hamburg, 1986.
13. Michael Hübl, 'Kunst im Netzwerk — Eine Ausstellung in der Kunsthall Hamburg als Denkmodell', *Kunstforum* 88, 3/4 (1987), 192–203.

Part II
ELECTRONIC IMAGING

2

Conventional Photography vs Analogue and Digital Electronic Imaging[1]

Anthony Hamber

The advent of photography at the end of the fourth decade of the nineteenth century has been to date the most revolutionary system of image manufacture, storage and dissemination ever invented by man. From the moment of the announcements made by Daguerre and Fox Talbot in 1839 this new imaging system was adopted by those wishing, for a variety of reasons, to record works of art. Indeed, there is evidence to suggest that Fox Talbot hoped to commercially exploit his invention through the production of copies of engravings, manuscripts and sculpture.[2]

Colour photography has evolved into one of the essential tools, often the primary tool, of those studying art for academic art historical, scientific and recreational purposes. That we do not necessarily agree with John Ruskin who wrote in early 1870 'I tremble to think what would happen if photographers were able to take photographs in colour, seeing what mistakes they make now when they have only monochrome to deal with'[3] is primarily due to the fact that as Ralph Evans, the eminent photoscientist, stated as early as 1943, 'one of the basic assumptions which underlies all theories of photographic colour processes is that a photograph *can* be made which *looks like* the subject.'[4] The phrase 'looks like the subject' is at the very core of the discussions in this article for it infers a level of acceptibility in image quality. The parameters of this acceptibility are coming under increasing examination and adjustment.

In spite of new, and potentially more comprehensive forms of colour imaging systems, conventional colour photography remains the benchmark by which others are judged. Of these new electronic imaging systems, electronic digital imaging has to date been the most influential. Its future potential for the study of art will be as significant as the inventions of Daguerre and Fox Talbot.

The first colour photographs were produced in the 1860s by the Englishman James Clerk Maxwell and two Frenchmen, Charles Cros and Louis Ducos du Hauron. It is interesting to note that both Cros and Ducos du Hauron photographed oil paintings, probably from their own or their family collections, as part of their experiments.[5] The basis of these nineteenth century colour photographic systems was the exposure onto black and white film of three separate images of the subject. One exposure through a red filter, one through a green filter and one through a blue filter. When projected in registration a full colour image appears. This is the additive colour system and it essentially has 'linear' characteristics, that is that it has a mathematically consistent pattern of behaviour; a unit change in the input causing a unit change in the output. However the practical difficulties of the additive system, particularly in terms of the long camera exposures required, led to the adoption of the subtractive colour system which uses the complementary colours to R, G, B, these being Magenta, Yellow and Cyan (C, Y, M).[6]

The first colour materials, such as the Autochrome produced by the French firm of A. Lumiere & Ses Fils from the summer of 1907, was the first practical single-plate colour film made commercially available. The Autochrome had many disadvantages, though it was commercially available until the 1930s. In 1912, the German art historian Aby Warburg showed a coloured 'Lumiere-Lichtbild' of a watercolour copy of a lost painting by Piero della Francesca when he spoke at the International Congress on Art History in Rome.[7]

The Kodachrome colour transparency film, introduced in 1936 with an improved version marketed in 1938, was the first film to successfully use the technology of the integral tripack based on the subtractive colour system. This film had the C, Y, M sensitive layers in one combination within a single emulsion and is the basis of current colour films.[8]

Conventional colour photography is still the most comprehensive and best quality imaging system yet devised by man. However electronic imaging is beginning to have a noticeably significant effect on this market as well as creating others. The video camera is one of these new markets. All the major conventional photographic firms are heavily engaged in research into electronic still cameras and although prototypes appeared as long ago as 1983, and selected photographers at the Los Angeles Olympics in 1984 were given the use of some of these cameras, they are as yet not readily available.

The majority of the electronic still cameras produced to date have used an image sensor known as a charged couple device (CCD). In spite of the use in the 1980s of CCD technology in electronic still cameras this image sensing device was designed in the previous decade. Where the CCD has had its greatest domestic impact to date is in the field of drum scanning for the printing and reprographics industry. Recently the video camera market has also seen the introduction of CCD technology.

The advent of these new electronic technologies has highlighted some of the distinct limitations of conventional colour photography. Many of these limitations are emphasized when the subject matter being photographed is a painting. Such limitations include the characteristics of the photo-sensitive dyes used; the gamut of reproducible colour; the limited contrast range; the ability to resolve detail in the original; the sensitivity of emulsion and their exposure characteristics; the stability and permanence of the photographic image and the accessibility of the image. An outline of each of these problematic areas will give an appreciation as to why conventional colour photography is often highly restricted as a form of archival imaging of works of art.

Colour, as perceived by the human brain, is a synthesis of physics, physiology and perceptual psychology in a combination unique to each individual. Though there is continuous research in all three disciplines, perhaps even the introduction of another which is called psychophysics, there are two overriding factors that have always had to be taken into account. Firstly, that even with much experience, coupled to practical as well as theoretical training, even the most attentive observer has no way of specifying colour in an absolute or quantitative sense.[9] The second factor is the very nature of a colour reproduction of an original; that it is a reproduction, an approximation and can never be identical to the original. Colour photographs are therefore approximations, albeit sometimes highly accurate ones. Optimizing colour reproduction is a highly complex synthesis of several scientific fields some of which are, by the admission of their respective leading experts, still in their infancy.

The psychology of visual perception is an extremely complex synthesis of subjective and objective criteria acting in mostly non-linear functions and often based on sets of analogies constructed by the idiosyncratic experiences of the individual. We perceive the world about us in different ways depending on the circumstances. Perceiving in isolation images which reproduce the world about us is disproportionately complicated and made particularly so by the variation of viewing conditions for both the original and for its image. This factor is one which bedevils all imaging systems and which is compounded by the concept of the 'acceptability' of an image. Still photography has to be more 'accurate' than the moving image which relies on the dynamic of motion to cover up a multitude of inexactitudes.

The first limitation of conventional colour photography is that the gamut of colour which can be created through the subtractive system is smaller than that possible using the additive system. This is primarily due to the fact that Red, Green and Blue are 'purer' spectral colours than Cyan, Magenta and Yellow. Neither additive nor subtractive systems can match the colour gamut of the human visual system. Furthermore, practical and economic considerations have meant that the dyes currently used in conventional colour film emulsions cannot, even in theory, produce colorimetric reproductions, that is that the reproduction is indistinguishable from the original in terms of colour.[10] The spectral sensitivity of the currently commercially available conventional colour films are the results of compromises based on many years of experience and are, in themselves, a synthesis of objective and subjective criteria as well as commercial considerations. The use of any particular dye with optimum spectral sensitivity as one of the colour sensitized layers may be made impractical by the effect of its combination with the other two layers. Indeed the secondary absorptions of light within the different dye layers of the film are often more influential on the colour reproduction than the primary absorption characteristics.[11]

Oil paintings and some works of sculpture are often far from being 'average' absorbers and reflectors of light. For instance many of the works of Titian, Rembrandt and other Dutch seventeenth century artists pose considerable problems when photographed. Similarly bronze sculpture, due to its very limited contrast range which is placed at one end of the contrast range of films, causes considerable photographic difficulties. A contrast range which seems quite average to the human eye may, photographically speaking, be far outside the contrast range of a film. A particularly apposite example is the interior of a medieval cathedral in which the contrast difference between the clerestory and ground floor level may be far greater than the ability of a film to effectively record. Shadow areas in paintings often absorb most of the light falling upon them. Conversely, white highlights in a painting reflect as little as 18 per cent of the light falling upon them. This light absorption/reflection factor must be taken into account when photographing paintings. A common mistake is to measure the light falling onto a painting as an indication of the camera exposure. This presupposes that the painting or object is an average reflector, which it may not be. What the film records is light reflected from the object, not light falling onto it. Reflected readings of luminance are more often than not the critical factors which determine camera exposure.

The limited contrast range of colour films can be counteracted by several techniques. The work may be selectively illuminated to balance up the luminances from the painting so that the film can record them within its contrast range by using a single camera exposure. This is a highly complicated and time consuming task which, in the case of small paintings in particular, is often impossible to carry out. Using large format cameras it is possible to cut cardboard masks which cover the highlight areas following a single camera exposure for the highlights. Then multiple flash exposures onto the uncovered shadow detail on the painting permit enough light to reflect back to the film to place both highlight and shadow detail within the film exposure range. Both these methods are subjective and imprecise. To complicate matters further, all colour photographic films suffer what is known as the failure of the law of reciprocity. This occurs either during very short or very long camera exposure times (for most films anything longer than $\frac{1}{2}$ a second or shorter than 1/10,000th of a second). Colour films then lose speed and change their colour balance and, in spite of use of filters and additional camera exposure, cannot be fully corrected to give optimum results.

Paintings often exhibit characteristics such as anomalous reflectance and fluorescence. Anomalous reflectance occurs when the film records an object as a different colour because it is sensitive to more and different wavelengths in the electromagnetic spectrum than the human eye. A common example of this is the notorious difficulty of photographing the flower the Morning Glory. Certain textiles also show signs of anomalous reflectance. Many modern twentieth century artists use synthetic pigments which cause extreme examples of this characteristic.

Fluorescence is a common factor and occurs when a substance absorbs electromagnetic energy at one wavelength and emits it at another. Blue/green fluorescence is frequently a problem when photographing paintings and is the result of a combination of many factors such as inorganic pigments, organic substances, varnishes, retouching or simply the integral effect of numerous layers of pigment on top of each other. Both anomalous reflectance and fluorescence can be predicted to a certain degree by experience. The paintings of Claude Lorraine often include blue/green fluorescence, presumably because of a certain pigment or a combination of pigments. The experimentation with pigments such as bitumen by artists such as Joshua Reynolds and the Pre-Raphaelite Brotherhood also produce some predictable fluorescence.

While experience can give some indication of the likelihood of these characteristics, little can be done about them. Firstly one must wait until films are processed before one can verify the appearance of these characteristics — and this lack of immediacy is one of the many limitations of the photographic process — and secondly, as with the failure of the law of reciprocity, the use of filters may change other elements of the overall colour balance.

Differences in films are numerous. Films vary from batch to batch; emulsions are produced to 'ripen' to a point at which they are at their integral optimum; temperature and humidity can be influential before, during and after exposure. There are essentially two film types. One balanced for 'daylight' and the other for 'Tungsten' light. 'Daylight' film has a wider spectral sensitivity than 'Tungsten' film which is less red sensitive due to the compensation necessary for the excessive red factor in the illuminant. Thus if a painting is photographed twice, once on 'daylight' transparency film and once on 'Tungsten' transparency film, and the two films are then processed together, comparison between the two finished transparencies will readily indicate differences which are most noticeable in terms of the colour.

The ability of colour films to record detail is a limiting factor. Some black and white films, such as those used for holography, can resolve as many as 1000 lines in one millimetre of the emulsion. The greatest resolution possible on colour film emulsions is in the order of 100 lines/mm. This may seem very impressive, and it is. However it is the detail resolvable in a reproduction of the original, say an oil painting, which is of relevance. Thus a 35 mm transparency (which has dimensions of 36 × 24 mm) could resolve 3600 lines in one direction and 2400 lines in the other. If the object being photographed has dimensions of 1500 × 1000 mm then when a full-frame transparency of the object is enlarged to the same size as the original there are approximately 2.4 lines resolved per millimetre of the original. The human eye can resolve about 6 lines/mm at a viewing distance of 340 mm.[12] Thus with a resolution of under 3 lines/mm one would, even in theory, have to more than double the viewing distance to at least 700 mm in order for the eye not to detect the structure of the reproduction. Other factors would result in overall image quality being extremely poor.

Using a larger format transparency will give more area to record the original but the problem centres around the interrelationship between the size of the original, the size of the photographic negative or transparency, the size of the reproduction from that photographic negative or transparency and its relationship with the original and the viewing distance from the reproduction.

Two characteristics of the photographic system have been particularly highlighted by the immediacy of electronic images. Firstly, when using conventional colour photography, it is not possible to examine the image during camera exposure stage of the photographic process. Using immediate-access materials (such as Polaroid) can give little information because it is not a like-for-like comparison. Secondly, however careful the calibration of colour film, the most decisive stage of the whole process can be development. Here again there is no immediate control or viewing facility. The result is that one must wait, often for several hours, before it is possible to make assessment of any photograph.

The question of stability and permanence has become a matter of considerable importance over the past few years both for manufacturers of photographic materials as well as consumers. All film manufacturers cover themselves from liability with a phrase such as 'colour dyes may change in time.' The stability and permanence of black and white materials pales into comparative insignificance when these characteristics of colour photographic materials are examined. Light, heat and humidity all effect both stability and permanence.[13] Changes in contrast and more noticeably colour can appear within six years in spite of archival storage. Furthermore, disregarding whether the transparency was ever an accurate reproduction of the original or not, there is no way in which the degradation of the image through the changes in the combination of dyes can be either quantitively or qualitatively calculated. This is of particular relevance to those who use colour photography for scientific measurement and recording of works of art.

Despite the fact that photography revolutionized the dissemination of images of works of art it is, by late twentieth century standards, a relatively inaccessible form of imaging. Direct satellite broadcasting has enabled events to be transmitted, real-time, to anyone who has a television with a suitable receiver. Yet a photographer must get exposed film processed before it can be televised and this takes a minimum of one hour, unless a Polaroid type material is used. Obviously the use of television has increased the dissemination of images based on photographic originals but, as yet, this has not increased their inherent accessibility. Furthermore, the quality of a televised photographic image is far lower than the original from which it was taken. In essence a photographic print or transparency can be viewed in one place at one time. Making multiple copies may increase potential accessibility but, without care, attention and expense, such copies are often not accurate reproductions of the original and are in any case failing to remove a fundamental problem. Picture libraries and slide collections are distinctly archaic forms of image storage and dissemination when placed in context with the current developments of the information technology revolution.

So far it has been shown that conventional colour photography, when used to image works of art, has distinct limitations. This is not to say that the accuracy of all colour photography of works of art is distinctly limited but that in certain respects and in certain cases problems will arise. Some of these problems are irrespective of whether the object is a work of art. What must now be looked at is the current role and future potential of analogue as well as digital electronic imaging systems.

On 15 July 1924, Dr H.E. Ives transmitted between Chicago and New York three colour separations of a photograph by Max Hofstetter of the star of the silent screen Rudolph Valentino. By using Bell telephone lines to send these three images Ives initiated a system which was to revolutionize the transference of images.[14] The age of the electronically transmittable colour image had arrived.

Ives' system of image transfer was aimed to assist those in the printing and publishing industries and it is in these two fields, rather than in the field of conventional colour photography, that we find the origins of the electronic imaging technologies which are today making such an impact on the society in which we live.

The developments in the scanning technology used by the printing and reprographics industries since the late 1960s have resulted in an explosion in colour reproductions, most noticeably in the magazine industry. These developments stem from a major breakthrough made in 1969 by the British firm Crosfield with the Magnascan 450 drum scanner. This scanner was the first to use digital techniques to produce enlarged and reduced colour separations which enabled faster and potentially more accurate production of publications with colour illustrations. The scanner output signal was converted to digital form thus enabling immediate reductions and enlargements. In 1976 Crosfield introduced the Magnascan 550 scanner which was the first machine to use digital technology for colour correction. This system, called a look-up table (LUT), was problematic in terms of speed and interpolation of dot output values. However the introduction of minicomputers has solved the speed problem and refined algorithms the difficulties with interpolation.

It was as recently as 1982 that Eikonix introduced the first colour scanner to utilize that charge couple device (CCD) which is currently the technology most favoured for electronic imaging both in terms of analogue and digital technologies.[15] Companies such as Crosfield, Scitex, Eikonix and Hell all currently produce digital scanning systems which allow great degrees of control over a photographically originated image. Anyone who has seen one of these systems working will have been more than a little impressed by the speed and flexibility which permits a single operator to change the size, shape and colour of an image. Corrections, such as the removal of unwanted reflections can be made in a matter of seconds whereas photographic retouching is highly skilled, expensive and time consuming. Many colour illustrations produced using this technology, most noticeably the glossy holiday brochure image of an 'Ideal' young couple lying beneath a 'perfect' palm tree on a seemingly deserted Caribbean beach, come perilously close to breaking the spirit if not the letter of the Trades Descriptions Act. It is almost certainly the case that the final image is an electronically concocted illusion. The beach was in fact littered with sunbathing tourists but by electronically removing groups of people or single individuals and then replacing the holes left with 'averaged' colour taken from the surrounding patches of sand an apparently empty beach has been produced. Then a photograph of a palm tree was taken and everything but the tree was digitally removed. The tree was then placed somewhere in the concocted beach scene. Any area of the original image which has been overlayed by the tree was removed. Finally two models were placed on a backcloth in a photographic studio and photographed in a typical beach pose. Again everything from the image save for the couple was digitally removed and the couple were placed beside the palm tree and supposedly on the beach. The final image could then be manipulated to produce an even light balance from a supposed single source of illumination, the sun.

The main limitation of these systems is that their output is primarily for hard copy printing but as William Gamble, editor of *Penrose's Annual*, wrote in the 1925 issue of the *Annual* while discussing colour printing: 'There is a public craving for colour, and the appetite grows as the means of feeding it increases.' More recently firms such as Crosfield and Scitex have produced systems which use high-speed array processors for tasks other than their previously central output of Lasergravure whereby the cylinders used for printing are engraved directly by digital proofing methods. Now systems convert the C, Y, M, and black data used for printing into R, G, B, for colour transparencies; carry out data compression algorithms for archiving or data transmission purposes and even convert video-frame data.

That such control over an electronic image is possible is due to the manipulable image being a digital one. The digital image is a precisely definable one based on the conversion of electronic signals into binary digits. This inherent precision is the key to the potential of future electronic imaging and it is relevant here to point out some of the essential differences between analogue and digital electronic images.

An analogue image is one stored as a constantly varying signal. The changes in intensity of this signal denote the brightness or darkness of the image. There is an analogue image as long as there are changes in the intensity of the electronic signal. The fundamental weaknesses in the system are twofold. Firstly, the system of sampling a signal in an analogue form is imprecise because it does not accurately record the temporal or spatial 'boundary' to each piece of information. Replay of this signal, which is normally the replaying of a magnetic storage tape, must be at exactly the same rate as during the recording stage. Secondly, magnetic storage tape is neither permanent nor stable. The power of an analogue signal diminishes as magnetic tape ages through both time and use. The changes may be small but they are taking place. In essence all images stored on magnetic tape are slowly fading away at a rate difficult, if not impossible, to precisely determine.

Digital imaging is based on the binary digit and a system of allocating a temporal or spatial boundary to each piece of information. Digital information is sampled and recorded as a set of precise on/off signals which are either there (and thus precise) or are not (which results in no reading at all). Thus digital imaging is accurate both in terms of signal sampling and recording and, given an archival storage medium, both stable and permanent.

There are several analogue and digital electronic imaging systems currently being used to record works of art. These include VHS, Betamax and U-matic video-tape, videodisc, compact disc and optical disc. A quick appraisal of the characteristics of these systems will indicate their relevant positions in current and future imaging systems.

The advent of the domestic VHS or Betamax video-tape player opened up a whole range of possibilities for the dissemination of images. Many households now own one of these machines. However, to date, few video-tapes exclusively dedicated to the visual arts have been produced. Those that have been produced have not been great commercial successes. Images stored on Betamax or VHS video-tape are of low resolution, unstable and impermanent. Random access on video-tape is impractical and general access times for image retrieval is slow. Video-tape is thus not a suitable medium for archival storage and overall image quality is low in comparison to colour photography.

The ultimate quality of any of these systems under discussion is determined by the limitation of bandwidth of the electromagnetic spectrum that is devoted to broadcasting the signal. The video signal for domestic television broadcasting is 4 MHz with another 2 MHz for the audio information. VHS video-tape has a video bandwidth of under 2 MHz. U-matic video-tape has a slightly larger bandwidth and videodisc video bandwidth is greater again being nearer 3.2 MHz. However none of these systems has a bandwidth the size of television broadcast quality and therefore all give poorer image quality.

Videodisc has become very popular as an image storage medium though the domestic market has not adopted the new technology either as quickly or in the numbers hoped for by manufacturers such as Sony and Philips, who invented the system.[16] The Dutch Open University makes extensive use of videodisc technology (see chapter 5). The advantages of the videodisc technology are the large numbers of still images which can be stored on a single disc, about 100,000, together with the rapid random access time of individual image recall. (Thirty minutes of moving images can alternatively be stored). A much heralded videodisc of images of Northern Renaissance painting produced by the German publishers Belser Verlag in collaboration with the University of Essen has yet to become commercially available, though a prototype was demonstrated at the 1986 Frankfurt Book Fair. It is believed that the question of reproduction fees may be the reason for its early demise. This is an interesting point since it is possible to encode a videodisc with 100,000 images (50,000 on each side) and the cost of even a token reproduction fee per image would result in an enormous amount for a single 'full' disc. Furthermore the general logistics behind the production of a videodisc are very considerable, particularly in terms of labour. The National Gallery of Art in Washington and The Mauritshuis in The Hague are currently producing videodiscs of paintings from their collections. The Science Museum in London makes extensive use of videodisc to display both still and moving images related to adjacent exhibits. This system is controlled by an 'in house' system using BBC Micro computers and is a good example of how to produce a most efficient and effective interactive video system from a limited financial budget.

The limitations of videodisc are again that overall image quality is poor when compared to colour photography. The information encoded for each image is normally sufficient to fill a domestic TV screen (i.e. 625 lines). Thus a great many poor quality, low resolution images may be stored on a videodisc. The technology is analogue based so is neither very accurate nor permanent. Archival stability of videodiscs are normally guaranteed for ten years but the actual life expectancy is unknown. The practicalities of producing a videodisc are enormous particularly in terms of selection, identification and indexing of the images. This often results in the image quality of the photographic originals on which the disc is based becoming a low priority. However, once made the videodisc can be re-used by simply changing the software interface; there are obvious analogies with the conventional use of a slide library within a teaching environment.

The electronic still camera technology, based on the CCD, has moved rapidly since the early 1980s, though often in fits and starts. However, it is nowhere near as advanced as the technologies used in drum scanning and in terms of image quality it can only just be equated with that of television broadcast quality and the conventional photographic 'disc' camera format. These two points perhaps indicate why, after the much heralded use of electronic still cameras by selected photographers at the Los Angeles Olympics in 1984, there was not an immediate flood of similar cameras for the domestic market into the electronic equipment discount stores in the High Streets. The fact that poor quality colour photographs of track events in the L.A. Olympics could be found on the pages of newspapers in Tokyo a mere two hours after the event was almost irrelevant. It was possible to see live all these events on domestic television, and record them at home. Similarly good quality colour photographs could be found in daily papers the following day.

The camera and film manufacturers now accept that the domestic market wants better quality hard copy prints than is possible from the 'disc' camera format. However, a new breed of 'TV-Photo' hybrid systems appeared within a year of the 1984 Olympics when the Fuji Photo Film Co. Ltd. began marketing in Japan a system whereby fifty standard colour prints could be electronically scanned and stored (as NTSC TV signals) on a 2 inch magnetic disc and displayed on television screens. Such developments are worth noting since such hybrid systems may well play a significant role in future electronic imaging systems. This role may be a temporary stop gap measure. Since in many areas electronic imaging has much ground to make up in order to match conventional colour photography the use of so far unmatched elements of photography within a hybrid electronic-photochemical system may be thrust on electronics manufacturers by market forces. An example of this is the technologies used to produce the interactive optical disc system at the Musée d'Orsay, Paris, which will be discussed below.

It is relevant to point out here that high definition television (HDTV), which has 1200 TV screen lines rather than the standard 625 lines in the U.K. or 525 lines of the U.S.A., has been a marketable reality for several years. However, the television manufacturers not only have to convince the general public to buy the 'new and better' product but also convince the television companies to buy completely new studios to be able to produce television programmes in the new format. The introduction of digital television in the not too distant future is another factor which the television manufacturers must take into account when considering marketing these various new technologies.

Electronic digital images (EDI) can be turned into transparencies or prints. The Mitsubushi G650 seven colour thermal-transfer computer printer has a resolution of 300 dots per inch and can handle up to A3 size paper. PC type computers can drive such printers and it is this type of hybrid system that will play a crucial role in EDI systems until electronic imaging can match and even surpass conventional colour photography in all areas. There are machines currently available which use cathode ray tube guns driven by electronic signals (converted from digital to analogue) to write images onto conventional colour film to produce 35 mm transparencies with 4000 line resolution.

Electronic still camera technology is severely limited in terms of the requirement of high speed image acquisition in order to capture moving scenes. The conventional camera shutter speeds are those aimed for. The CCD electronic still camera works on a system of having a matrix of light sensitive picture elements (pixels) in an area array. When light hits each pixel a electrical charge is created which needs to be transported, processed and stored. In 1985 these CCD area arrays had little more than 400,000 pixels (i.e. a matrix of 500 × 800 pixels) while a disc film frame has about one million pixels and a 35 mm film frame some 12.6 million.[17] By early 1988 Videk, an Eastman Kodak Company, was advertising but not selling (!) an area array CCD camera supposedly 1350 × 1035 pixels. It is believed that Eikonix, another Eastman Kodak company, has produced area arrays far bigger than this but only as part of US Defence Department contracts for military satellites. In all these cases there are problems with the speed of image acquisition, processing and storage. The speed of photo-chemical latent image acquisition is unlikely to be matched by electronic imaging for some time.

When camera shutter speed times are not the determining factor the other system of using a linear array can be used. It is this system which has been used in the scanning industry with great success. Still electronic cameras can also use this system to build up images. The linear array, which can now be as long as 6000 pixels is stepped several thousand times and exposures taken each time. This can, however, be very slow particularly when colour images are required, for the CCD array must either make three exposures (R, G, B) at each stopping point using a colour filter system or scan the image three times, one scan for each primary colour. Eikonix CCD cameras tend to use this latter tri-scan system. However, each scan can be out of registration by as much as 1.7 pixels. It is possible to electronically re-register the three images, but this is a complex and time consuming process. Furthermore, in order for an image with very high resolution of detail in the original to be acquired a system of multiple scanning is necessary. This consists of moving a linear array sensor up and down in a series of strips and then mosaicing the strips together to make the complete image. Such a system requires a very high degree of accuracy since the beginning of each scanned strip much be made to register with the previously scanned strip. Such accuracy is known but is only used over small areas. Zeiss claim that the addressability of the digital motor moving one of their microscopes over its image field is accurate to within 0.25 of a micron of its starting position. This means that it would be possible to accurately return to a pixel when scanning at a resolution of 250 lines/mm. However the Zeiss microscope mentioned has an image field of only a few square centimeters. For a large image area, such as 1500 mm × 1000 mm, a two level system would have to be used. Firstly there would be a 'crude' repositioning device to take the camera/scanner back to a localized area and then a second positioning motor would make the refined repositioning. Such technology currently exists though the times for repositioning are long, often requiring many minutes.

The advent of the CCD, the flatbed scanning systems and new computer hardware and software technologies have given rise to the possibility of a new system of imaging works of art, far superior to that of photography. The control at all levels of image manufacture, storage and retrieval is considerable. It should be pertinent to discuss the merits of the new technology in respect to the limitations of conventional colour photography.

Firstly, tricolour scanning using the additive system is possible and thus a greater gamut of colour can be recorded. Furthermore, it will be possible to use different illuminants from very precise bands of the electromagnetic spectrum. This will permit x-ray, ultra-violet, infra-red as well as 'visible' spectrum recording to be made at a single time. Each pixel can be addressed, measured and calibrated through the use of computer software giving an accuracy hitherto unknown.

The ability to view an image as it is being manufactured is one of the central advantages. A principle element of this electronic immediacy is an insect like acronym named 'WYSIWYG' which stands for 'What-You-See-Is-What-You-Get'. To some experts, the very term 'WYSIWYG' is a misnomer since electronic digital imaging currently relies on analogue CRT monitors to display the images while they are being manufactured. CRTs are based on a system of using bands of red, green and blue phosphors, in what are called triads, to produce a full-colour image. The colour gamut possible using this technology is limited, being far less than the human visual gamut or the gamut possible through the use of conventional colour photography or four colour printing. An increase in the numbers and colours of phosphors would increase the gamut of reproducible colour as does an increase in the number of colours used in the printing industry.

What is perhaps more crucial is that the calibration and definition of the colours produced by emissive screen technologies, such as the CRT, is still very much in its infancy. Committees to advise about international standards are appearing almost week by week. Currently any electronic imaging conferences wishing to have credibility must have an entire session on the topic of calibration of colour monitors. Steps are being made in the right direction but much work must be done before 'WYSIWYG' can become a workable reality. Such a reality is one of the fundamentals necessary for a colorimetric electronic imaging system for two reasons. Firstly, the CRT display is currently the only form of viewing, real-time, an image taken from a CCD device and stored on a computer. Accuracy of the digitally stored data relies to some degree on the accuracy at the display system. It is possible to display images in a numerical form to identify the accuracy of input data. Thus a CCD sensor can be calibrated so that a standard colour or general grey-level reflectance value gives a set numerical reading. Thus 18 per cent reflectance (which is the equivalent of photographic 'mid-gray' card) might give a value of 56 when an 8 bit gray-scale is used. Secondly, CRT displays will in the foreseeable future play a key role in the display of recalled images. Accurately calibrating CRT monitors will enable more accurate evaluation of the image displayed.

The complexities of constructing international standards for colour CRT displays is indicated by the fact that, as yet, it is not known how to compare an image formed by transmitted light (a transparency on a light-box) with an image formed by emissive light (a CRT monitor).[18] Such difficulties in comparison of images produced by transmitted, reflected and emitted light have always existed. Human visual perception has enabled comparisons to be made. However, given the future potential of electronic digital imaging systems, a much fuller and clearer understanding of human visual perception is necessary so that calibration of the various forms of hard- and soft-copy output devices produced from electronic information may lead to optimum image quality.

However, very high quality results are possible using colour CRT monitors for qualitative image analysis as can be testified by the briefest of examinations of the glossy colour magazines which litter the shelves of newsagents. The degree of control and manipulation of a digitized image on a CRT monitor as used in the scanning systems designed by Scitex and Crosfield is not only phenomenal but also one which indicates the potential of electronic digital imaging for the recording and study of works of art. By using computer software during the electronical scanning of works of art, immediate examination and control of the image becomes a reality.

Such interactive control of image acquisition would permit the identification and correction of anomalous reflectances and fluorescence. Furthermore, since each image sensing pixel in the CCD can be addressed and controlled it would be possible to removed extraneous highlight reflections. Similarly, the problems of a large contrast range could be removed. The computer can store a greater contrast range than is the case with conventional photography and a CCD can be calibrated to accept such a range. It is possible in extreme cases, such as a Rembrandt, that two scans would be necessary, one for the highlight areas and one for the shadow areas. The two images could then be electronically merged to produce an overall view with a contrast range closer to that perceived by the human eye than is currently possible.

In terms of image resolution, electronic digital imaging is limited by the number of pixels in the image sensor and the number of exposures made by that sensing device over the object being scanned. The longer or bigger the CCD array and the greater the number of 'strips' (or 'patches' when using an area array) imaged the higher the resolution of detail in the original. One limiting factor to consider is the limit to the resolution of CRT monitors. It has already been stated that HDTV CRT display has double the number of lines of the current European TV 625 line standard. Specialist colour CRT monitors with 2000 lines are produced by firms such as Conrac, Barco and Sony but these can only display the resolution made possible by the type of CCD-based scanning systems outlined above by displaying details from the overall image. Image framestores can display larger images on such 2000 line monitors but only by the monitor acting as a 2000 line 'window' onto a larger 'background' image. Panning around the overall image is thus possible but the capacity of the framestore and the ability of the central processing unit of the computer (CPU) to process the information required for 'window' display and 'background' is currently a limiting factor. However, theoretical and applied research into the ergonomics of the resolution of human visual perception should indicate the optimum resolution required for colour monitors. The crucial parameters are the size of screen and the viewing distance.

A major consideration for any high resolution electronic imaging system is the type of storage medium and the forms and systems of image recall. The amount of digital information that may be gleaned from a painting using a linear array CCD sensor travelling over its surface could be enormous. It has been estimated that 14 megabytes of storage space would be required if a 7 × 9 cms colour transparency was scanned using Red, Green and Blue illumination at a resolution of 40 lines/mm. The ImagiTex monochrome scanner which uses five CCD focal plane linear arrays, each containing 4096, to cover an area 457 × 624 mm at a rate of 44 samples/mm using 8-bit data, produces half a Gigabyte of information. It is important to appreciate that images require considerably more storage space and are more complicated to store than alphanumeric information.

At present optical disc is being promoted as the cheapest and most effective form of mass archival storage. Since the electronic digital image of a painting will not need to be changed in any way (indeed the accuracy, stability and permanence being a fundamental and hitherto unknown reference point) the information will be recorded once but then read many times. Such WORM (Write Once Read Many) systems already exist and coupled to compact disc read only memory (CD-ROM) they are being marketed as the ultimate in mass archival storage. Hitachi produce a CD-ROM capable of storing 552 Megabytes of information (sufficient for the Post Office to store all 23.5 million private and business addresses in the U.K. onto a single compact disc). The 1 Gigabyte write-once 12 ins optical disc is now readily available and 5 and even 10 Gigabyte discs should be commercially available in the not too distant future.

In 1987 the U.K. Public Record Office initiated a pilot project using a Data General optical disc storage system. This development was seen as being an important step in giving optical storage media governmental approval. However, the Central Computer and Telecommunications Agency (CCTA), a unit set up to advise government on applying new technology, has yet to formally approve the new storage medium. The reason behind this is primarily one of the certainty of optical disc stability and permanence. Considerable efforts are made to detect and correct hardware and software errors by special encoding systems on optical discs. On some optical discs, in 14 bits there may be only 8 bits of information while the remaining 6 bits are divided between error detection and correction.[19] Possible disc corruption could be disastrous and such problems have already taken place in Washington D.C. There the Library of Congress started to use an optical disc WORM system but had such considerable data corruption problems that a change from plastic to glass medium discs was necessary.

Currently lifetime guarantees on optical discs are for more than ten years and some, such as those produced by OSI, are guaranteed for as many as thirty years. Claims that discs may remain stable and uncorrupted for as long as 100 years are irrelevant if one imagines the advances in mass archival storage which have taken place over the past few decades or certainly in the thirty years since 1958. However, the market aimed for by optical disc manufacturers is normally a business one where legal requirements about keeping company records (normally in the region of ten years) are paramount and longer disc lifetimes are not a prerequisite.

Recently a new form of digital mass storage has become available with the arrival of digital audio tape (DAT). DAT has sent shudders through the electronics industry. In particular those firms which committed vast amounts of capital to set up the production of compact discs are worried that DAT may take over from CD audio and CD-ROM. DAT may have the advantage of digital encoding but it still has the problems of the stability of the magnetic tape.

Currently the most advanced electronic digital imaging system used within the field of the visual arts is the optical videodisc system at the Musée d'Orsay, Paris which opened to the public in a blaze of Gallic glory in the winter of 1986. From its inception under the aegis of President Pompidou the d'Orsay was seen to be an opportunity to produce a benchmark for innovative museum display techniques for the 1980s and 1990s.

The brief set out for the Musée d'Orsay project stated that there should be a database of 16,000 images from the museum's collection together with some related works from other collections. Textual information should also be available. The system as used by the public would consist of two screens using a single keyboard. One screen would display the image while the other text. Images should appear on the screen within ten seconds of being selected.

The firm chosen to produce the d'Orsay system, and who have subsequently set up two other similar systems in Italy, was Process Systems (also known as PSY) of St Cloud. PSY chose a British image processing hardware system named TOPAZ, manufactured by Primagraphics, as a central part of the overall system which includes an Eikonix 78/99 camera with a linear array of 2048 pixels, a VAX 11/785 computer, and ATG optical Gigadiscs for storage.

By the summer of 1987 just over 4,000 images had been recorded from both flat reflectance copy as well as large format colour transparencies. It has been found that digitizing transparencies is easier than digitizing reflectance copy which is becoming less and less frequent. Digitizing is carried out by placing transparency on a Super Chromega E box which is essentially the light source used in colour enlargers in photographic printing. This light source has dichroic filters which enable it to produce 'white' light which can be minutely adjusted. The Eikonix camera is mounted above the box on an enlarger stand. The first step is to set the light box to 'white' light and then calibrate the camera to this light source. Once this has been done the transparency can be placed onto the light box.

Digitizing is resolved at 1200 × 1024 by stepping the linear array over the image plane of the camera. Such resolution is considerably less than is possible with the 2048 pixel CCD linear array camera. The determining factor is the system of image recall, in this case CRT monitors with a resolution of 1280 × 1024 pixels. The actual resolution of the displayed image is in fact only 1000 × 1000 pixels, the remaining area being a border to the image. This resolution of 1000 × 1000 can theoretically be increased by interpolation algorithms, that is adding between adjoining pixels an extra pixel made up from an average of its surrounding pixels. This is the converse of some image compression algorithms used as a method for reducing storage and for image analysis. In this method a matrix of pixels, say an array 5 by 5, is averaged to produce a single pixel. Both interpolation or compression algorithms are highly problematic.[20]

Each transparency is scanned though a red, green and then blue filter and these separate images appear in sequential overlay on the monitor. The three colours are scanned at 8 bits per colour and then reduced to 16 bits, that is 5 bits per colour per pixel and one bit left — either for addition to a particular colour or for controlling software. However, the addition of the spare bit to one colour does not necessarily produce better overall colour quality since the combination of the three primaries as 5 bit information need not be enhanced by a supplementary bit of information to any one of the colours. Furthermore, though the CCD has far better reciprocity characteristics than conventional colour film these are not totally 'linear'. The level of full brightness possible with the Super Chromega E is often not sufficient for the pixels in the Eikonix camera to record a signal which will reproduce as a good quality colour image. This is often caused by the density (darkness) of the transparency being scanned. The practice is to individually boost each of the three colour signals to use the full 1–255 range of 8 bits of information per colour. Such adjustments may not take into consideration the original interelationship of the three colour signals. Thus when the three boosted colour signals are recombined the colour balance may be very poor indeed.

One example of the problems encountered with scanning transparencies is that of the painting *The Funeral at Ornans* by Gustave Courbet. This painting appears very dark to the human eye even when brightly lit on a Parisian summer's day. The transparency of this painting used for scanning was very dark. Particular care was taken to recalibrate the overall colour using the boosted colour signals. However, members of the curatorial staff were convinced that the overall fidelity of the image was poor, particularly in terms of its apparent darkness. Thus the image of *The Funeral at Ornans* was calibrated to appear on the monitor as a far lighter image showing more detail than the human eye can perceive in 'real life'. The results of such subjective decisions repeatedly appear in the colour reproduction of works of art in many publications. They indicate problems of both the subjective nature of colour memory as well as objective considerations such as the practical problems of reproducing a photographic transparency without being able to compare it with the original. This is of course made even more difficult by what has been already mentioned concerning the problems faced when trying to compare images produced by reflected, emissive and transmitted light. Therefore the subjective correction of colour, contrast and overall appearance which is possible using the d'Orsay system is problematic.

The digitized images made from the photographic colour transparencies have been stored onto optical discs (each holding 1 Gigabyte of information) which have been linked together into what is called a 'daisy-chain'. This system alleviates some of the problems encountered when having to constantly increase the amount of storage space made available for image storage. At the time of writing, the current d'Orsay 'daisy-chain' of optical discs is nowhere near full. The main advantage of using this system is that while each of the optical discs is mounted in a separate cartridge the cartridges do not need to be selected and moved as is the case when using the so called 'juke-box' system. In this 'juke-box' system individual unmounted discs must be mechanically moved and played. Information recall and access times can be as much as fifteen seconds for unmounted cartridges though this can be reduced to about four seconds for a mounted system. The primary disadvantage of a 'daisy-chain' system is that in order to remove the necessity for slow moving and mechanical optical character reading components, only one side of each optical disc may be used for storage.

The d'Orsay system has primarily two parts. The VAX 11/785 computer, the optical disc storage, the scanning system and the textual database software system are all in one corner room above the museum's main entrance facade. The public access to the system is almost as far way as it could be in the other corner of the building, placed on a mezzanine gallery. Here one finds several 'workstations' each consisting of two monitors and having a keyboard built flush into the flat table top and under a thick, flexible plastic covering.

The system is menu driven and has an 'adult' and 'children' mode. As is so often the case many children are far more computer literate than their parents and invariably end up using the 'adult' system while it had been known for some academic grown-up art historians to become enthralled with the system designed for 'children' which is based on a game of French 'hangman'! One member of the CHArt Committee recently spent most of his first use of the machine playing the 'hangman' game and quickly concluded that the answer was always Degas or Cezanne!

The 'adult' system uses the two monitors to display an image on one and text (mostly based on a standard, if somewhat restricted, museum or gallery catalogue) on the other. Searches can be made to discover what images are on the database. Several fields can be called up so that one might ask how many paintings by Cezanne with tables, apples, women and a mirror are on the database. The answer is displayed as a text list and the images can then be called up as required. Obviously more sophisticated software could be written for the system. However, there is some hesitancy from museum and gallery curatorial staff in general to make such a system into a complex and comprehensive image and text database. This hesitancy is centred around the belief that the public may well spend more time playing with the electronic images than looking at the real thing in the museum. The design of future electronic image display systems for other museums has alrady taken this into account. Indeed it looks likely thst one way of encouraging the public to go and look at the original objects is to have low resolution display monitors.

Elementary mistakes at the scanning stage have not helped image quality. The images, as displayed, are only 1000 × 1000 pixels and the viewing distance is close (being about 60 cms). Some transparencies or reflectance copies were not scanned full frame. The result is that as little as 50 per cent of the screen is filled with the image, the remainder being an 'off white' background. Some of the questions from the menu driven control sometime necessitate a caption or inscription on the image to be read. This is sometimes quite impossible for the resolution is insufficient.

As has been indicated above, the calibration of colour CRT monitors is a highly complex matter. The 'off white' background chosen for the d'Orsay displays was selected from 100 electronically generated colours by subjective testing methods. The colour chosen is rather imprecise and distracting since one perceives it as being very impure and an indication of the overall image quality. The use of a 'cleaner' looking white for the border would help perceived image quality. The CRT monitors are calibrated only once a week and on the author's two visits to the d'Orsay to look at the system it was visibly noticeable that no monitor matched another in terms of the colour of the border surround.

Although the Musée d'Orsay system can enable images to be summoned within six or seven seconds (well within the contract stipulations) this is not always the case. The system works with one graphics controller for two monitors/workstations. Thus if the same image is called up simultaneously, a 'queue' forms and the recall time lengthens. Quite how long this image recall time might be if every workstation was asked to call the same image simultaneously is not clear but there is no doubt that it would be a problem.

The innovation of the Musée d'Orsay system is that it exists; that it has found its way across the drawing board into the public domain. However the success of the system is tempered by the lessons which have been learnt. Firstly, for all its power and sophistication, the VAX 11/785 is not the most suitable computer for such a system. This is not to say that it could not handle the task, indeed during 1987 only two or so of the shutdowns of the entire system could be found to have originated in a fault in the VAX, but that other computers could have handled the recall of images more efficiently and thus more quickly. Subsequent systems will have to use far more precise overall design specifications for the selection of all hardware and in particular the computer which runs the whole show. Similarly, the use of single graphics controllers for two workstations was not appropriate.

The third lesson learnt is perhaps the most pertinent one. When the system was on the drawing board it was decided to locate the core in the corner room of the main facade. It was pointed out that it would be difficult to control the air-conditioning in this area and this has proved to be the case. The humidity levels in this room have lead to several automatic shutdowns of the entire system. Furthermore, the public workstations in the mezzanine gallery have also had to be shut down several times, again due to humidity level. The digitizing screens are shut down first because they produce most heat. While it may be possible to improve the main computer and optical disc rooms the perennial problem of humidity levels in a general public gallery are almost impossible to fully cater for. How can the humidity level in a public gallery be kept under control when forty rain soaked visitors may arrive en masse, walk through many galleries and then stand in front of a painting, or in the case of the Musée d'Orsay a computer, for twenty minutes?

This paper has been a highly selective overview of the current relationship between present electronic imaging technologies. It is neither comprehensive nor exhaustive for the simple reason that the interelationships between art and these scientific developments have hardly yet been forged let alone been given a clear direction in which to take the study of art into the twenty-first century. The Musée d'Orsay system has been described at length not because of its use of any new technology but because it is currently the most advanced of any type being employed within a visual arts environment. No theoretical or applied research was necessary to construct this system. Nevertheless, this system in many ways heralds the dawn of a new era not only in the dissemination of images of works of art but also the possibilities of computers to produce a new tool for those who wish to study art either as amateurs or professionals. The possibilities of such a technological tool to synthesise images and text into a new form of visual communication is an exciting expectation.

Quite how academic art history, the discipline from which the author has approached computers and electronic digital imaging, will be influenced, perhaps directed, by computers will perhaps become apparent by the end of the twentieth century. From its inception, the discipline of art history has been racked by insecurities. These insecurities have in part been brought about by sensitivity to the often strongly stated scepticism of more ancient, and in some respects more clearly definable disciplines, such as history, towards a form of academic training which is in essence not much more than one hundred years old. Art historians continue to ponder over how to define the discipline in which they find themselves. Their quandary is that art history's greatest strength, that being that there is no other academic discipline or area of human interest which cannot be related to the study of the history of art, is also ironically its greatest apparent weakness. How can one be a master of such an imprecise academic discipline when being an intellectual jack of all trades is an impossibility?

This is neither a new concept nor, more importantly, one restricted to the academic study of art. Yet art history has been until very recently reluctant to delve into the scientific disciplines in order to build a more comprehensive methodology which would not only give far more substance to the discipline as a whole but also perhaps remove some of the elements at the root of the insecurities mentioned above. One such scientific area is that of photography. Given that photographs and the photo-mechanical reproduction are such essential tools of the art historian, it is more than a little surprising that practically no emphasis is placed on the understanding of the essentials of the science of photography or how they should be used within the methodology of the discipline of art history. In many respects, art history has never fully come to terms with the use of photography as an essential tool. One is almost led to despair when one hears that in 1988 some of the most eminent art historians on the planet are convinced that in order to properly study the history of art in a truly academic way one must use black and white photographs since they are always 'more accurate' than colour photographs!

In certain respects this is methodological water which has passed long ago under the bridge of academia. Art history once again faces new technology which may substantially change the course of its history. The arrival of computers and the possibilities of electronic digital imaging for the recording, study and dissemination of the world about us and works of art in particular should be seen as most exciting. Just as in the Victorian era the blending of the sciences with the arts was seen as the norm rather than the exception, so those studying art either in an amateur or professional capacity should adopt and adapt the new technologies to open for exploration hitherto unrecognized avenues. The complexities of the technology should not be seen to be a hindrance. One does not have to know how to design and build a Grand Prix racing car in order to drive and enjoy the possibilities of a more conventional road going machine.

Notes

1. This article is based on a paper given at the April 1985 meeting of CHArt and a paper titled 'Electronic Digital Imaging and Art History; Advantages and desirability' presented at the symposium on Colour Imaging Systems held at Clare College, Cambridge 22–26 September 1986. For a more detailed account of electronic digital imaging one may consult A. Hamber, 'Colour Photography vs Electronic Digital Imaging As A System for Recording Works of Art' in *Journal of Photographic Science* Vol. 35, 1987 pp. 200–8. It has not been possible to reproduce the illustrations to either of these papers in this article.

2. J. Ward and S. Stephenson, *Printed Light: The Scientific Art of William Henry Fox Talbot and David Hill with Robert Adamson*, Edinburgh, 1986 p. 89.
3. Quoted from the *Photographic Journal* by Alex Strasser in *Immortal Portraits*, London and New York 1941 and cited in A. Scharf, *Art and Photography*, London 1968 p. 334. This quotation is from an interview between Frank Sutcliffe and John Ruskin in the early 1870s.
4. R.M. Evans, 'Visual Processes and Colour Photography', *Journal of the Optical Society of America*, Vol. 33, No. 11, November, 1943 pp. 579–614.
5. In the collection of the Musée des Beaux-Arts, Agen there are several colour photographs by Ducon du Hauron of paintings. (I am grateful to Anne-Marie Esquirol for this information.) The International Museum of Photography at George Eastman House, Rochester has a colour photograph by Charles Cros of an eighteenth century portrait. Aaron Scharf, in *Art and Photography*, London, 1974 p. 362, cites a letter from Cros to Edouard Manet thanking the artist for the loan of a painting which he (Cros) had photographed in colour.
6. Magenta is a equal mixture of red and blue. Yellow is an equal mixture of red and green and Cyan is an equal mixture of green and blue.
7. Quoted from A. Warburg, *Gesammelte Schriften*, ed. G. Bing, Berlin, 1932, I, 253 by T. Fawcett in 'Visual Facts and the Nineteenth Century Art Lecture', *Art History*, Vol. 6 No. 4, December 1983, p. 457.
8. The most readable account of the history of colour photography is still Brian Coe's *Colour Photography: The first hundred years 1840–1940*, London, 1978.
9. S.J. Williamson and H.Z. Cummins, *Light and Color in Nature and Art*, New York, John Wiley, 1983, p. 15.
10. N. Ohta in *Photographic Science and Engineering*, Vol. 27, No. 5 September/October 1983, pp. 193–201.
11. Yu. N. Gorokhovskii, *Spectral Studies of the Photographic Process*, London, 1965.
12. D. Levinstone and R. Kee, 'Overview of System Requirements for Electronic Still Photography' in the *Advanced Printing of Paper Summaries for Electronic Imaging '85*, Exposition and Conference, Boston 7–10 October, 1985, pp. 29–37.
13. J.H. Townsend and N.H. Tennet, 'The Photochemical and Thermal Stability of Colour Transparencies' in *Colour Imaging Systems* (ed. M. Pointer), The Royal Photographic Society, 1987 pp. 117–23.
14. L.W. Sipley, *A Half Century of Colour*, New York, 1951 pp. 65–6.
15. G.G. Field, 'The Evolution of Colour Scanner Technology' in *Colour Imaging Systems* (ed. M. Pointer), The Royal Photographic Society, 1987, pp. 62–8.
16. For a general account of videodisc technology see R.S. Adrain, C.R. Davis, T.W. Russell and W. Burns, 'Laser Video Disc Archival Storage' *Journal of Photographic Science*, Vol. 35, 1987 pp. 97–106.

17. D. Levinstone and R. Kee, 'Overview of System Requirements for Electronic Still Photography' In *Advanced Printing of Paper Summaries for Electronic Imaging '85*, Boston 7–10 October 1985, pp. 29–37.
18. One colorimetry-based metric for emissive displays (i.e. colour CRT monitors) was accepted in 1986 in draft form by the American Standards Committee for Human Factors Engineering of Visual Display Terminal Workstations (ANSI Standard HFS–100).
19. D. Archer, 'Project Quartet-information exchange in the Research Community'. Paper presented at colloquium on 'Optical Mass Data Storage' at The Institute of Electrical Engineers, London, 22 December, 1986.
20. See A. Hamber, 'Review — "Art analysis: probing beneath the image IEEE Spectrum June 1986 0018-9235/86/0600-0066"' *CHArt Newsletter*, 3, Summer/Autumn 1986 pp. 11–3 and J.F. Asmus 'Digital Image Processing in Art Conservation', *BYTE*, March 1987, Vol. 12, No. 3, pp. 151–68.

3

Art History Core Videodisc Retrieval Project

Julie Hausman

The University of Iowa has long been a leader in the field of educational applications of videodisc technology. Weeg Computing Center's Computer Assisted Instruction Laboratory (CAI Lab) has sponsored a number of videodisc projects since the mid 1970s, including a pediatrics diagnostic project, an educational classroom behaviour record evaluation project, a LeMaze instruction project and a film editing instruction project. Several of these projects have won major awards. There was also a pilot project with the School of Art and Art History in which 1,000 images of Dürer and Raimondi prints from the School's Bartsch Collection were placed on videodisc with a computerized retrieval program. While this project was small in scope and application, it did demonstrate the feasibility of such projects when applied to a subject like art history. It appeared that issues such as image quality, ease of use, and length of retrieval time could be satisfactorily addressed.

I had read the report on this project prior to accepting my present position as Curator of Visual Materials in the School of Art and Art History. When Joan Sustik Huntley, a research specialist at the CAI Lab, approached me in my first week on the job about the possibility of doing a second project with Art & Art History and several other departments, I enthusiastically agreed. This began another major project under Weeg's CAI Lab sponsorship.

We selected the Core collection of slides as a basis for the Art History project. The Core collection is a 'mini' collection from which introductory art history classes are taught. It is comprised of the monuments of art history as illustrated in introductory text books. These slides cut across the range of the entire collection. Thus they would provide a test of the feasibility of constructing a database for the whole slide collection at some future time. The slides in the Core collection, being most in demand, are consequently the most restricted in use. Only Core class instructors are allowed access to them. Other faculty or students are not allowed to use them. Multiple copies of a permanent, nonfading videodisc could give access not only to faculty and teaching assistants in all departments of the University but also to students. These images also have the largest potential for classroom application, not just in art history but in other areas such as English, comparative literature, foreign languages, history, etc. (In fact, the Communications Studies program is already using the disc, even though it was only mastered in December 1985, when the database was not yet complete.)

I began selecting material for the disc in 1983 in conjunction with a project to evaluate and upgrade the Core colection. I conducted a survey to see what we had and did not have with respect to several art history texts with special attention to Helen Gardner's *Art Through the Ages*[1], which is the text currently used in our survey class. As a result, we made about 1,000 new images for this joint project.

There was no preconceived limit to the number of slides to be used in the project. A videodisc will hold up to 54,000 images on a side. We had originally estimated 8,000 to 11,000 slides anticipating 14,000 to 18,000 total images on the disc when details and close-ups of slides were included. These estimates were made when the selection process was only partially complete, after the first half of the Core class slides had been surveyed. Insufficient allowance was made for the fact that the second half of the course covers more material, especially in the area of architecture. We wound up with 30,000 images.

A number of criteria were used in the selection of slides:

1. We considered significance of the represented work in the history of art. Is it a major monument or of some special significance?
2. Slides were selected for the utility of a particular view or detail. If a work was selected, attempts were made to include significant details. In the case of sculpture and architecture, multiple views, interiors, exteriors and plans were included. If a work was significant enough to include, we attempted to give it fairly complete visual documentation.
3. The quality of the slide was considered although no slide was

eliminated simply because it was low quality. If the slide showed something not included in any other slide it was used on the videodisc regardless of its quality. The project is also viewed as archival and thus represents the slides that are available in the collection regardless of quality.

4. If the work was illustrated in a major art history text we attempted to include slides of it on the videodisc. Texts considered were Gardner,[1] Janson,[2] Hartt,[3] Honour & Fleming,[4] Canaday & Taylor.[5] All are either in use at Iowa, or favourites of art history instructors there.

Slides from all sources were used including original slides, copywork and commercially produced slides with the majority being from copywork. We were advised by the University lawyer that if the disc were not distributed or used off campus we should be covered by the educational 'fair use' guidelines. We sought permission from commercial vendors whose slides we wished to include. In some cases we received no response which we took to indicate there was no objection. Only one vendor was so restrictive in conditions that we decided to not to use their slides. Most others granted permission, and we are deeply grateful to all of them.

Because there was no accessioning system for slides at the University of Iowa when I came and since the cataloguing system is not discreet, it was necessary to implement an accessioning system both for the sake of the collection and the requirements of the project. Each slide had to have a unique identifier. Slides from the collection were given accession numbers as they were selected for the project along with all new slides added to the collection.

The transfer process which produced the master tape for the videodisc was done by the University Video Center as part of a larger CAI project completed by a Video Production Grant designed to support campus video needs. The Office of Educational Development and Research provided funding for assistantships in Art History to prepare the slides for the transfer process and to research on the database.

Slides were loaded into carousel trays for the transfer. Each tray was accompanied by a list of the slides in the tray. Each slide was identified by accession number and a brief description. Extra sheets were included giving directions for detail shots including slot number, accession number and description of desired close-up.

Some compromises were necessary to accomplish the transfer

process. Initially the Video Center requested that slides be divided into horizontal and vertical images. This requirement was later dropped because it did not save the time they thought it would while it was extremely time consuming for the staff. Since many slides were being used in classes, we could not always schedule production to keep slides in either chronological or catalogue order. Thus Roman material comes before Greek material, for example. Once the initial tape was made we lacked the funds to re-edit it, so logical order was sacrified on the disc itself. We did not view this as a major drawback since the disc is designed to be computer controlled.

Just before production was scheduled to begin the videodisc of National Gallery, Washington, D.C. came out. We had already decided that each slide would be shown completely with a border, with close-ups to be made if desired. The National Gallery disc convinced us that a grey rather than a black border added measurably to the overall image quality. The grey border significantly reduces contrast problems. While adding grey borders involved a major amount of video production work, we felt it was an important enhancement to the disc.

A further problem we encountered was the amount of conservation work necessary to prepare the slides for the transfer. Dirt, Newton rings (an optical interference pattern), fungus, precipitates, even fingerprints can show up on the videotape and subsequently the disc. The slides must be clean for the transfer process. Portions of our collection spent many years in storage in a basement room where the humidity was very high. In these areas extensive cleaning was often necessary. This added considerably to the amount of time necessary for the preparation of slides.

The transfer process itself was done by projecting the slides onto a matt white surface. The image was recorded using a Sony M3A video camera with a modified lens for computing exposure control and an Ampex VPR-3 Still Frame Storer. The grey border is generated electronically and adjusted manually. A grid is superimposed on the slide to serve as a guide.

Consideration and decisions for the database began at the same time as selection of the slides. Initially, I made a rather long list of what I would like the database to do. We were able to incorporate much of the list into the project. We wanted to make the database as flexible as possible within the limits of what was available to us. We realized that variable length text fields would be ideal to handle certain items desired in the database like subject and commentary on the work. INFOtext which runs on the Prime minicomputer was the only choice of the text management software available. None of the availiable software for microcomputers was quite adequate for our purposes. Thus the issue of whether to have a self-contained system housed in the Office of Visual Materials or to use the University's time shared computer system was resolved for us by the choice of INFOtext. Besides offering variable length text fields, INFOtext permits indexing down to the word level producing a dictionary which makes searches speedier. It allows use of a synonym file which can be used to handle alternate spellings, abbreviations and synonyms.

The retrieval categories or items in the database are of three different types. The first are fixed length character and integer fields which contain basic information about the work of art including artist, title or description, scope, medium and materials, dates, location, and subclass or style. The second are fixed length character and integer fields which contain indexing material about the slide including videodisc frame number, accession number, classification or catalogue number, source of the slide and detail information (portion). The third type are variable length text fields for subject, texts and comments. Subject can include key subject terms and a visual and iconographic description of the work. The text field will initially include references to the textbooks listed earlier, but could be used to include as many references as desired. The comments field can be used for a variety of purposes including remarks about the work itself such as provenance and condition to critical remarks to commentary directed to specific university classes.

The equipment for the project includes the Prime minicomputer in the Computing Center where the database is stored. IBM-PCs are used as terminals by means of an emulator program developed at Weeg Computing Center for this application. The PCs were chosen because they can be used as stand alone micros when not in use as terminals. They are equipped with two asynchronous communications cards, one to communicate with the Prime via a Sytec cable and the other to communicate with the Pioneer LD-V6000 industrial videodisc player. Pioneers were chosen because of their excellent playback capability and their record for reliable performance. The images are displayed on a Sony Trinitron 1271Q colour monitor. Costing about $700.00, it gives as good resolution as I have seen under $5000. This is our current equipment configuration. We have Tandy 100 model computers to control the videodisc in the classroom where access to the database is not necessary. Also for classroom use are two Sony 722Q1 colour video projectors.

Central to the project are the programs for accessing the database and videodisc at the same time. We have two different menus, an administrator's menu and an end-user's menu. Both are designed to be 'user friendly'. The user's menu allows one to search the database and display records. The administrator's menu does everything the user's menu does, and has options to add data, update data or exit to the programming level. Both menus allow for the printing of data.

The heart of the disc and the database is the search menu. The search fields are listed down the screen with command options listed across the bottom of the screen. To search any field the user enters the number of that field. This causes the cursor to move to that field and the value to be searched for is entered. The search option is then selected. A status line at the bottom of the screen informs the user that the computer is searching. Once the search is complete it tells how many records have been selected. The search menu can search more than one field for multiple values simultaneously. In addition to searching any of the fields in the database, a free-form search can be done where all indexed fields are searched for the listed value(s). The user may then select the display option to view the selected records and images.

The display menu shows the basic record while the image is shown on the monitor. By selecting options at the bottom of the display screen the user can view other information about the image including location, subject, comments, text and indexing information. The user may also go forward (or backward) through the selected group of images either one at a time or by any number desired.

For classroom use, a Tandy 100 model computer can be programmed to show pre-selected groups of images in any order desired. While Art and Art History has not been able to use the disc in the classroom yet because the equipment was slow in arriving, Communications Studies which has a brand new facility is already using it in the classroom.

We are now past the half way point. Since 1982 when the decision to do the project was made we have selected the slides, designed the database, produced the disc, completed most of the programming and begun data research and data entry. Currently we have 2,326 records in the database.

There remain 28,000 images to research and enter. We are also in the process of producing a 'mini index' to the disc for use until the main database is complete. This index should be done sometime in early 1988. We expect to be using the disc in art history classes later in the spring or by the fall of 1988. Some minor programming changes remain to be done and a method for allowing other departments access to the database and programs must be installed. Finally we must evaluate the project for its effectiveness and impact.

Because of the current economic depression in agriculture in Iowa which has drastically reduced state revenues and consequently regents' funding, it is not clear when the University will be able to commit funds to complete the project. Outside funding is being sought and work will continue as rapidly as we are able.

Notes

1. Gardner, Helen, *Gardner's Art Through the Ages*, 7th ed. rev. by Horst de la Croix and Richard G. Tansey, New York, Harcourt, Brace, Jovanovich, 1980.
2. Janson, H.W., *History of Art: a Survey of the Major Visual Arts from the Dawn of History to the Present Day*, rev. and enl. ed., London Thames & Hudson, 1977.
3. Hartt, F., *A History of Italian Renaissance Art*, rev. and enl. ed., London, Thames & Hudson, 1980.
4. Honour, H. and Fleming, J.A., *A World History of Art*, London, Macmillan, 1982.
5. Canaday, J.E., *A History of Western Art*.

4

Electronic Images: The Aga Khan Program for Islamic Architecture Videodisc Project

Lisa M. Kamisher

This paper discusses the work being carried out in the Aga Khan Program for Islamic Architecture's department of Information Services and Technology. The basic research agenda is to create a deliverable system that combines computer software and optical disc technology for the study of historical and contemporary Islamic architecture. This effort culminated in a project called Images System.

The topics addressed cover the concepts, design premises, components and operation of the original prototype system. It also examines new development using techniques for image digitization. The paper concludes with a look at future enhancements and opportunities.

Concepts and design premises

The Aga Khan Program for Islamic Architecture is a graduate level academic, library and research program carried out jointly by Harvard University and the Massachusetts Institute of Technology. It was established in 1979 under a permanent endowment from His Highness the Aga Khan to promote the study and teaching of art, architecture and urbanism. Funding was also made available for limited term research in the Information Services and Technology department. Since 1981 a variety of projects have been carried out resulting in the Images System.

In conceptualizing the objectives of the Images System it was decided to create a prototype that integrated textual and visual information. The logical choice for entering, maintaining and searching printed information was a database. On the non-print side, videodiscs were attractive because of their archival characteristics, replicability, dense storage of colour images, and random access to single frames.

We knew that videodisc images could not replace the high quality of original 35 mm slides and photographs. Instead, they would serve as a reference to the original material. In the final assessment we opted for merging technologies that could handle high speed retrieval of images with the ability to search and display text. The result was a computer controlled database and optical videodisc presented to the user through a menu system.

In order to build a new resource tailored to the subject area of Islamic architecture the system was developed in close association with intended users. This community included students and faculty in architectural design and history as well as managers of visual materials. Our objectives included creating a model that could be installed and tested at the two universities in the Aga Khan Program; the Massachusetts Institute of Technology's Rotch Visual Collection and Harvard University's Fine Arts Library visual collection. We did not undertake work in the area of picture transmission. Instead, we assumed storage of the images at the installation site through local distribution of the videodisc.

Finally, the information had to be transportable to other sites within the Islamic world that may vary in the level of technological sophistication and resources. This led to a sequenced videodisc that can be used as an electronic picture library functioning independently from the computer. The videodisc is arranged by geographic location, building type, and alphabetically by building name. To support this use a printed index listing brief descriptions for every image is provided.

Components of the system

The user builds a search through a menu driven system that results in a series of images. These pictures are displayed on a monitor along with associated information shown on the screen of a personal computer.

Informational elements in the system are in two formats: text and pictures. The pictures are stored on a twelve inch laser reflective, optical videodisc. It is mastered in the NTSC American format and contains over 30,000 still frames from 35 mm slides and black and white photographs. Most of this material was gathered from the Aga Khan Program Archives, a repository that holds the right to reproduce the pictures for educational purposes. Copyright clearances were obtained for the rest of the original photography so that the disc could be distributed. Title slides of place and monument names, as well as maps, were generated through the use of a computer paint system.

The text information is primarily a database that prodvides basic identification for 85 per cent of the images. The remaining 15 per cent are described in-depth. Each image in this 15 per cent subset is individually indexed with over fifty fields of information including: building identification by name, type, location, date, dynasty, patron and architect; subject analysis of the picture's content, along with construction materials; bibliographic references; and record keeping data.

When utilizing the prototype Images System the user can search only on this subset of fully indexed data. However, if one moves to any image on the videodisc minimal, if not detailed, identification is shown. To insure a standardized use of terminology for indexing and retrieval of the architectural images, a controlled vocabulary of over 5,000 terms was established.

The system is composed of multiple software and hardware components. The software that controls the system combines off the shelf and custom designed programs. The two commercial packages are PC/FOCUS, a hierarchical database, and GEM, a graphics package. The custom software consists of a set of programs written in the C language. These programs are implemented to create a menu system that makes the command language of the database searching transparent to the user. It also enables the user to build a search strategy and customize the results.

The hardware consists of an IBM XT or AT personal computer with a mouse input device; a videodisc player and monitor for display of images; and a printer for producing hard copy of the text. The configuration does not include equipment to produce photographic prints, slides or paper copies of the pictures.

Operation of the system

The Images System is set up as a public access tool in a library or visual collection. It is currently being subject to a limited period of testing and evaluation. LEARN, SEARCH, FRAMELISTS, SCAN, SYSTEM, and EXIT constitute the major modules of the system (Fig. 1).

LEARN is an interactive tutorial designed to demonstrate standard

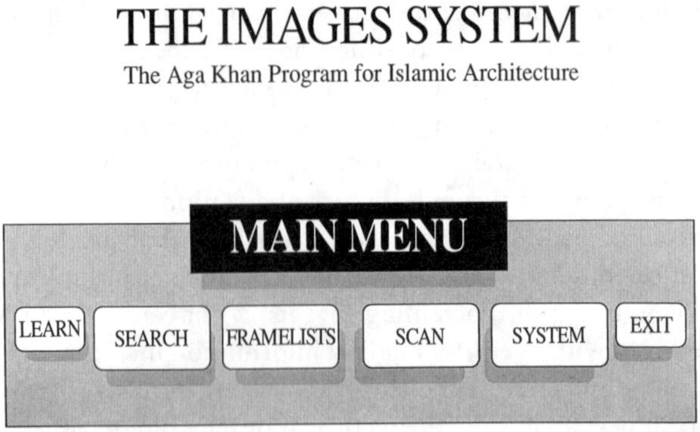

Figure 1.

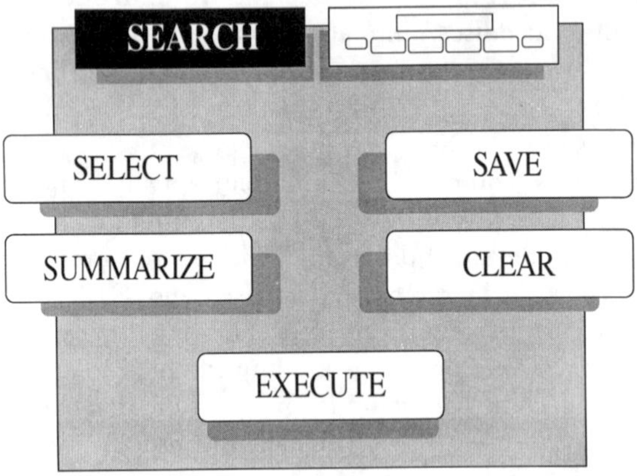

Figure 2.

conventions for operating the menu driven interface through use of a mouse and minimal keyboard entry.

SCAN is the mode for browsing the videodisc randomly. Alternatively, SEARCH offers retrieval of images based on a set of user defined criteria. It includes selecting search terms from authority lists of valid descriptors, summarizing the strategy and executing it (Fig. 2).

FRAMELISTS lets the user work with the results of a search by reviewing images and text. At any point in the review process a user can save the list of images, on a diskette, for presentation at a later time. Framelists can also be transferred to an on-line order form for

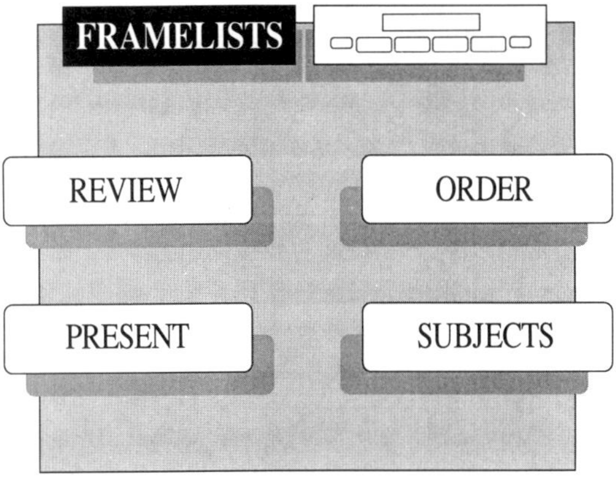

Figure 3.

requests of reproductions of the original 35 mm slides and photographs (Fig. 3).

While reviewing, the user can rearrange, add or delete images on the list of results. Related visual material such as plans and elevations are accessible immediately and additional information including historical data, bibliographic references to publications used in indexing and terms used to describe the images are available. This descriptive text can be annotated with personalized comments about the image and both indexing and personal data can be printed (Fig. 4).

SYSTEM provides a means for managing files of framelists and search strategies. SYSTEM offers saving, loading, merging and erasing functions (Fig. 5).

New development

Users of the videodisc want the ability to directly control the visual presentation of information within the system. However, in its present state the Images System only permits viewing single images in succession. To create subroutines for manipulating images we have experimented with digitization techniques. An AT&T TARGA graphics board captures the analog signal on the videodisc and translates it into digital information that can be computer controlled.

The software to support this development in the Aga Khan Program is called LightTable. It is a paradigm intended to simulate the flexible environment of viewing and sorting slides on a light box. The

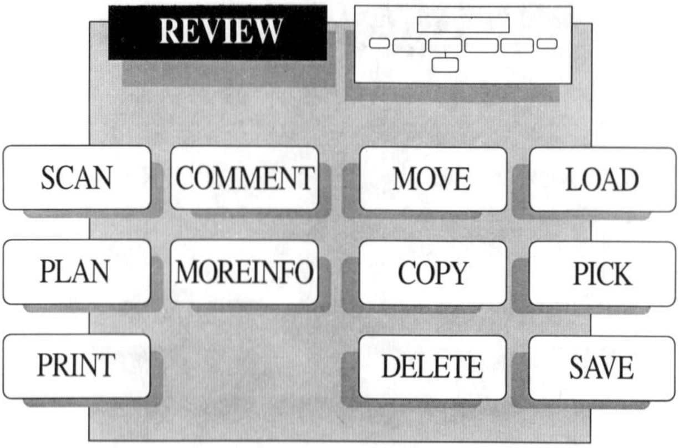

Figure 4.

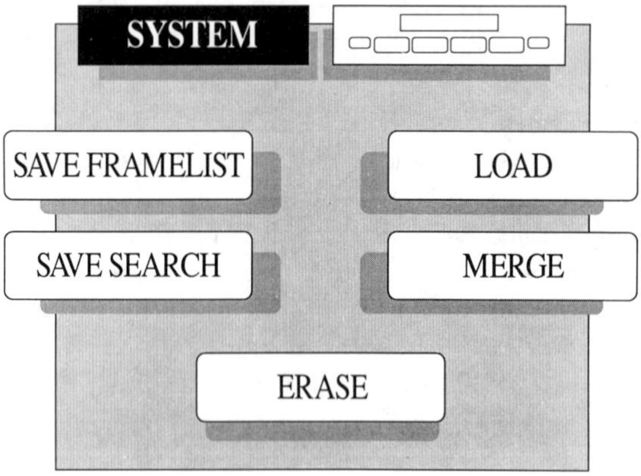

Figure 5.

programs for the system are written in the C language. The primary features are designed to shrink videodisc images so multiple frames can be compared and contrasted, to rearrange and annotate the small images, to enhance the clarity of line drawings, and to control the display parameters of the visual information.

LightTable functions are performed through a series of pop-up menus that contain commands. The Main menu accesses a Videodisc menu that contains actions for control of the disc, step forward and step back, one image at time, browse at a fixed rate, search for a particular image by its frame number, and display or remove the frame number on the monitor.

To shrink an image and make a 'slide' the create command is selected from either the Main menu or Videodisc menu. Slides can be continuously added to the LightTable and the list can be named, saved, and reloaded through commands on the Main menu. Delete allows the user to eliminate one slide at a time or all slides currently on the LightTable.

The clarity and contrast of line drawings on the videodisc are not optimal. However, digitization is particularly appropriate for addressing this situation. The drawing can be translated into pure black or white pixels and the user given the choice of selecting the desired level of contrast. Once this selection is made the 'enhance' on command is executed to create a high contrast slide image.

To change the order and location of the slides on the LightTable, all menus are clicked off by the mouse. An image is made 'active' by pointing the cursor and clicking the mouse again. Any 'active' slide can be dragged to another position on the monitor. Once a slide is 'active' the 'more info' command allows the user to annotate it with a very brief caption.

Customization of the display parameters include clearing the background image on the videodisc so that only the small slides will be shown. Once this is done the solid gray background can be changed to another colour. Conversly, all the slides can be removed, leaving only the full size videodisc image. If the monitor has more slides than can be viewed on a single screen the scroll up and scroll down commands will move the display.

Future enhancements

The Aga Khan Program would like to transform the operational prototype into a robust turnkey system designed for distribution to learning centers in the Islamic world. While this requires a certain amount of reprogramming, to improve performance and insure maintainability, it offers new opportunities for enhancements in the areas of visual display, a revised approach to indexing and user supplied data.

One major improvement would be the integration of LightTable with the rest of the system. This would link search results to display and manipulation of multiple images and create a more flexible environment for handling visual information. Another significant change would be to make all 30,000 images searchable by place, building name and type.

Experimentation with item level, in-depth subject indexing for pictures led to the conclusion that it is extremely labor intensive and subjective. In order to create a more production oriented system only basic level indexing should be provided. Yet, it is important to maintain the potential for augmenting the information.

In its first iteration the controlled vocabulary was implemented as a cataloging tool. If it is installed on-line it can become part of a personal workspace where the user could reference the information and assign validated terms. These terms would also be searchable. For example, if an urban planner determined that the presence of vehicular traffic is an important feature in a series of images, he or she could assign the term and then find all instances of vehicular traffic, where designated.

Such a controlled manner of indexing and retrieval would be offered in conjunction with the ability to search user supplied comments of free text. In this scenerio trained cataloguers would provide basic information while scholars and practicioners augmented the data according to their own research requirements.

The Images System is a functional prototype currently installed in two university settings. An evaluation process is underway to assess the scope of work necessary to create a more robust version that includes the enhancements we have targeted. During 1988 the Aga Khan Program is looking forward to meeting the challenge of producing this improved system for distribution.

5

The Dutch Open University Visual Arts Videodisc Project

Wim Jansen

Introduction

Interactive video can be defined as the integrated use of interactive computer programs and audio-visual materials. To give the computer random access to both audio and visual data, this information is put on a videodisc.

The use of this integrated medium in education is now emerging. In the founding charter of the Open University of the Netherlands as an institute of higher education a special objective was formulated towards 'developing innovations in Dutch higher education'. It was felt that a new institution with a strong emphasis on the educational sciences, both in didactic and educational technology, would be able to give a new impetus to teaching in higher education in general. Dissemination of these stimuli would be guaranteed because the Open University has strong working relationships with all Dutch universities and a growing number of higher vocational schools.

This Visual Arts project is the first to be undertaken in the Cultural Sciences department of the Open University.

The Dutch Open University

Characteristics of distance education

The Dutch Open University provides higher education in the form of courses for seven academic disciplines. These courses comprise of between 50 and 250 study hours and consist of modules, mostly of 100 study hours. During the founding stage of the institution, the conditions for 'open' learning and, as a consequence, the conditions for teaching and course development, were stated as encompassing four characteristics of 'freedom':

> *Freedom of admission*: Although there is a minimum entrance requirement, no formal qualification is necessary to enrol at the university.
>
> *Freedom of time*: Students may choose where and when to study and are limited only by logistical constraints.
>
> *Freedom of place*: Students can study where they please, here again only being limited by necessary logistical constraints.
>
> *Freedom of subject*: There is no fixed curriculum. The student can chose from a number of well-defined courses, although, of course, not every combination of courses leads to a regular degree.

The practical realization of the above characteristics is that self-contained printed material is sent to the student's home. Audio-visual and computer-based material together with — to a lesser degree — personal tutoring is utilized where learning goals are unattainable through the sole use of the printed materials.

It should be emphasized that these media (printed materials, audio-visual and computer-based materials) were not meant to be seen as alternatives, one replacing the other. Courses can and often are effectively taught through the use of printed materials. Specific and especially didactic requirements can induce the need for the utilization of one or more of the other media, but 'only' as a functional and complementary addition to the course. Consequently no single medium is regarded or put forward for use as a separate entity but all media used are part of an interdependent and integrated 'mediamix'. This implies that the selection, design, development, production and tuition of both the content and the media-formats for any given course are also taken up in an integrated (team) approach.

At present all the non-printed material is centred within a number of study-centres, spread throughout the country. The locations are chosen in such a way that most students live within 30 kms of a study-centre. These study-centres are envisaged as 'facility-houses'. They each contain video-, audio- and computer-systems and have a small library. The study-centre is the first encounter between (prospective) students and the university. Counsellors can help students in making their choice of whether and what to study. Tutoring within the university is seen as a marginal activity, covering the issues that are impossible to teach with only the use of the self-contained printed, audio-visual and computerized packages.

The role of interactive electronic media

The choice of electronic media is decided by the educational technologist in collaboration with other members of the course-team. Operational criteria for the use of the Interactive Video in courses are a combination of the criteria stipulated for the use of audio-visual media and of those necessitated by the interactive use of the computer.

Audio-visual material is needed as a functional addition:

- when certain processes or phenomena are being taught and are essential as a substitutional experience; as, for example, when these experiences cannot be dealt with in reality because of problems of time, distance or even because of physical dangers.
- when processes or phenomena, because of their dynamic and/or complexity cannot be easily explained in words.
- when processes or phenomena can be explained in words, but cause severe problems for the target group because they do not match their experience.

Interactive use of computers in needed:

- in situations of periodical self-testing of knowledge and skills, including feedback or assistance with shortcomings.
- as a substitute for tutorial teaching: particularly the use of Computer-Aided Learning systems (CAL).
- in simulations and more complex learning and practice programmes.

Instrumental use of computers is needed if students have to learn to use the computer as an instrument (data processing, information retrieval, control etc.). Simulations provide an abstract model of reality which is sufficiently valid to enable users to study, manipulate and forecast the behaviour of that reality.

Interactive Video is gaining increasing priority in the Open University distance educational setting because it permits operational use of computers. Moreover, Interactive Video provides possibilities to reduce the foreseeable problems which can arise when students must be offered 'real life' practicals.

The Interactive 'Visual Arts' Videodisc

The videodisc and the software will be available with the printed course material of the 'Visual Arts' foundation course which deals with seven art historical disciplines:

painting
sculpture
architecture
minor arts
printing
film and photography
industrial design

These subjects are presented in introductory chapters together with themes such as sociology of art, psychology of art, iconology, form and function in art, reception, perception and philosophical themes such as the theory of light, ideas and the ideal, the sublime etc.

Following the introductory chapters, the themes are then discussed from a historiographic point of view. Different themes in art history, from the Middle Ages to modern times, are studied in subsequent chapters.

In over fifty chapters the student is acquainted with a large amount of information. Different parts of different disciplines are discussed in numerous places within the printed material, without giving the student the opportunity to examine the works of art carefully — only 10 per cent of the pictures are in colour — or providing them with tools to make interpretations. To overcome these problems it was decided to implement a videodisc in the course.

The aims of the videodisc project

1. To offer the students the possibility of exploring a catalogue of images based on:

a. art historical disciplines;
b. historicism (chronology and thematic);
c. periods and styles;

or a combination of these fields.

By placing the images and their descriptions together and offering the students a free choice in the way in which they may examine the database it can be expected that the students will gain insights into the different aspects of art history.

2. To offer the students the skills to make the interconnections through the different art-historical approaches in order to attain an insight into the relationships between theory and historiography.

The videodisc project

The videodisc project is divided into three parts:

a. The catalogue of images containing 15,000 works of art.
b. A database for retrieving and providing test information on the images.
c. The self-test.

The catalogue of images

The catalogue of images consists of 15,000 works of art, including details. Only half of them are used in the Videodisc course (the other half will be used in the next course on art history dealing with Dutch painters and their paintings in the seventeenth century).

This means that the disc being produced is generic. There are numerous advantages of a generic disc. For example:

- A multi-purpose disc is created.
- The production costs are reduced since only one disc has to be made.
- The bigger the database, the more useful the catalogue becomes for art historians.

The only constraint is the number of frames which can be stored on one side of a disc (about 54,000).

The retrieval system

The retrieval system offers two options; exploration of the visual database, and a learning environment.

1. Option one allows the student to explore the visual database and to

choose freely between the different disciplines, style periods and historical periods. When the selection from the combination of criteria has been made, the system shows the pictures responding to these criteria, and next to the pictures the retrieval system projects, in overlay, the information about the pictures, such as name of artist, name of object, date of creation, location, disciplines and style period. If more specific information is required, the 'description' option can be selected. In this case a new page is generated by the computer with information about the iconography, form and function, reception, perception etc. of this particular work of art.

In addition, the user can go further into the system by selecting details of the picture or other pictures by the same artist, or pictures made by artists who lived in the same period (see Fig. 1).

2. The second option offers a learning environment to the student — this does not mean that the exploration option does not create a learning environment; it is more a question of labelling. If this second option is chosen, the computer generates random pictures, posing questions such as 'Who made the painting?', 'What is it called?', 'What style/period is involved?' and 'By whom was it comissioned?'. The student answers these questions by displaying the correct answer using the scroll bars on the screen. Mistakes are noted by the system and feedback is given about each mistake. If the student is wrong a second time, the computer will give the second answer and offers the user the possibility to ask for a description.

The computer logs the results of the student's efforts at the end of each learning session, enabling the student to see on which areas of his subject more study is required.

The self-test

This part of the programme aims to give the students an insight into the relationships between theory and historiography, by posing questions which make cross-references through the course materials. For example, the student is shown different pictures of works of art, of which only one demonstrates the theory of the symbolism of light. The student is then asked to indicate which picture is the correct one. If the answer is correct, the next set of pictures is shown with new questions. If the answer is wrong, the student is given some help. There are two standard help options:

1. More information is given about the subject in the question. In this

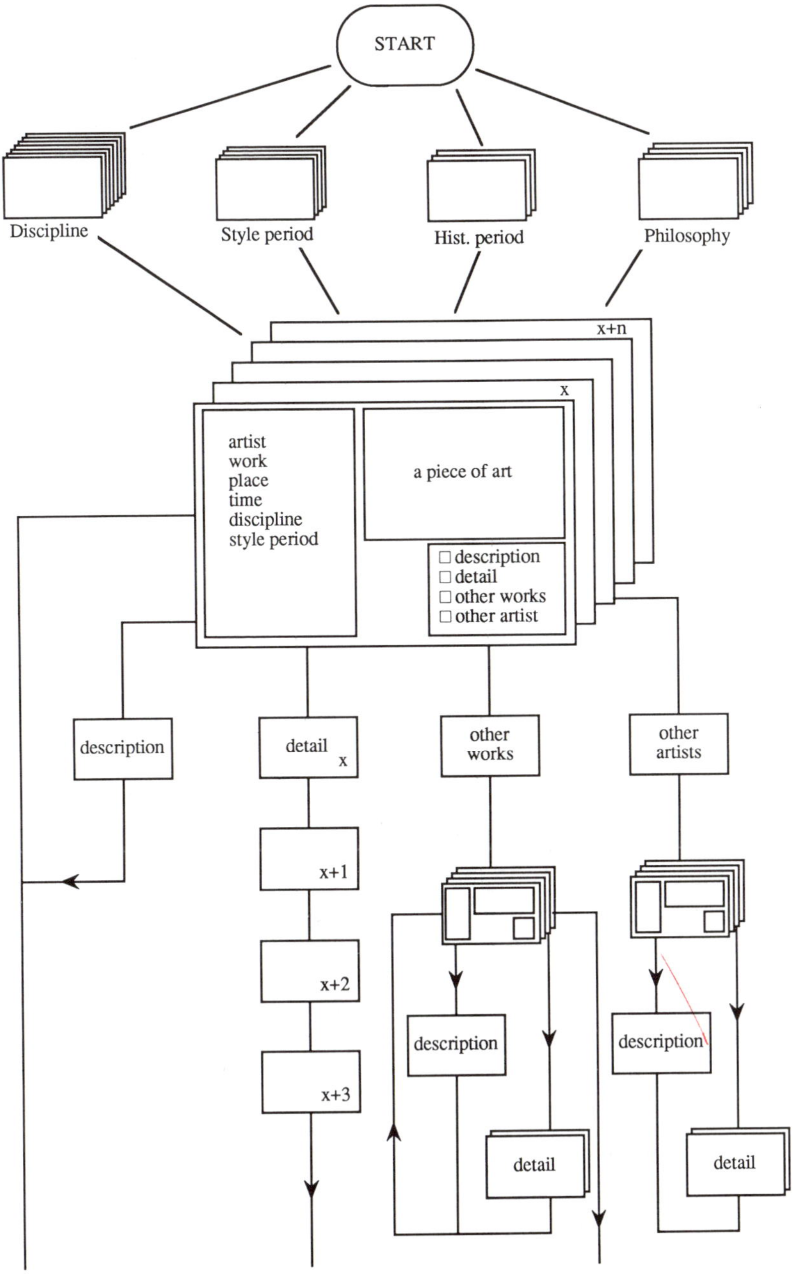
START
Discipline
Style period
Hist. period
Philosophy
x+n
x
artist
work
place
time
discipline
style period
a piece of art
description
detail
other works
other artist
description
detail
x
other
works
other
artists
x+1
x+2
x+3
description
description
detail
detail

Figure 1.

case it means there will be a brief description of the theory of the symbolism of light. The same question is then asked again.

2. The student is given information about the picture he indicated as correct but which was in fact wrong. The feedback given will be such as 'Sorry, but your answer is wrong. This picture was made by X in the Y century, and the iconography indicates a Z theory.'

The programme-control

The use of computers is relatively new in art history. Some museums have produced their own videodiscs with some first level interactivity (e.g the possibility to skip from one frame to another, alternating from picture to text, etc.). Other users find the quality of the picture on the screen too poor and would rather use new techniques such as digitization to store and retrieve their works of art. The Dutch Open University had above all educational aims in mind in producing a videodisc on art history. We wanted to offer our students exploration facilities and to supply them with skills so that they could make interconnections through the material. These aims are more important to us than the absolute quality of the picture, or 'state of the art' videodisc. By doing so we had to overcome the problem that most of our art history students had never seen a computer before. To most art historians computers are 'magic boxes'.

To make the use of interactive video acceptable to the students we had to give extra attention to the user interface. Screen design and a fool-proof program became important issues. We decided to use a window technique to build this program. As an experiment there will be two demo versions of the program: one using MS-windows and the other using drop-down menus created with Turbo-Pascal, although only the best version will be implemented. By using window techniques and the use of a 'mouse' as an interface we believe that the students can use the program with a minimum of knowledge of computers and their operating systems.

Production

In this project the whole spectrum of activities has been undertaken by employees of the Open University. The overall planning of the project was carried out by an art historian and an educational technologist. The educational technologist developed the education design of the program, carried out the project planning, the programme flow and estimated the costs, as well as producing the videodisc. The art historian was responsible for the quality of the content of the program. The programmers are responsible for the production of the software.

The 'Visual Arts' Videodisc should be available to students by the spring of 1989.

6

Paintings by Number: Art History and the Digital Image

William Vaughan

This paper sets out to consider the potential of the digital image as an aid to the study and preservation of works of art. It will begin with a general survey, and will conclude with a particular consideration of the 'Morelli' project that is being carried out in the Department of History of Art at Birkbeck College, University of London.

As such it might be thought to be dealing essentially with technical matters. However, issues involving computers are rarely that straightforward these days. Before going on to the main theme, therefore, we will first look briefly at the wider implications of the application of the new technology to the subject.

Over the last decade the use of computers has become so widespread that they now constitute a social as well as a technological phenomenon. The subject of the history of art is no different from virtually every other academic discipline — whether in the sciences or the humanities — in experiencing their impact. Like practitioners in most other arts-based subject, historians of art have found the introduction of computers particularly problematic because they seem to encourage practices alien to the traditions of the discipline. They seem to promote intransigent and insensitive methods in areas where intuition and subtlety have been prized. A few have responded with enthusiasm — perhaps too much enthusiasm — to the possibilities opened up. But the more customary reaction has been that of opposition. This has tended to take two forms. Either there has been outright hostility — a refusal to engage on any level with the new barbarism: or else there has been a more subtle subversion; the suggestion that the whole matter is a trivial one — one that involves no more than technical means — something that is no different in effect from such useful devices as the typewriter. The fact that the most common experience of computers is through word-processing helps to strengthen this last assumption.

In many ways this second reaction is the more problematic. For if the enthusiasts and the outright opponents over-estimate the significance of the change, those who regard it as a merely 'technical' issue severely underestimate it. The patterns of thought generated by the use of computers have become too widespread to be regarded any more as trivial. Like other mechanizations of human activities, it has come to affect the process it set out to simulate. Just as the photograph transformed our perception of the image or the airplane our sense of motion, so the computer has affected our conception of both thought processes and the nature of knowledge. In day to day terms this can be seen in the way that words like 'database', 'mode' and 'program' have entered our language. At the specialist level it can be seen in the activities of those philosophers and psychologists who — for nearly a generation — have been using computers to generate models of human mental behaviour.[1]

The impact of the computer on our view of human nature (the ultimate topic of the humanities) has become too profound to be ignored. And it is far better to approach this problem from a position of knowledge than of ignorance. Significantly, it was those in the know, the computer scientists themselves who first drew attention to this situation. Joseph Weizenbaum's book *Computer Power and Human Reason* (1976) provided a pioneering critique of the implications of computers for our thought processes and use of information.[2] Many of the problems that he raised have been echoed more recently in the chapter on 'Knowledge in Computerized Societies' in Jean François Lyotard's book *The Postmodern Condition.*[3] As the title of this work by the French philosopher suggests — the experiential impact of computers is now accepted by cultural analysts as an integral part of the contemporary predicament. Perhaps most important of all is the way that Lyotard emphasizes the change that computers have brought about to the structure of knowledge.

The main engagement of art historians in this area has been not amongst those working in academic departments, but amongst those working in art galleries, museums and archives. Here, the physical and management problems relating to the care and classification of the actual objects that the art historian studies and the documents that he uses has given an urgency to the consideration of the new technology. This difference of response has, in its turn, tended to augment the growing rift between academic art historians and conservators and curators. The increasing inclination amongst academics to explore those dimensions of art that engage with social history has turned attention away from the classification and analysis of the objects themselves and towards the consideration of the circumstances of their origin, their reception and their use as symbols of cultural power. I do not wish to criticize this tendency — which is one that has certainly affected my own work. But I do think that it is unfortunate that it has sometimes led to a discounting of the need for the close reading and study of imagery. It is my hope that the new possibilities offered up by computers may — if responded to appropriately — help to heal what seems to me to be an unnecessary rift. Be that as it may, it remains the case that most of the current projects that contain methodological innovation are to be found in museums, archives, and conservation studios, while the academic art historians, on the whole, do not go beyond the application of packages worked out for other problems to their own work. I do not wish to belittle such work. It is of course making an important contribution to scholarship. But — and this is important — it is not leading to the development of new practices.

But why, it may be asked, should innovation in this field be important? There is certainly no point in innovating for innovation's sake. This is true: but there is also another significant point to consider. This is that unless specific demands are made that emanate from the needs of the subject, computers are unlikely to develop in ways that will be most valuable to it. It is worth remembering that computers have only evolved in the directions that they have because of the changing expectations people have had of them. Certainly few of their original creators can have envisaged such phenomena as word-processors or personal computers as the likely products of their endeavours. If they sidestep the challenge of computers, academic art historians will not only fail to make use of a valuable resource. They will also limit themselves to having to accept the second-hand products of initatives from other disciplines. For like it or not, they will still end up by using computers. Only the computers will be dictating to them rather than the other way around.

This is why it is of such importance that art historians consider the ways in which computers currently handle images. For the description and analysis of imagery — whether at a technical or a critical level —

remains central to the practice of art history. Furthermore, it is the principle aspect of the subject that distinguishes it from other forms of historical and critical enquiry. The digital image offers the art historian a specific challenge; as well as a unique opportunity to make an innovative contribution to the use of computers in historical and critical studies.

In view of this, it is indeed striking that so little attention has as yet been paid by the academic art historian to the digital image. The largest listing of art historical projects using computers is the *Census* organized by the Scuola Normale Superiore in collaboration with the J Paul Getty Trust at Pisa in 1984.[4] One hundred and sixty-two projects involving works of art are listed. Yet while there were fulsome sections on cataloguing, thesauri, iconography, documents and sources, and bibliographies, there was none on either imaging systems or pictorial analysis. A few projects using video discs or digital imagery did get into two sections at the end called (respectively) 'Computer as a Tool' and 'Special Uses of Computer'. By and large these were projects that were not being run by art historians. It was in fact a non-art historian, the mathematician Russell A. Kirsch of the U.S.A. National Bureau of Standards, who attempted to map out the methodological issues in an article entitled *Making Art Historical Sources Visible to Computers: Pictures as Primary Sources for Computer-based Art History Data*.[5] Kirsch demonstrated some fascinating possibilities. He showed, for example, how an image, once it has been digitized, can be manipulated to afford otherwise unobtainable views. But mindful of his own position as a non-specialist, he also made it clear that it was up to art historians themselves to take matters further.

Since 1984 there have indeed been some significant developments. The digital image has at least made a public appearance as a form for storing and recalling reproductions of works of art — perhaps most spectacularly in the installation at the new Musée d'Orsay in Paris. There have, too, been some spectacular uses of the resource by conservationalists as a means of recovering information about the former states of pictures. But it is true to say that any use of it as an aid to critical or historical analysis is still in its infancy.

Before going on to give some further account of this primal world, it might be helpful to consider what exactly a digital image is. This account must, of course, be necessarily brief, and will dwell on those features most relevant to their application as means of reproducing and analyzing works of art.

All us are now aware of 'digital' as a concept, if only from digital

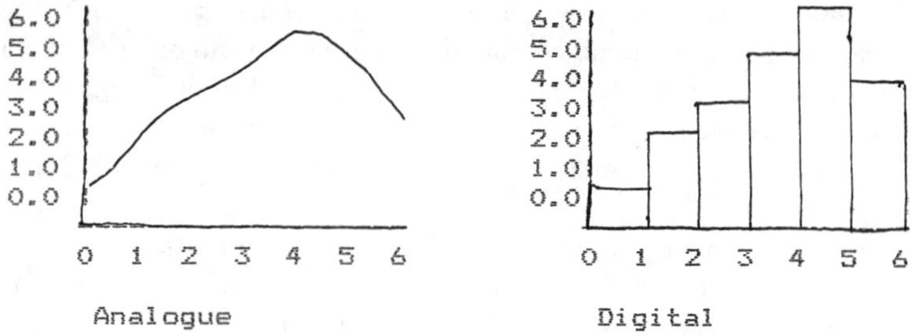

Figure 1. Diagrammatic representation of 'analogue' and 'digital' signals.

watches. The main point is that it is a method of recording phenomena, whether time, sound or light, as a series of regular measurements.

Digital measurement is to be distinguished from non-digital measurement — which is usually known as 'analogue'. The 'analogue' measurement attempts to reproduce the phenomena being observed by copying it as exactly as possible, without subdividing it into intervals and values. Figure 1 may help to make this clear. The measurement on the left shows a curve, the one on the right the same curve reduced to a set of measurements at regular intervals.

A 'digital' image, is an image that has been recorded by such a process. Figure 2 is a detail of the painting *The Toper* by Frans Hals in the Rijksmuseum in Amsterdam after it has undergone a process of crude digitization. In this case the picture has been divided into a matrix of rectangles and the average of the tonal and colour values for each area has been recorded. This type of process is familiar to most of us through our daily experience of images rapidly being reduced to matrices of squares by editors of television programmes.

Later in this paper we will consider what the opportunities are that such a process offers. But first I want to cope with what might seem from the example given to be a crippling limitation. This is that in the process of digitization, information is lost. Nobody would for one second accept this image of Frans Hals's *Toper* as an acceptable 'reproduction' of it.

But the point to remember here is that the quality of the digital image depends entirely upon the number of observations that are contained in it. If they are sufficiently numerous and subtle in their measurement they can exceed the degree of detail perceptible to the human eye. At that point, the image produced from a digital record of

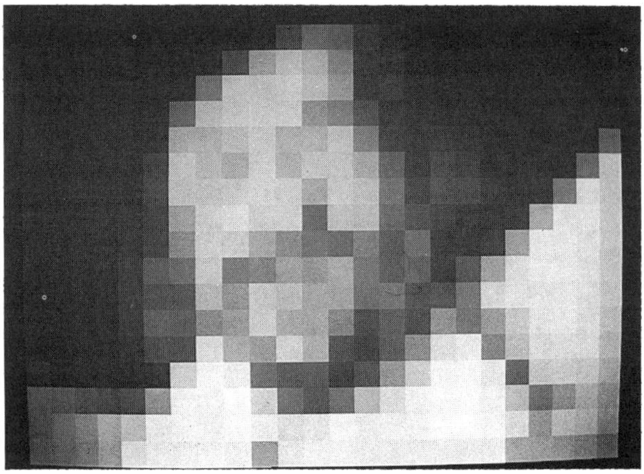

Figure 2. Digitized reduction of detail of Frans Hals' painting *The Toper* in the Rijksmuseum, Amsterdam.

a picture will be able to match or even surpass the quality and resolution of any reproduction made by conventional photographic means.

The digital image, therefore, does not need to imply any loss of significant information. At the same time it offers many characteristics that reproductions taken by other means do not. The fact that it is based on quantifiable measurements produces three great advantages:

1. It is STABLE
2. It is TRANSFERABLE
3. It can be MANIPULATED.

There are, of course, a considerable number of problems as well. The 'stability' of the digitized record is based on the fact that it is a series of measurements. Numerical values are far less susceptible to change than an 'analogue' signal, which attempts to mimic the actual effect of the original. It is for this reason that digital signals are used increasingly in telecommunications and in sound recordings. But the digital signal still has to be stored, and it is here that the problem arises. For no system of electronic data storage can as yet provide any guarantee of long term stability.

But this leads to the next point; transferability. The digitized record does not have to be kept in one particular place. It can be 'downloaded' as numbers (or indeed any other convenient system of symbols). Nor need this 'permanent' record be electronic. It could be printed out, and then re-entered automatically be means of an optical character reader. The record would, it is true, be prodigiously long. The resultant 'text' might well be as voluminous as a Dickens' novel. But if we allow such length for a work of literature, why not for a work of art?

Finally — and perhaps most important of all — comes manipulation. For this allows features of pictures to be isolated and analysed. The common television experience of cavorting images should not obscure the real usefulness for such procedures. They are used in medical research, for example, to isolate abnormalities and diseases, and by the police to help in the identification of fingerprints. Indeed, it is hard to find any form of enquiry that makes use of images that does not now exploit the manipulative power of the digital record to aid it in their analyses.

Any form of enquiry, I might have said, except for the history of art. For here the usages are still sporadic and rudimentary. It is tempting to see this simply as a product of an inordinate resistance to change; but this would be a too negative interpretation of the situation. The types of analysis used by critics and art historians are elaborate and complex. They cannot be reduced to a set pattern of procedures in the way that say a criminologist would when looking for the points of comparison that would establish the identity of two fingerprints. Nevertheless, even in this field there are useful activities that could be undertaken now, and which would undoubtedly lead to the opening up of new possibilities.

An account of one of these activities — the 'Morelli' project — is given later in this article. But first I wish to give a brief overview of the three main areas in which digitization is having — or is likely to have — an effect.

1. The reproduction of images

The issue of the reproduction of images might seem to be a straightforward one. But it is central to a unique problem concerning the visual arts. This is the fact that, with the partial exception of the print, they exist in unique form. Unlike works of music, literature, film and drama, they have a single manifestation that can only be 'reproduced' not repeated. This problem is one that causes concern, both because of the limitation placed on the perception and analysis of the reproduction, and because of the mystique that it creates around the original object. The latter can all too easily become the focus of a cult of elitism.

This has implications for the analytical study of art, as well as for its appreciation. For, like other historical and critical subjects, the study of the history or art must use examples which it can 'analyse'. For most practical purposes, this is mainly done with reproductions, and the art historian must largely discuss what is perceptible in these. It has long been recognized that the nature of the reproductions available has had a determining effect on the evolution of the whole subject. It is well known that, before the emergence of mechanical reproduction in the mid-nineteenth century, historians were limited in the kind of critical analysis that they could bring to images. The detailed comparison of forms, the so-called 'objective' discussion of style, the whole of the comparative method established by the great art historian Heinrich Wölfflin at the end of the last century was dependent upon the availability of photographs of works that could be placed side-by-side.

In those days, of course, only black-and-white photographs were available, and it is noticeable that Wölfflin's own set of comparative procedures concentrate solely upon form and tonality — the things that could be perceived in a photograph. Since that time, photographs have become the principle sites for most investigations. However much we emphasize the need of direct study of works of art, however much we take students on gallery visits and field trips, we are nevertheless usually facing photographic reproductions in our classes, and often when we discuss direct visual points with colleagues. There must be few of us, too, who are so confident of our memories, that we do not feel that our recollections of a given work of art are being corrupted by constant exposure to reproductions of it. This danger is all the greater now that colour reproductions have become the norm. Colour memory is notoriously fickle. Often I am staggered when I look back through a catalogue of an exhibition where I have got used to taking the colour reproductions as being more or less 'correct' to look more closely and finds notes that I made to myself at the time containing messages like 'the browny red is really light pink' or 'this green is blue'. Added to the problems of distortions brought in at the time of printing, are those that grow as the reproduction decays. This is particularly noticeable with slides where any colour will, with time and use, end up as a reddy brown.

The recording of works of art by means of digitization certainly offers the possibility of obtaining reproductions that are more accurate in the first place, and less susceptible to decay in the second. The problems behind establishing the appropriate method for achieving this are immense. They are, however, being tackled in a pioneering project that is described in Anthony Hamber's paper elsewhere in this book.[6]

The project does not rest on the naive expectation that reproduction will ever be an exact science. For there is no such thing as a single image of a picture to be reproduced. It is well understood that the perception of an object is dependent upon the workings of the individual mind. The term 'psychophysics' has recently been coined to pinpoint the fact that the nature of what we see is a subtle blending of expectation and input; but the observation itself has been a commonplace in the psychology of vision at least since the time of Pascal and Descartes. What the project is seeking is to provide accuracy and stability for essentially two purposes. First, for the scientific investigation of the physical properties of paint and the use of optical physics for this by the scientific departments of galleries. Second, to provide a source for the study of pictures which, while not claiming to be absolute, at least can claim stability, and hence function as a clear reference point.

It is the stability of the digital image that is the first of the properties that makes it so useful in this scheme. For, as we have already seen, once the record has been made, and the scale of the record is known, then this image can remain absolutely unvarying — provided, of course that it is kept in a form where it will not actually physically destruct.

Apart from the mere fact that it offers stability of a kind not currently known in reproduction, the digital image opens up some interesting problems. First — and this will be returned to later — is the fact that paintings themselves are constantly changing. Sometimes the changes are dramatic, and sometimes they are subtle. At the moment we already use photographic reproductions to remind us of the dramatic changes — for example when a picture gets destroyed or badly damaged.

But when it comes to subtle changes, such as the gradual change in colour emission of a pigment over centuries, then we are virtually helpless. However, the digital image, because of its unvarying nature, could provide a stable account of the colour and tonality of an image at a precise point in its history. As time went on, and the picture changed, the digital image would maintain a record of how the picture had been rather than how it is. This could create interesting issues. For which would be truer to the original — the actual physical object as it is now, or the record taken at an earlier time? Up till now it has been impossible for the art historian to separate object fetishism — the worship of a work simply because it is 'the original' — from authenticity — the idea of coming closest to the actual effect intended. I do not believe that the new situation would lead to people actually valuing the historical digital reproduction above the decayed original. But it would at least clarify the distinction between object fetishism and the search for information.

This is perhaps a rather esoteric issue. More to the point is the fact that a digital image can be copied endlessly without loss of quality. This again is due to the nature of electronic reproduction which one might say 're-performs' rather than reproduces the record that it has. At the moment, with the use of conventional photography, there is a constant need to rephotograph works to maintain a source of undegenerated reproduction. This need would be obviated if digital recording became the norm. For not only would it no longer be necessary to get a 'closer' image of the 'original'. It would also be possible for a high-level digitized image to provide the source for every other imaginable kind of reproduction — whether slide, colour transparencies for reproduction or whatever. A 'bank' of such images could greatly reduce managerial problems related to reproduction — as well as establishing a more accurate source.

In the above section I have had to speculate, because what we are looking at is something not yet in being. We are only at the very beginning of the use of digital images for the reproduction of works of art. There are, it is true, projects like the digitized archive of masterpieces of Tuscan art,[7] or the use of digitized images in the Musée d'Orsay. But — valuable though they are — none of these projects are yet using images of the degree of fidelity and precision to make a fundamental difference to our use and understanding of reproduction. It may be some years before truly 'high resolution' reproduction becomes a norm. Yet when it does come in it is as likely to have as profound an effect on our responses to works of art as the photograph did in the last century.

2. Conservation

The situation in the world of conservation is very different. Here the impact of digital methods has been felt for many years. But once again it is the stability and manipulative potential of the digital record that have proved to be their principle attractions.

It is self-evident that if pictures did not change there would be no need for conservationists. But change they do, either through the external force of destruction or by the internal agency of the gradual metamorphosis of its constituents. One might describe the conservationist's task as being both to reduce such variations to a minimum and to discover the nature of the changes that have already taken place. For both to be achieved one needs knowledge of the media that the picture is made of. Such knowledge comes of course from many sources — from chemical analysis and the observation of physical structure. Digital imagery has led to a vast number of extensions of the traditional means for investigating such phenomena.

An example of the aid that digitization can provide for chemical analysis of pigments is the work being carried out by David Saunders, Scientific Officer at the National Gallery, London.[8] Dr Saunders has been making digitized records of paint samples in order to study the ways in which pigments change over a number of years. This method promises to be far more precise than the conventional types of spectroscopy previously employed.

Dr Saunders' project provides an example of the value of the stability of the digital record when it is necessary to chart change. The manipulative power is also used by conservationists. In this case it comes into its own where reconstruction is required.

The technique has been used to enhance those penetrative methods whereby the conservationist is able to probe beneath the surface of the paint to find what lies underneath. One particularly ingenious example is the work of the scientific department of the Soprintendenza ai Beni Artistici e Storici in Venice. A normal procedure for reading beneath the surface of pictures is by photographing them in infra-red light. Giorgione's famous *Tempesta* have been photographed by the Soprintendenza in this way. The infra-red rays penetrate the picture surface to reveal covered details. But the problem is that there is still some of the surface image left which interferes with the image of what lies underneath. The scientists of the Soprintendenza are able to sharpen their reading of images that lie beneath the surface by 'subtracting' the digitized surface image from the digitized infra-red image. The result is that — unlike normal x-ray and infra-red photographs — the subtracted image greatly reduces the interference provided by the surface image to the reading. By these means, for example, it has been possible to detect clearly the shape of a tower in the landscape of Giorgione's *Tempesta*.[9] This technique, therefore, can provide critical information about the history of a painting that is undiscoverable by any other means.

Digitization can also help in literal reconstruction — where there is a need to replace areas of paint that have actually been lost. One notable example is that used in the restoration of the great Cimabue Madonna that was wrecked in the Florence flood of 1967. By means of digitization, it was possible to average out the tonalities of the paint areas that surrounded missing pieces and thereby suggest a median tone for the missing piece itself that would be compatible with its surroundings.

The widespread usage of digitization in conservation and restoration projects is a direct consequence of the involvement of trained scientists in such work. The kinds of projects mounted, and questions asked, moreover, have direct analogies with those in other scientific disciplines, where precise answers to clearly formulated problems are expected. In the last section of this paper I shall be looking at a very different environment — that of pictorial analysis for historical and critical purposes. Here all the problems of applying computer methods to the complex modes of thought of the humanities pertain.

3. Pictorial analysis

As has already been remarked, the concept of 'a priori' pictorial analysis — that is, analysis of images in terms of absolute visual factors — has few defenders in the art historical community today. Analysis — whether formal or iconic — tends to be contextual, and is dependent upon extensive reconstructions of the intellectual, social and political milieu in which the images were generated. As I hope I have already made clear, I do not find myself at variance with this development. But I still feel that it is necessary to introduce a close reading of the object into such analyses.

At the present level of development the particular analytical strength of the digital image lies in its ability to assess formal relations between different images. It is relatively easy to use it to establish, for example, the different tonal gradations used in a particular work, the spectrum of colours, the disposition of forms. It is very poor, by contrast, in being able to address complex cultural associations. It is even extremely difficult to get it to make the simplest of iconographical identifications. To tell whether a given oval is, for example, the head of a Madonna or a new potato would require the most elaborate amount of programming. There are those who feel in consequence of this that there is little point in pursuing investigations in this area until the science of Artificial Intelligence has progressed to the point where such complex recognition patterns become possible.

While accepting that the automated iconic or culturally-related reading of images is not likely to progress much in the near future, I do not agree that this a reason for abandoning the use of digital images in pictorial analysis. I think that what is called for is the consideration of other types of investigation that are made possible by it.

One obvious and highly exciting area is that of reconstruction. This is closely related to the kinds of reconstructions made by conservationists already alluded to. The difference is that here they are manipulated to provided evidence of effects that could perhaps not be guessed at by any other means. It is possible, for example, by a regulated shifting of tonalities, to see how a picture might look under different lighting effects (say candlelight for an altarpiece now in a museum), or a sculpture at different angles. There have even been some impressive reconstructions of whole buildings, such as that by the IBM image research group of the lost Saxon Minster at Winchester, in which it is possible to simulate the effect of being inside a defunct edifice.[10]

Fascinating though such reconstructions are as aids to imagination, they do not properly constitute any form of descriptive analysis of images. They are not analogous to those formal explorations of texts that have become so well known and controversial in musical and literary studies.

But here we meet another problem. For the computer to effect such analyses, it is necessary for it to have some fundamental unit to make its computations with. Such an element is lacking in visual communication. As has frequently been pointed out, one of the features that separates images from music and literature or mathematics, is this absence of any indentifiable basic unit. There is no equivalent to the sets of words or notes or numbers of the other discourses. There are, it is true, many theories of vision that would seek to establish a group of primaries. But these remain theories, and are not an accepted set of conventions whereby visual records are conveyed.

There have, it is true, been a number of interesting attempts to classify pictures into formal elements. Such activities take their inspiration from formalist criticism of the early twentieth century and the well-known claims of Gestalt psychologists that there are primitive form-recognizing faculties in the mind. In recent years these claims have been updated and revised — notably by Marr in his 'computational' theory of vision. Marr himself has used digitization as a means of simulating a 'primal sketch' which he believes to be at the basis of our ability to recognize form.[11]

Some analysts of pictures have seen the reduction of images to computerized 'primal sketches' as being the road towards a new syntax. In his article in this book, Lutz Heusinger reproduces some examples of essentialized compositions.[12] These, and similar kinds of image reduction in terms of outline have in fact been the principle area explored by those who have taken an interest in the subject. It may well be the case that such reductions do present some early stage in our recognition of form. But however interesting they are for developing a theory of vision, it is hard to see as yet what practical help they can provide for the comparative analysis of works of art.

My own approach has been a more pragmatic one. I have sought to explore avenues that are already open, ones that work using the syntax of vision actually employed to construct the digital image itself. It must be remembered in this context that the digital image does in itself perform an analysis on an image. It divides it into a series of units. As it happens (and I cannot believe that this is coincidental), the categories used for these do correspond to the three basic areas of pictorial experience mentioned by Renaissance art theorists, namely design (or disegno), colour, and tonality (or chiaroscuro). Design is recognizable by means of the mapping of positions on the grid of horizontal and vertical matrices that the digitization process creates across the surface of the picture. Colour and tonality can be derived respectively from the chromatic and 'gray-scale' values assigned to the individual picture elements or 'pixels'.

The pixel is, indeed, the fundamental element of the digitized image. Each one has an address locating its position on the matrix and a value, and it is from the information provided by these that the image is constructed. Working directly with such measurements may not allow us to interpret the subjects of pictures. But it does enable us to quantify many of their physical properties. We are able to distinguish them from each other and to classify, analyse and compare them according to strictly formal characteristics. It does, in fact, provide new and more powerful ways of pursuing those investigations into the identity of pictures and pictorial styles that have traditionally been the province of connoisseurship. But I do not believe that the matter stops there. It also allows us to quantify and classify pictorial types and motifs in ways not previously attempted. From this it might be that a precise syntax of visual forms will emerge.

It was with a view to exploring the potential of the digital image for such analyses that I set up the system called *Morelli*. Historians of art will recognize in this name a reference to Giovanni Morelli, the nineteenth century Italian doctor and connoisseur who attempted to establish an objective system for the recognition of the styles of different artists. Basically his method worked on a principle familiar to most scientific forms of classification. He compared features common to all the objects he was classifying. As he was working with artists who habitually depicted the human form (namely those of the Italian Renaissance), he chose to compare the ways in which they treated different parts of the body. One particular feature that he paid attention to was the distinct ways in which different quattrocento artists habitually depicted ears.[13]

Morelli himself achieved some remarkable results — though it is uncertain to what extent his system was actually responsible for the identifications that he made. By and large art historians have steered clear of Morelli's system. They have shown more interest in his contributions to the psychology of vision than the application or adaptation of his method. However, it should be noted that while art historians have dismissed Morelli's system, it has been used to advantage by archeologists in this century as one means of classifying the hands of anonymous craftsmen. Professor Beasley's classic work on Greek pots is based on the Morellian system, while a more recent practitioner of the method is Michael Roaf in his analysis of the reliefs at Persepolis.[14] Neither Beasley nor Roaf, I hasten to add, made use of the Morellian method exclusively. It is simply one tool that they use alongside many others.

My 'Morelli' is not a literal attempt to reproduce the Italian connoisseur's method in automated form. But what it does share is the principle of comparing forms. Like Morelli's method, too, it is seeking to establish identities on the basis of direct visual analogy. I have already given some account of the system elsewhere.[15] My description here, therefore, will be brief.

The object of the system is to provide a universal method for identifying, classifying and comparing pictures. As it seeks to include all kinds of pictures it cannot, as Morelli did, depend upon the isolation of specific motifs like ears. There is not much point, after all, in trying to identify a landscape by looking for its ears. What it does instead is to use the analysis that digitized reproduction automatically performs on a picture to derive specific types of measurement.

Essentially, what it does is to reduce the information about a digitized reproduction of each picture massively in a regular manner, by automated means. The result of this process is a set of numerical variables that can be compared. Since the intention is to have a system that can scan the measures of millions of images, there is obviously a premium on reducing that about each one to a minimum. I have been working to a factor of 64 bytes of information per picture; that is, the amount of storage normally required to record about one line of text. I have found this to be perfectly satisfactory for the purposes of basic identification. What one gets for this is a system that can do the following:

a. *Individualize different paintings*
In effect what it does is generate a 'unique identifier' for each picture by automated means.

b. *Recognize (within 'reasonable' limits) that different reproductions of the same picture refer to a single image*
This is a very important point. Every reproduction of a picture is different. Sometimes the differences are great, sometimes they are small. When making comparisons the Morelli system cannot therefore rely on a process of absolute matching. It has to have a more flexible process that will quantify degrees of match and arrive at a conclusion.

Figure 3 is a printout from the process in its original form, which I wrote using a BBC Micro. This shows it matching up different reproductions of a painting by the Sienese fourteenth century painter Duccio. The actual images given here are crude digitizations of the original reproductions and are only there for reference purposes. Even these however, are enough to show that the reproductions being compared differed considerably.

c. *Differentiate manual copies of pictures from the originals*
This is an equally important issue. If the system can relate different photographic reproductions of an image to each other, might it not confuse a manual copy of a picture with the original? What does it do, for example, with a situation like the one presented by Figures 4 and 5? Figure 4 shows a painting by Raphael — the portrait of Castiglione in the Louvre. Figure 5 shows a copy of it by a later artist, the great Flemish painter Rubens. Superficially they look quite similar — certainly every bit as similar as the different reproductions of the Duccio on the other screen. But the system is, nevertheless, able to decide that they are different paintings. The reason why it can do this is basically because manual copies, however carefully made, will show irregular variants of form that do not occur in photographic copies, however clumsily the latter are made.

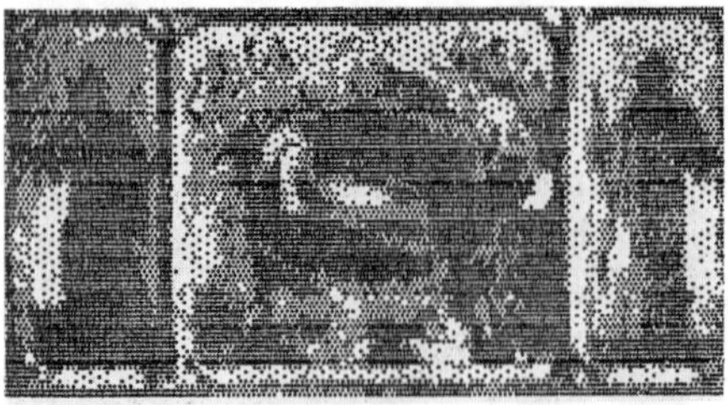

:0 DIGIM.200.176
DUCMAN2
Comparison — 100%
Actual Image

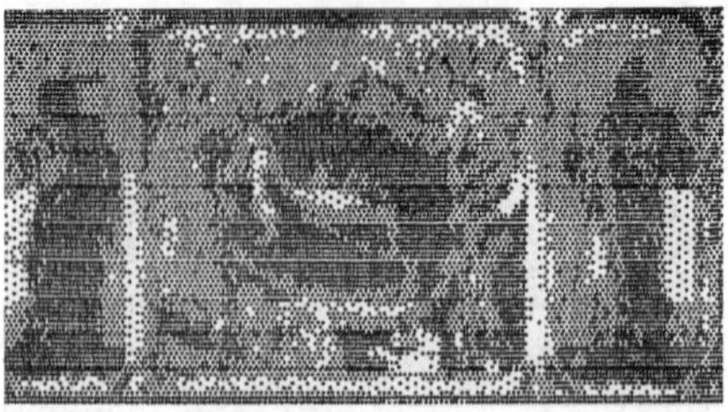

:0.DIGIM.200.177
DUCMAN3
Comparison — 77%
Same Image, Different
Reproduction

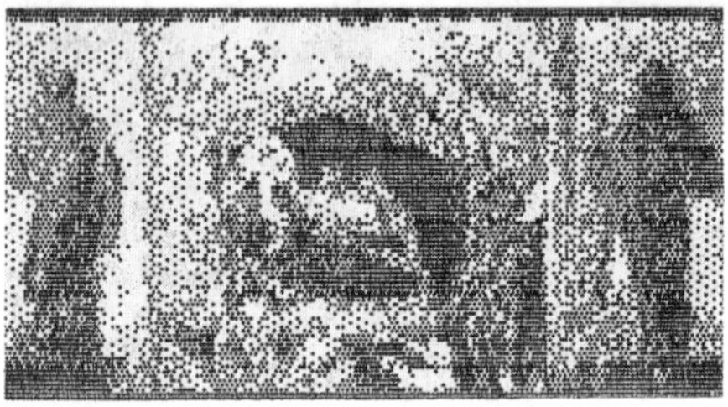

:0.DIGIM.175.175
DUCMANA
Comparison — 71%
Same Image, Different
Reproduction

Figure 3. Printout from a 'Morelli' search. Search image — Duccio, *Nativity with Isaiah and Ezekiel* (National Gallery, Washington).

d. *Associate pictures that are formally similar with each other, without actually confusing them with each other.*

It is not enough, for example, simply to say that the Rubens version of Castiglione is not the Raphael. It is also necessary to establish that it is a *version* of it. It is also of interest to know which other pictures resemble it, albeit less closely. 'Morelli' provides a means of ranging images in relation to a given source picture. Figure 6 gives an example of this in another printout from a Morelli search. Here the machine has first ranged differing reproductions of Rembrandt's self-portrait of himself in the National Gallery, London. It has then found another picture —

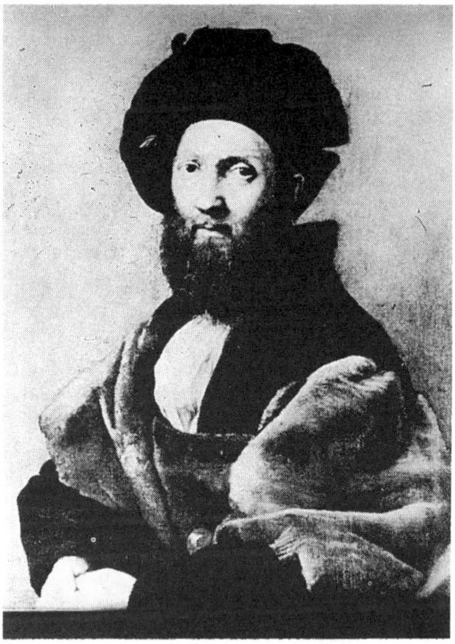

Figure 4. Raphael, *Portrait of Castiglione* (Louvre, Paris).

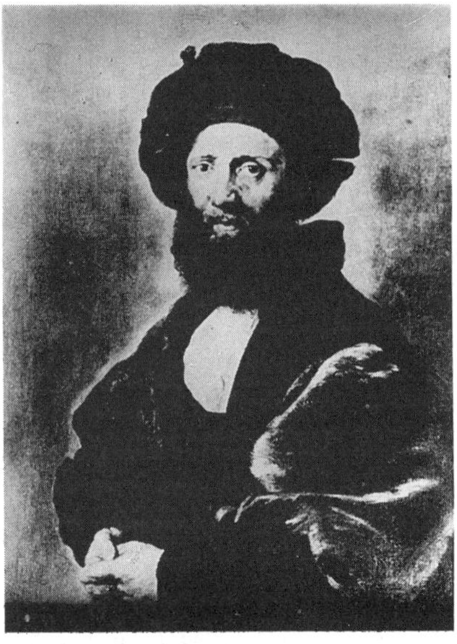

Figure 5. Rubens, *Copy of Raphael's Portrait of Castiglione* (Courtauld Institute, London).

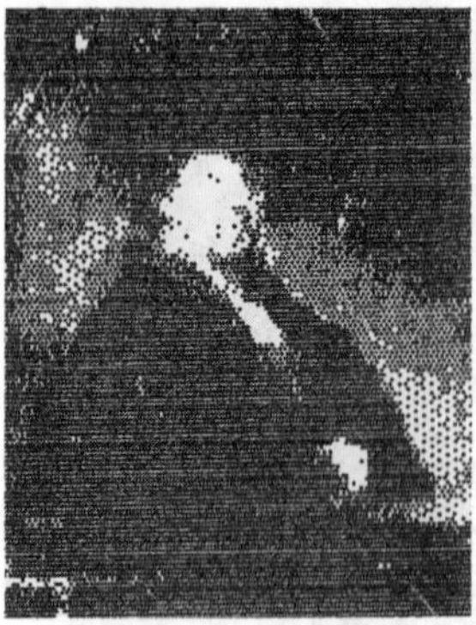

:0 DIGIM.25.22 REMSP-5
Comparison — 100%
Actual Image

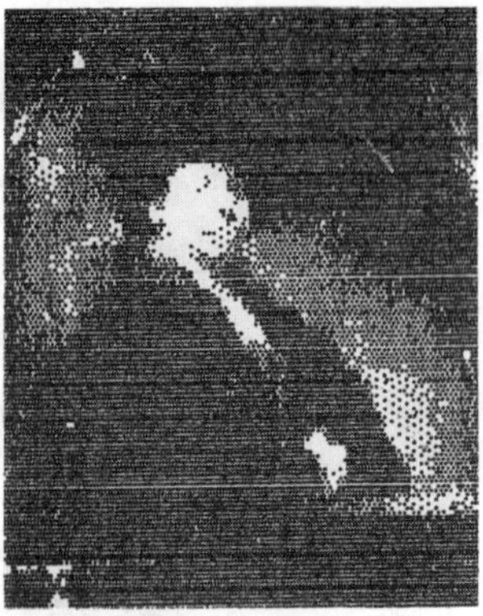

:0.DIGIM.50.33 RSP-6DA
Comparison — 73%
Same Image, Different Reproduction

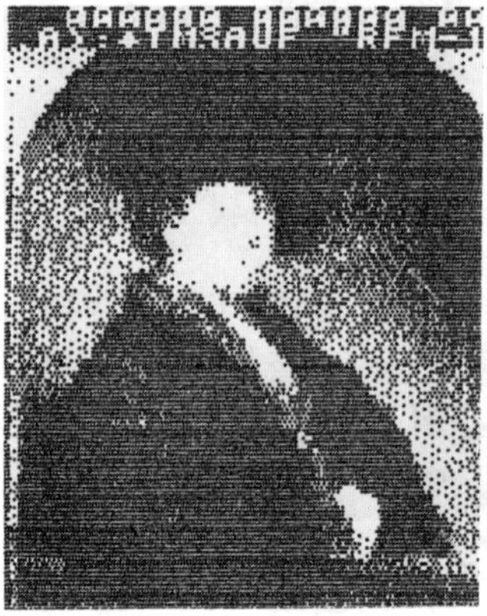

:0.DIGIM.50.28 REMSP-1
Comparison — 60%
Related Image

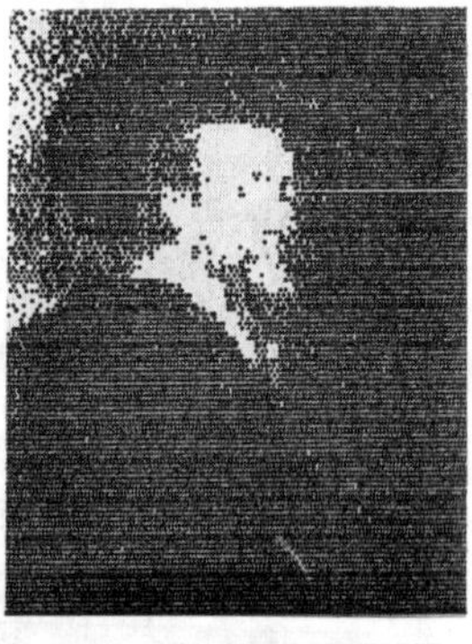

:0.DIGIM.75.60 RUBENSP
Comparison — 34%
No Relationship

Figure 6. Printout from a 'Morelli' search requesting reproductions of specified picture and of the picture in the system that was compositionally closest to it. Search image — Rembrandt, *Self Portrait at the Age of 34* (National Gallery, London). Compositionally closest image — Rubens, *Self Portrait* (National Portrait Gallery, London).

a self-portrait by Rubens. This last picture is included by the machine in the search as it was the one in the system that was compositionally closest to the Rembrandt self-portrait. As well as including this reproduction, correctly ranged after the varying reproductions of the actual Rembrandt, the system also offers the comment that, while having some compositional affinities, the Rubens self-portrait is clearly a different picture to the Rembrandt. The machine produced this information on this occasion because I required it to look for the 'nearest related' composition in its memory as well as the versions of the actual picture I was scanning. But this was a choice that I made. It is up to the user to decide what degree or type of association he or she wishes to pursue.

The system itself is a 'learning' one. That is, the system stores information about each picture that is entered, and can use this to group and comment on the works already in it. Every new picture added to the system enhances its ability to compare and discriminate. It stands to reason, therefore, that such a system would be at its best when it has absorbed the resources of a whole picture library containing millions of images. This has not as yet been done — though a trial of the system at the Bildarchiv at Marburg in West Germany is being planned.

Many people who have seen the system have been sceptical about it being workable on such a large scale. At the present I have no way of being able to counter this scepticism with proof. However, there are two factors that weigh in its favour. The first is the empirical fact that the system has already — in a group of a thousand images — been able to distinguish works that are very similar — including ones that are in fact manual copies of pictures. Indeed, I chose as a base for my prototype 500 half-length portraits — on the grounds that this is a genre in which there is very little formal variation. Not only did I find that the system was able to differentiate such works on very little information with relatively little difficulty; it also brought home to me the fact that images that seem to us to be very close when we view them without any form of measurement, turn out in fact to be very distinct when one 'overlays' them. This is one of the areas where 'computer vision', if it can be termed such, is much more precise than ours. For a deviation to the right or left of one pixel can be immediately picked up, whereas to the naked eye it would be invisible.

The second cause for optimism is that the amount of data for each image that I end up with might be relatively small — but it is still capable of a truly astronomical amount of variation. Sixty-four bytes of computer memory is the space conventionally allocated to store about a line of printed text. But if one thinks of this as a number, it can rapidly be appreciated that we are talking about a figure that — on the decimal system — would have over 100 digits in it. Even if one was assuming that the system was linked to an archive of, say, 10,000,000 images (considerably more than any of those currently in existence) — the chances of an overlap between one set of data and another occuring would be astronomically small. And even if such an overlap did occur, it would be so infrequent as to have no serious impact on the general workability of the system.

What would such a system be used for? The uses could be many. Indeed, I believe that they would grow as the facility became generally available. But immediate uses would be to check the identity of a given image, and to look for variants and associated works. As such it would work pictorially very much like the 'word-search' procedures that help scholars to find titles of publications relevant to their work. This would be made possible because the system is extremely rapid. It would literally be capable of scanning the relevant information about millions of pictures in a matter of minutes. Searches that currently take art historians months — even years — to complete could be undertaken in a matter of hours. I would envisage that the presence of this facility would encourage new ways of dealing with images — particularly in dealing with them on the scale that would enable the creations of group classifications. What would also be novel and exciting about the system, would be the fact that it would be visual associations that would be guiding the comparisons. For the first time, art historians would have ways of classifying pictures visually, rather than verbally.

The idea of making such visual identifications is not, of course, new. There are countless examples of the use of image recognition systems in scientific disciplines. Perhaps one of the most analogous is that developed recently at the University of Edinburgh for recognizing fingerprints. This system both demonstrates the practicality of creating automated image sorting systems, and the need for developing different ones for different purposes. The fingerprint system is far more sophisticated than mine — and has a much finer task to perform. One of the consequences of this is that it has to store nearly ten times as much information per image. Furthermore, the measures that it takes from each fingerprint are uniquely relevant to the structure of fingerprints and do not have application to other types of images.

The Morelli system, by contrast, takes general measures that do not relate to one type of image more than to another. In other words, it has been designed to sort widely varying types of pictures, rather than make discriminations within one group of highly similar images.

Finally I would like to emphasize again that, because I have been using a general system, my method of classification is not based upon any theory of vision. Rather, it simply uses the means of evaluating position and tonal intensity that are established conventions in the creation of a digitized matrix. It is the arbitrary nature of the measurement that is, in my mind, the reason why it can handle such a plurality of images with equal effectiveness.

My main interest in developing this system has been to provide a referencing tool for art historians. But since developing it the point has been made to me that it might have applications for other groups who work with large archives of images — such as textile manufacturers and photographers.

So far I have described what has been done. The aim has been to achieve identification with the minimum amount of information. But it will also be clear that, even using this limited information and a crude system of numerical comparison, a descriptive element is at play. Even as it stands 'Morelli' groups images interestingly according to certain formal similarities. It will find associations, for example, between the flat expansive landscapes of the seventeenth century painter Koninck and those of certain abstract expressionists. It can suggest, too, the degrees of continuity within the compositional practices of different artists. It will come as no surprise to any art historian to learn that 'Morelli' finds a greater degree of compositional continuity within the *œuvre* of Vermeer than in that of Rembrandt. But what is perhaps more interesting is that these degrees of relation can be quantified, and can be discussed in terms of measurable patterns. There are also suggestions that the characteristic distributions of tonal values can be found amongst the output of different artists. It may be that from such features a 'thesaurus' of forms could be established, or even that the individual styles of different artists could be described. Alternatively — and this, from my point of view would be every bit as interesting — it might be established that there is no physical basis for individual style. It might be found — as is sometimes claimed — that the concept of the personal style of an artist is a chimera, that each artist can have many styles that are used for different purposes and have no fundamental association to each other. It might be found, similarly, that the idea of different countries producing 'schools' with distinct features is equally incapable of substantiation — that the concept of a national school is no more than a cultural construct which ignores the real similarities and distinctions between works. The point is that the system would provide a tool for testing such hypotheses. Until such tests are made it would be foolhardy to predict their outcome.

Such developments, however, require higher quality images than those that are already being used in the system. The existing referencing system has to work with poor quality images to be practical; namely those that already exist in archives. Analyses of styles and grouping of types will need information of considerable refinement. Now that we have our new high quality equipment — thanks to the support we have received from University College and Birkbeck — we will be in a position to procede with this side of the project. We will not, of course, lose sight of the further development of the referencing facility, since this has a clear practical function that can be immediately implemented.

Whatever the outcome of such activities, they will at least help, I hope, to emphasize the need to explore the potential that digitized images have for certain kinds of pictorial analysis, and encourage more art historians to become involved in this field. Ultimately it is this involvement that I wish to promote — far more than any particular product that I might have an interest in. For the point is that the digital image will within the next decade or two become the normative image. As this happens it is likely to have as profound an effect on the subject as the introduction of photography did in the mid-nineteenth century. At the moment the situation is still sufficiently fluid for the consumer to have an impact on the way the digitizing process is developed and applied. But this opportunity may not remain for long. Soon will come the period when the technology has become standardized and changes will be harder to effect. Art history is a small discipline and will have much greater difficulty making a contribution at that stage. This is the time at which an opportunity is being offered. It is one we should not miss.

Notes

1. A notable example is the computational theory of vision formulated by D. Marr. See D. Marr, *Vision: A Computational Investigation into the Human Representation and Processing of Visual Information*, San Francisco, 1982.
2. J. Weizenbaum, *Computer Power and Human Reason*, London, 1976. See especially pp. 128–34.

3. J. Lyotard, *The Post-Modern Condition*, London, 1987.
4. *Census: Computerization in the History of Art*, Vol. 1, ed. L. Corti, Pisa, 1984.
5. In *Automated Processing of Art History Data and Documents*, ed. L. Corti, Pisa, 1984, Vol. II, pp. 275–90.
6. See Chapter 2: A. Hamber, 'Conventional Photography versus Analogue and Digital Electronic Imaging', pp. 23–49.
7. V. Cappellini, M. Bacci, C. Conese, 'Digital Methods and Techniques for Analysis and cataloguing of Works of Art' in *Automated Processing*, op. cit, p. 220.
8. See Chapter 7: D. Saunders, 'The Investigation of Colour Change by Digital Imaging', pp. 98–116.
9. 'Riflettoscopia All'Infrarosso Computerizzato' in *Quaderni della Soprintendenza ai beni Artistici e Storici di Venzia*, Venice, 1984, pp. 48–53.
10. A description of the IBM 'Saxon Minster' Project was given at the 1986 CHArt Conference by Dr Andrew Walter (see *CHArt Newsletter*, No. 3, 1986, p. 7.
11. See note 1 above.
12. See Chapter 1: L. Heusinger, 'Computers and the History of Art', pp. 1–22.
13. For a discussion of Morelli's method see: R. Wollheim, 'Giovanni Morelli and the Origins of Scientific Connoisseurship' in *On Art and Mind*, London, 1973, pp. 177–201.
14. M. Roaf, 'Sculptures and sculptors at Persepolis' in *Iran: Journal of the British Institute of Persian Studies*, Vol. XXI, 1983. See especially p. 10 for reference to Morelli.
15. W. Vaughan, 'The Automated Connoisseur' in *Computers and History*, ed. Denley and Hopkins, Manchester, 1987, pp. 215–21.

7

The Investigation of Colour Change in Digital Imaging

David Saunders

Introduction: changes in the painted surface with time

The problem of the deterioration of paintings is not new, indeed it is evident that many artists have been deeply concerned about the permanence of their work. Much attention was paid to thorough preparation of pigments, media and the support onto which a mixture of these was to be applied. Despite this methodical approach, which was the result of many years of practical tradition, changes were often noted within the lifetime of the artist. In a few cases it is suspected that alterations made to the painting some years after their completion were an attempt by the original artist to compensate for unintended changes in appearance.

There is much practical advice offered as to which pigments to avoid. For example, Cennino Cennini (late fourteenth century) in his 'Il libro dell'arte' cautions against vermilion: 'But bear in mind that it is not its nature to be exposed to the air . . . because, in course of time, from exposure to the air it turns black.'[1]

It would be impractical to include here a comprehensive survey of the ways in which the surface appearance of paintings may be altered. The examples that follow illustrate a number of types of colour change that occur frequently in oil and tempera paintings, and that may be shown easily without colour plates.

Fading is probably the most common type of colour change. It is often difficult to detect these alterations in colour since the original

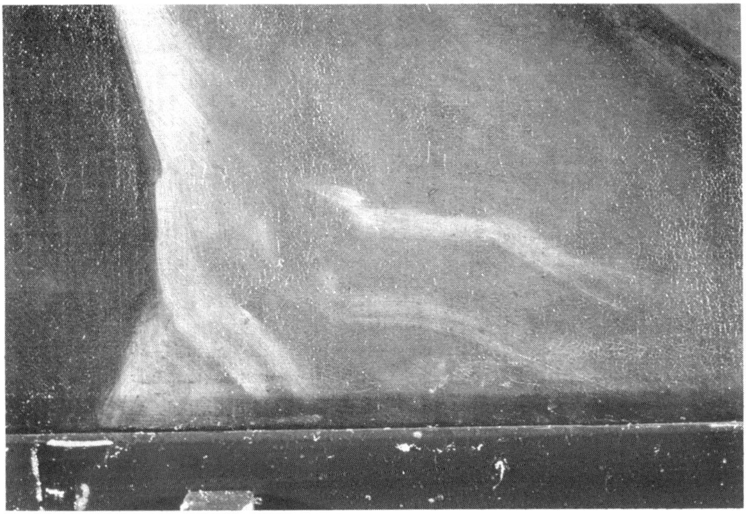

Figure 1. Sir Godfrey Kneller, *Portrait of William Congreve.* (The National Portrait Gallery, London. No. 3199). This detail shows an area of the sitter's coat that has been protected from light.

colour is not always known. In certain cases, however, part of an area may have been protected from the damaging effects of excess illumination by the frame in which the picture was displayed, by retouching at an earlier date or by an overlying layer in the original composition. If the painting is subsequently removed from the frame, cleaned of retouchings or suffers the loss of an upper layer then the original colour may be revealed in an area adjacent to the faded pigment. Figure 1 shows the bottom edge of a portrait by Kneller which was been displayed in a frame which protected the bottom 1.5 cm of the painted area, whilst Figure 2 shows an area of the background of a portrait attributed to the studio of Hans Holbein which had been over-zealously retouched at an earlier date. Cleaning has now revealed an unfaded portion of the original background colour containing the blue pigment indigo.

The unfaded area of the portrait in Figure 1 contains a red lake pigment. Lake pigments are organic colorants derived from insect or plant matter which have been precipitated onto an inorganic substrate. There pigments are generally red or yellow and are known to be very

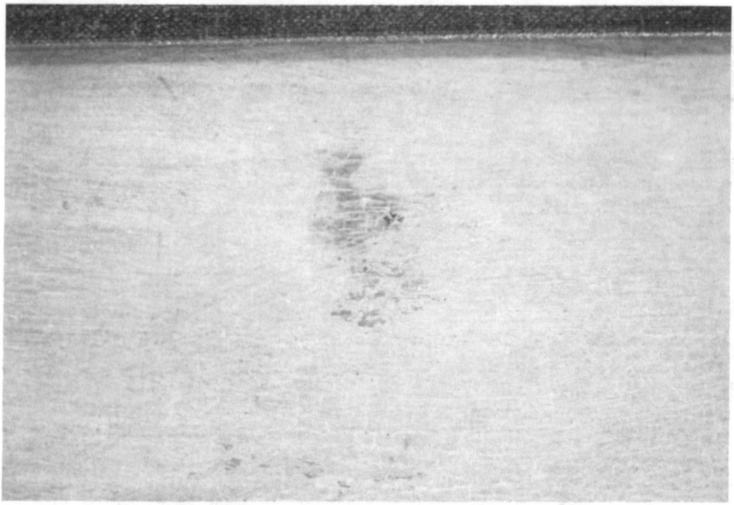

Figure 2. After Hans Holbein, *Portrait of Sir William Butts*. (The National Portrait Gallery, London. No. 210). This detail of the background shows an unfaded area which, until recent cleaning, was protected by a retouching.

sensitive to fading on exposure to light. This loss of colour has been well documented. Cennini in 'Il libro dell'arte' warns: 'Beware of this type ... (it) does not last at all, either with temperas or without temperas, and quickly loses its color.'[2] Later, Mason in his account of the colouring technique of Reynolds notes 'Northcote endeavoured to persuade Sir Joshua to abandon those fleeting colors, lake and carmine .... He did adopt it (vermilion) in his later works, however, finding by experience the ill effects of lake and carmine.'[3]

The fading of lakes can have two effects. Firstly, there may be a simple loss of colour, as illustrated in the painting by Kneller in Figure 1 and in many other examples. The second type of change of colour arises when the lake pigment has been used in conjunction with other colorants either by mixing or by applying the lake as a glaze over another layer. When the lake pigment fades the colour of the other pigment will predominate. Certain green areas in a number of seventeenth century Dutch paintings are thought to have been produced by use of a yellow lake applied over a blue underlayer. The fading of the lake has left a disturbing array of blue foliage.

A second group of quite common colour changes arise from physical

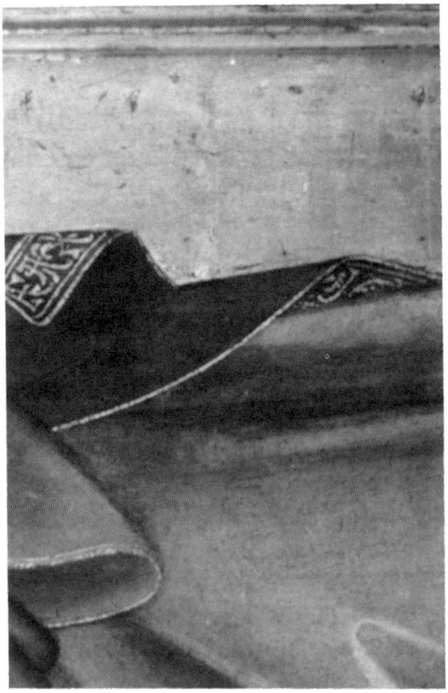

Figure 3. Nardo di Cione, *Three Saints*. (The National Gallery, London. No. 581). Detail of the robe of St Peter showing blackened vermilion.

or chemical changes to the pigment. A dramatic example of this type of change is the blackening of the red pigment vermilion. This is illustrated in Figure 3 which shows a detail of the robe of St Peter from *Three Saints* by Nardo di Cione. The lining of the robe is painted using vermilion, some areas of which have undergone a colour change from red to black. The blackening is due to the light induced change in the crystalline form of the mercuric (II) sulphide from the red (alpha) to black (beta) form. This was noted by Cennini who, as already mentioned, attributes the change to 'exposure to the air'.

The landscapes of many paintings, particularly some of the Italian school, appear brown and parched. In some works this may be intended, but in many cases it has been revealed that beneath the browned surface the paint layer is green. These areas had been painted using a colorant known as 'copper resinate', a generic name for a

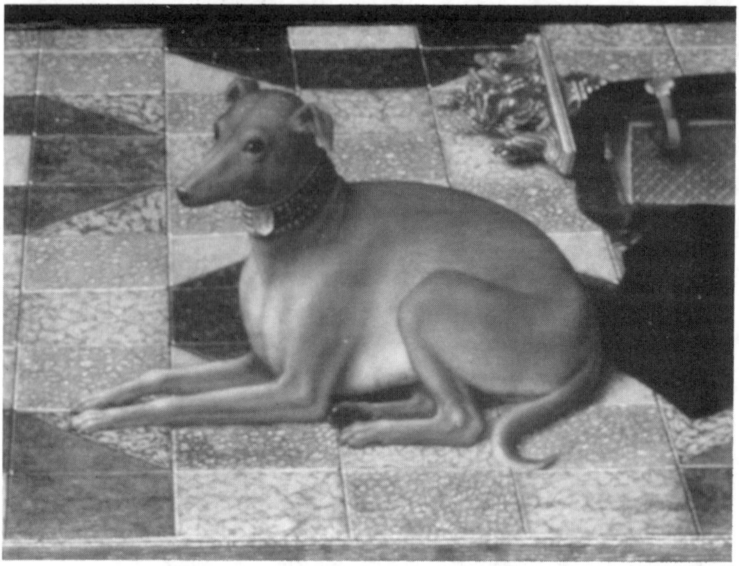

Figure 4. Gerard David, *The Virgin and Child with Saints and Donor.* (The National Gallery, London. No. 1432). Detail of the dog, showing the increased transparency of the paint layer.

group of pigments which comprise a copper salt (often copper acetate) dissolved in a resinous material, typically Venice turpentine. The action of light upon these causes the material to brown at the exposed surface creating the observed colour change.

As the medium in which the pigment particles are contained ages, its refractive index may increase. The result is that a previously opaque layer can become partially transparent and so reveal lower layers of paint of a different colour. In Figure 4 the dog was painted onto the completed tiled floor. Due to a change in the opacity of the paint used, the pattern of the tiling is now visible through the dog.

Many of these changes are believed to be catalyzed by light, with sources containing a high proportion of ultra-violet radiation being the most detrimental. To prevent completely any light induced colour change, it would be necessary to store the paintings in the dark. This is hardly compatible with public exhibition, so in practice a compromise is reached between the need to exhibit and the need to preserve the work.

The need to monitor colour change

As stated above, lighting conditions within a gallery are necessarily a compromise between those which are ideal for conservation purposes and those best for viewing. Within the National Gallery, London daylight is admitted to the rooms only after passing through diffusing glass which absorbs a majority of the harmful ultra-violet radiation. Light sources are selected to give good colour-rendering with minimal ultra-violet emission. The level of illumination is controlled by dimming the artificial lights or by using adjustable louvres to restrict the amount of daylighting.

In order to assess the success of this régime, however, it is necessary to monitor the colour of the paintings over a long time period. In many cases the damage has already been done, colours have changed to such a degree that their identity can only be determined by intrusive forms of analysis. In other paintings the changes are incomplete, and it is desirable to prevent further deterioration of the colours. For paintings executed in modern media there is the added problem that little is as yet known about the permanence of the materials employed.

Measurement of colour change by reflectance spectrophotometry

The first programme of colour change measurement, and indeed as yet the only such programme, began at the National Gallery in the mid 1970s. At this time there was no suitable commercially available equipment which fulfilled the criteria imposed by the nature of the study. The main requirements were that the technique should not be intrusive and that colour should be measured *in situ* without the measuring device making contact with the painting surface. The area of measurement should be sufficiently small to afford uniformity of colour. Lastly, it was necessary for there to be some method of accurately returning to the same position on the painting surface for measurement after a number of years had elapsed.

To fulfil these requirements a spectrophotometer was specially designed and constructed by Professor W.D. Wright (then of Imperial College, London). A similar instrument was also provided for the use of the Courtauld Institute.[4] The optics of the instrument have been described in detail in previous publications,[4, 5] but broadly consist of a monochromator to provide monochromatic light at 10 nm intervals throughout the visible region of the spectrum, and a measuring head to

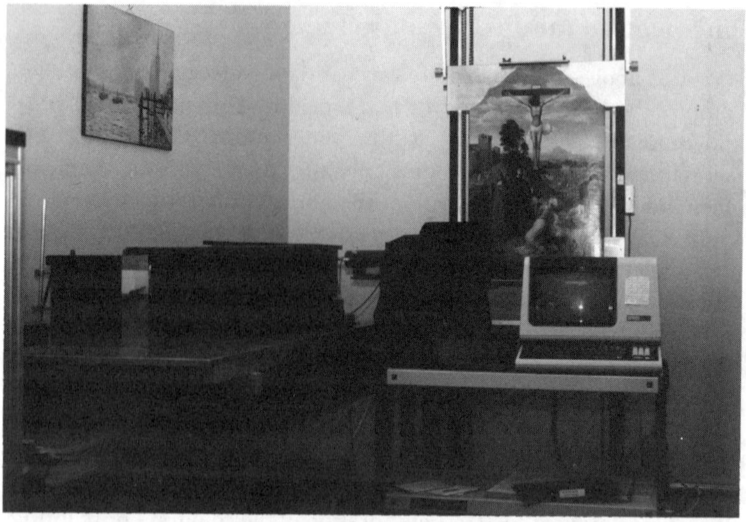

Figure 5. The Wright reflectance spectrophotometer.

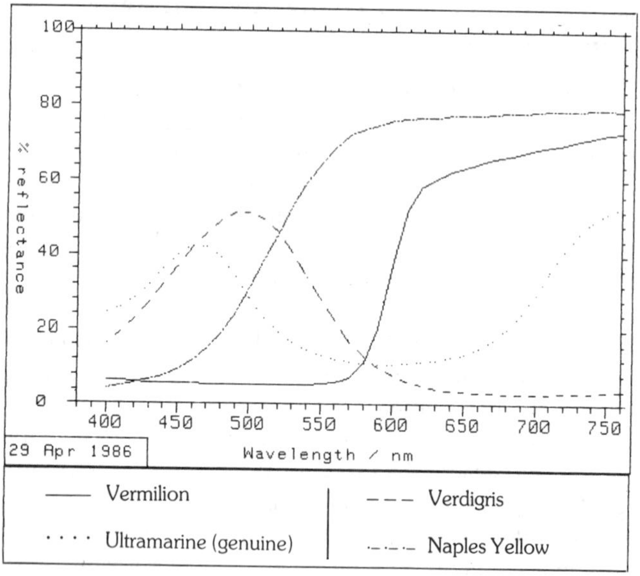

Figure 6. Reflectance curves for pigment standards: vermilion, ultramarine, verdigris and Naples yellow.

focus this light onto the painting surface and to measure the reflected light. The monochromator and measuring head are illustrated in Figure 5. Within the measuring head there is the facility to compare the quantity of light reflected by the painting with that reflected from an internal standard. The photomultiplier is connected to a digital ammeter which is directly linked to the department's Hewlett Packard computer. The computer makes the necessary dark current and reflectance corrections before storing a spectrum for the sample area.

The spectra may then be compared either graphically or numerically. The latter yield an expression for the colour of an area in terms of L*, a* and b*, the three colour coordinates of the 1976 CIE (Commission Internationale de l'Eclairage) system. Comparison of the coordinates after a five year interval gives the colour change in terms of ΔE where

$$\Delta E = ((a_1^* - a_2^*)^2 + (b_1^* - b_2^*)^2 + (L_1^* - L_2^*)^2)^{0.5}$$

A colour difference (ΔE) of unity corresponds to a just perceptible colour change.[6]

Figure 6 illustrates some typical reflectance spectra for common pigments, whilst Figures 7 and 8 shows the results of some recent measurements. In the first example the spectra are all for an area of coloured paint and were recorded at five year intervals. The increased reflectance at the red/yellow end of the spectrum with time is consistent with a yellowing of the varnish. In the second example, three spectra recorded over an eight year period show that no significant colour change has occurred in an area of a red flower.

The reflectance spectrophotometer has been used to measure both long-term colour change,[5, 7] and to assess the colour changes which may accompany certain conservation treatments.[8, 9]

Digital imaging: the prototype system

It has always been recognized that the system of colour change measurement afforded by the use of the reflectance spectrophotometer is not without many drawbacks. The major disadvantage of this technique is the necessity to select, at the outset, the exact areas to be monitored: There is no possibility of recording the colour in retrospect if an area seems to be of interest at a later date.

The first solution to this problem made use of the computer generated image processing equipment then available. The prototype system is shown schematically in Figure 9, and comprises a

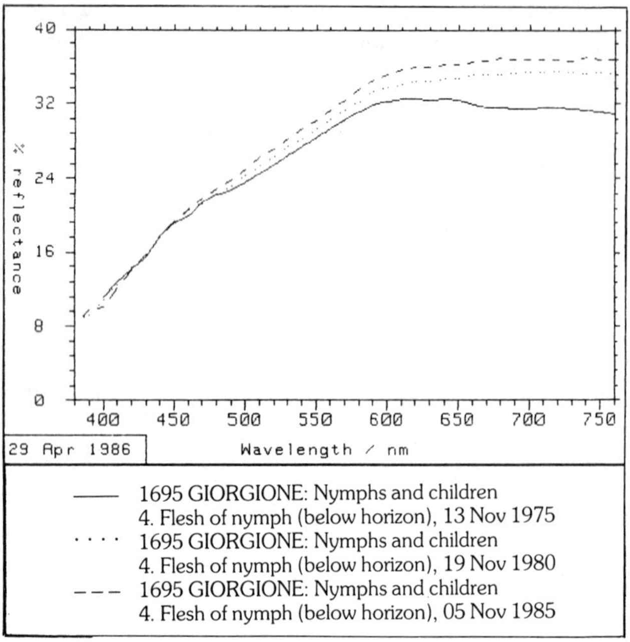

Figure 7. Three reflectance curves for a flesh coloured area in The National Gallery, No. 1695, recorded at five year intervals. The spectra show a yellowing with time, probably due to a colour change in the varnish layer.

monochrome TV camera connected to a computer by way of the 'digivisor'. Images may then either be stored on disc or else displayed on a TV screen via the 'supervisor'. In order to acquire images which contain information about the colour of the painting, colour separation filters are placed in front of the camera lens.[10]

The TV camera functions by breaking up the image into a number of horizontal bands. A standard European television picture is made up of 625 such bands. The band is transmitted by the camera as a continuously varying voltage (analogue signal). The voltage at a given time corresponds to the brightness of a particular point on the image. At the TV monitor the 'flying spot' darkens or brightens according to the applied voltage thus reproducing the intensity pattern of the image.

It would be possible to store this analogue signal, on magnetic tape for example, but in order to make use of the ability of the computer to

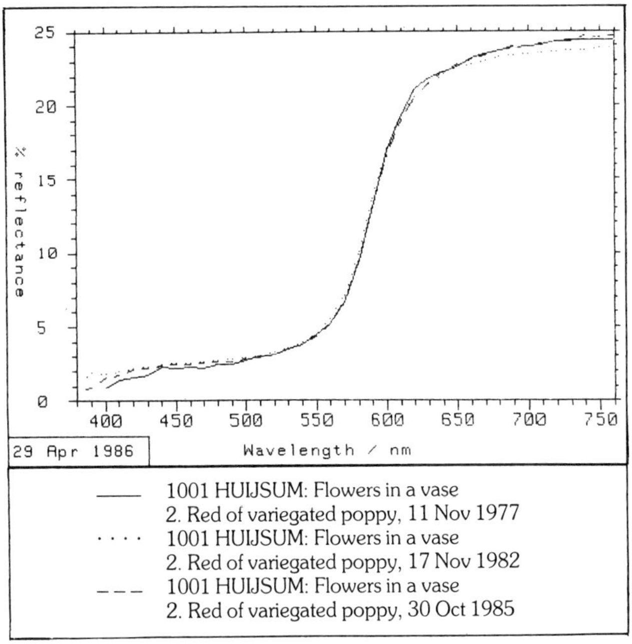

Figure 8. Three reflectance spectra for a red coloured flower in National Gallery No. 1001 recorded over eight years. The spectra indicate that no detectable colour change has occurred.

store and manipulate the data it is best to convert the analogue signal to a digital form compatible with the computer. To digitize the signal it is necessary to break up each band within the image into a number of individual picture elements or pixels. Each pixel is then assigned a numerical value which corresponds to the voltage of the analogue signal at that point, and ultimately to the brightness of the painting at the corresponding location. A pixel with a high number corresponds to a light area and vice versa. The area of the painting covered by a pixel will depend upon the distance between the TV camera and the object. Typically a pixel will represent an area of between 1 mm square and 1 cm square.

The task of digitizing the analogue signal is performed by the 'digivisor' which then passes the data to an array or matrix in the CPU. The matrix size chosen was 256 × 256. Although this is below the

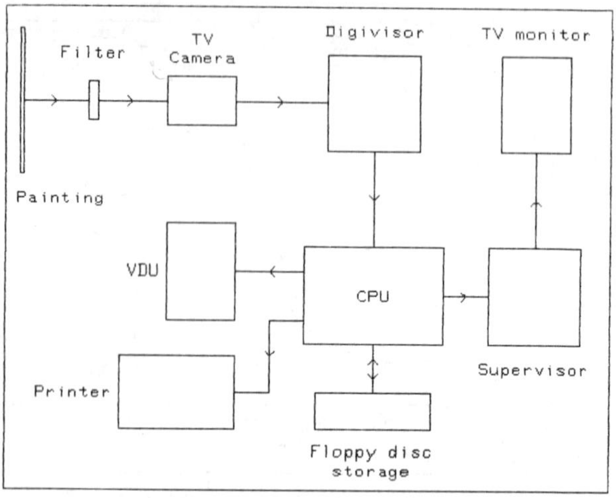

Figure 9. Schematic representation of the prototype image processing system.

resolution of a 625 line monitor it represents a fairly manageable array of ca. 65,000 elements. Once the data are allocated to such an array it is possible to store the data on magnetic media or perform mathematical operations upon it. To record colour the image is acquired three times, each time through one of a set of three 'Wratten' colour separation filters.

The detection of colour change using such a system requires that the image be recorded again after a suitable time has elapsed. In order to make meaningful comparisons it is necessary to have exact superimposition of images. Once this not inconsiderable problem has been overcome the colour separated images may be compared to give information on colour change. Clearly if such information is to be of use, corrections must be made for variables such as uneven illumination, spatial distortion and deterioration of the colour separation filters.

Despite these hurdles the prototype image processor was established and is illustrated in use in Figure 10. Unfortunately, problems with noise and with the non-linearity of response of the TV camera used led to a decision to abandon this system in favour of a digital imaging system based around a CCD (charge-coupled device) camera and a

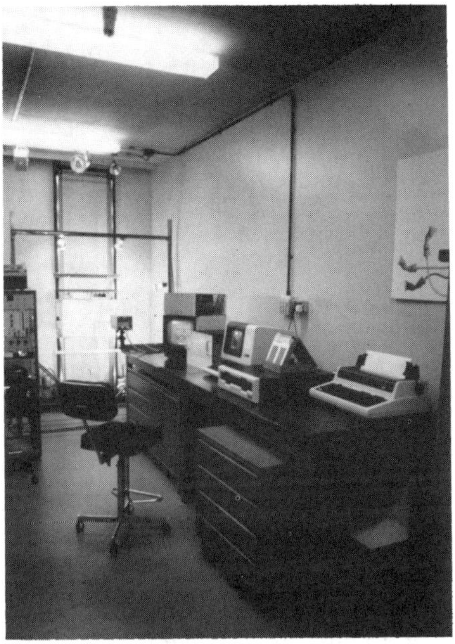

Figure 10. The prototype image processing system in use.

computer with a larger CPU than the DEC machine used with the prototype apparatus.

The present system

As mentioned above, the decision to develop a replacement system stemmed from the dual problems of the poor performance of the conventional TV camera and the need to use a computer with a sufficiently large CPU to accommodate at least two image matrices; the DEC computer used for the prototype system had only been capable of processing one eighth of the available data for an image and had performed image subtractions on one sixteenth of the image before storing the result to disc.

At this time the development of CCD or CID (charge injection device) cameras had reached the stage at which arrays of 256 × 256 or 512 × 512 were available, but the higher resolution devices currently on the market had not been developed. The decision to use a device with a 256 square array was based on the ease of handling the resulting

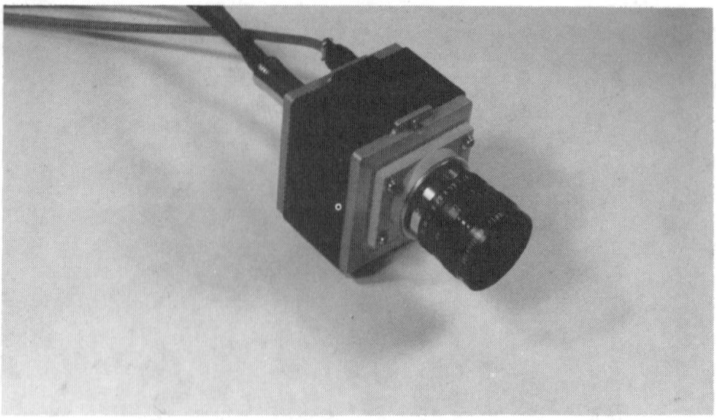

Figure 11. The CID digital camera used in the current image processing system.

data on a micro-computer. The CID camera chosen is illustrated in Fig. 11.

In a CID (or CCD) camera the image is focused directly onto the surface of the array. In this way each of the individual elements in the array corresponds directly to an area on the painting being imaged. The signal generated by each microscopic element is then digitized in much the same way as the analogue signal from the TV camera. It is, of course, possible to combine the signals from the individual elements to give an analogue signal, but this must then be sampled and digitized in the same manner as that generated by the conventional TV camera. Such a system would incorporate many of the disadvantages of the TV camera.

In order to overcome this the frame store to which the camera is attached provides the time-base signal for the camera. This allows the acquisition from the individual elements to be precisely controlled. The value for each pixel is then digitized and stored in an array in the frame store. The frame store is illustrated in Figure 12. The signal is digitized to a value between 0 and 255, giving 256 levels of grey. This corresponds to a binary code of eight bits or one byte, chosen because this is a convenient unit of information for the computer to store.

When the CID camera is functioning in a 'live' state the data in the frame store are constantly updated by new information from the camera. On a command from the computer, which is connected to the frame store by a parallel interface, the transfer of information to the frame store may be stopped and the digital image in the frame store

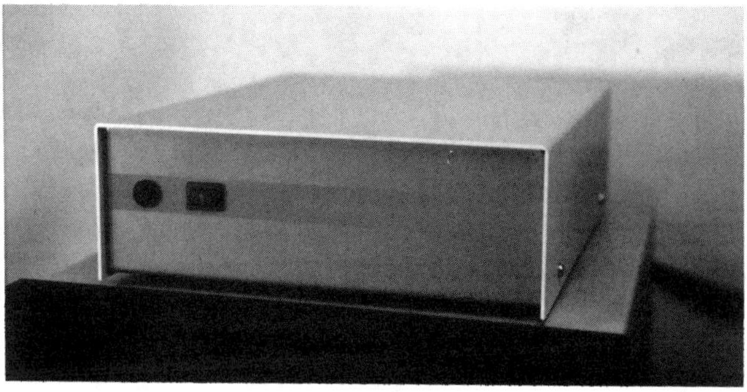

Figure 12. The frame store used in the current image processing system.

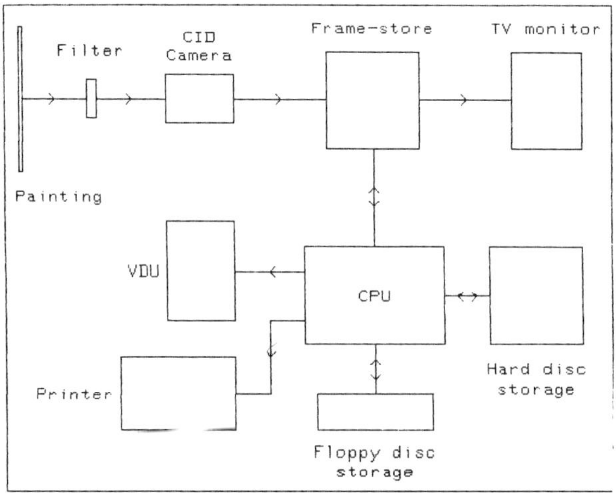

Figure 13. Schematic representation of the current image processing aparatus.

is 'frozen'. A further command from the Hewlett Packard computer causes the digital data for the image to be transferred to an array in the CPU or onto a hard disc for temporary storage. The current system is shown schematically in Figure 13 and in operation in Figure 14.

Images which have been recorded previously may be loaded from magnetic disc into the CPU. The data may then be transferred to the frame store to be viewed on the TV monitor. The TV monitor will

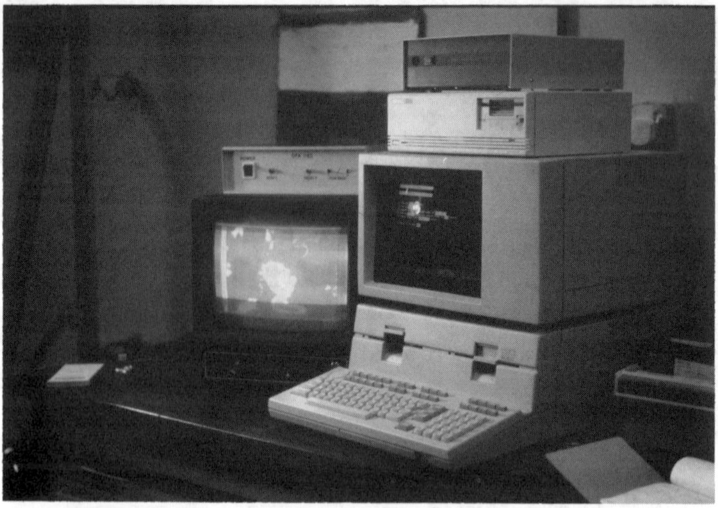

Figure 14. The current image processing system in use.

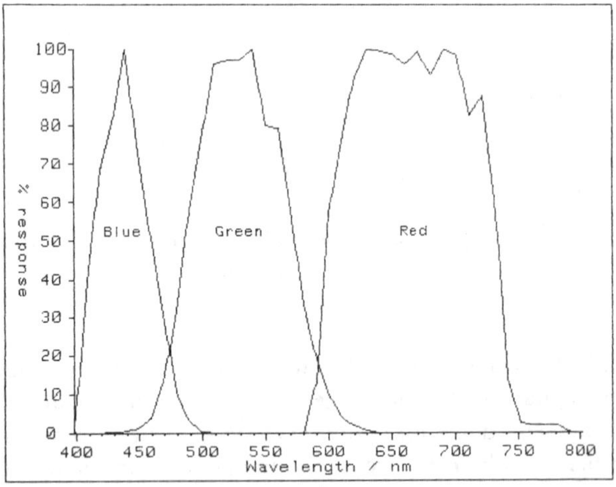

Figure 15. Spectral response characteristics of the CID camera with each of the three colour separation filters.

always show the image currently residing in the frame store. The larger available memory in the CPU (1.6 MByte) allows several matrices to be manipulated simultaneously. This allows image comparisons, subtractions and differences to be calculated reasonably rapidly.

To allow colour change to be detected the painting is again imaged through three colour separation filters in addition to the monochrome image. Three 'Wratten' filters are used, each in conjunction with an infra-red blocking filter. The latter is necessary since the CID array is sensitive to radiation in the near infra-red region. The spectral sensitivity curves for the CID array combined with the three filter sets are shown in Figure 15.

The procedure for measuring the colour of a painting

If the painting is to be measured for the first time then the problem of exact relocation does not arise. If the painting is being imaged for a repeat measurement then it is first necessary to ensure a pixel by pixel match of the two images.

To facilitate the relocation procedure one of the possible variables, the distance from the camera to the painting is standardized by fixing the position of the camera relative to the mechanical easel onto which the paintings are to be placed. It is then only necessary to manoeuvre the painting in the plane perpendicular to the line from camera to object. Two subroutines have been designed to assist in this process. To achieve a rough match between the position of the painting during the previous imaging session and the current position, the data for the previous image are retrieved from disc and stored in the CPU. The computer then alternately displays the 'live' image and the recorded image on the TV monitor. The painting is moved in the horizontal and vertical directions until a reasonable match is obtained. The second subroutine is then used to give accurate relocation. This subroutine gathers the 'live' image and calculates the difference between it and the stored image. Differences in position appear on the TV monitor as dark or light 'shadows' of the image. The painting is moved until the 'shadows' disappear leaving a uniform grey screen, indicating an exact match.

Once the painting is in the correct position the monochrome image and three colour separation images are recorded. Each image is the average of at least sixteen individually acquired images. This averaging removes the effects of noise and variation in the strength of the illumination at the exact moment of acquisition. To allow for the possibility of uneven lighting, a white card is imaged through each of the filter sets. The resulting images are then used to make a correction to each of the colour separated images before these are archived.

The two sets of images may then be compared to indicate any colour differences. As this project has not yet reached the stage where paintings are being imaged for a second time it is not possible to say how obvious changes in colour will be in the data for the colour separated images. Subroutines have been written to perform subtractions of one image from another, and these have been tested by 'doctoring' prints of National Gallery paintings to simulate colour change. Further subroutines will need to be developed to correlate changes in, for instance, the blue image with those in the red and green images. A comparison of changes in the three coloured images will give a more exact indication of the nature of the colour change.

Future development of the system

Any future system will undoubtedly be based on image storage and retrieval at considerably higher resolution. CCD cameras are now available with arrays of over 4,000 elements which are capable of stepped scanning to give an image composed of over 20,000,000 pixels. The handling of such large arrays will require greatly increased computing power. The current system operates on a computer which is also used for general computing tasks within the department; a future system is likely to require its own dedicated machine. In addition, such high resolution images demand high resolution monitors. At present the resolution of the best monitor is considerably less than that of the images acquired by the camera described above, although this is an area of active research.

The use of digital images is now well established in the colour reprographic industry and is currently being considered by a number of museums and galleries as a method for presentation. It would be a great advantage if a new system was capable of recording and storing images for scientific, educational, research, archiving and reprographic purposes.

Digital imaging: Other research programmes

In addition to the work described in this paper, digital imaging systems are being used by a number of groups throughout the world working in the museums and galleries field. The brief list that follows is intended only as an indication of the areas of research and not as an exhaustive survery.

In Venice research into infra-red reflectography has been aided by using digitized images recorded in visible and infra-red lighting conditions. The digitized visible image can be scaled and subtracted from the infra-red image to reveal pentimenti or underlying compositions on the same canvas.[11]

A collaborative project between the Metropolitan Museum of Art in New York and The National Gallery of Art in Washington, D.C. has been using a computer based system to combine infra-red reflectograms. Previously, these reflectograms were photographed and a mosaic assembled from the individual photographic prints. The digitized images can, however, be assembled and corrected using a computer to produce a unified infra-red reflectogram for the whole painting.[12]

A joint project between restorers in Florence and a computer centre in Rome has used digitized images to predict 'global colours' to replace areas of paint loss in panel and canvas paintings. The information so obtained is used as a guide during restoration.[13]

Work at the Ecole Nationale Supérieure des Télécommunications (ENST) laboratory in Paris has examined methods of enhancing digitized images of X-radiographs by removing the contours caused by stretchers, canvas weave and wood grain.[14]

Finally, the Musée d'Orsay in Paris has installed a digital imaging system, developed by commercial companies, to allow visitors and researchers to gain access to images of works related to the collection through an interactive computer programme.

Notes

1. Thompson, D.V., 'The Craftsman's Handbook. ''Il Libro dell'Arte of Cennino d'Andrea Cennini'' ', Yale, 1933, p. 24.
2. Thompson, D.V., op. cit., p. 26.
3. Cotton, W., ed. 'Rev. W. Mason's observations on Sir Joshua's method of coloring' in *Sir Joshua Reynolds' Notes and Observations on Pictures* . . ., by John Russell Smith, London, 1859.
4. Wright, W.D., 'A mobile spectrophotometer for art conservation', *Color*, 6 (1981), pp. 70–4.
5. Saunders, D.R., 'The measurement of colour change in paintings', *European Spectroscopy News*, 67 (1986), pp. 10–18.
6. Commission International de l'Eclairage, 'Recommendations on uniform color spaces, color-difference equations, psychometric color

terms', Supplement no. 2 to *Colorimetry* (E-1.3.1) 1971, CIE Publication no. 15, Bureau Centrale de la CIE, Paris, 1978.

7. Bullock, L.J., 'Reflectance spectrophotometry for measurement of colour change, *National Gallery Technical Bulletin*, 2, (1978), pp. 49–55.
8. Staniforth, S. and Bomford, D., 'Lining and colour change: further results', *National Gallery Technical Bulletin*, 9, (1985), pp. 65–9.
9. Staniforth, S., 'Retouching and colour matching: the restorer and metamerism', *Studies in Conservation*, 30, (1985), pp. 101–11.
10. Thomson, G. and Staniforth, S., 'Identification and measurement of change in appearance by image processing', in *Science and Technology in the Service of Conservation*, ed. by N.S. Brommelle and G. Thomson. Preprints of the IIC Washington Congress, 1982, pp. 159–61.
11. 'Riflettoscopia all'infrarosso computerizzata', *Quaderni della Soprintendenza ai Beni Artistici e Storici di Venezia*, 6, (1984).
12. Wecksung, G., Evans, R., Walker, J., Ainsworth, M., Brealey, J. and Carriveau, G., 'Assembly of infra-red reflectograms by digital processing using a portable data collecting system', ICOM Committee for Conservation, 8th Triennial meeting, I (1987), pp. 107–10.
13. Casazza, O. and Franchi, P., 'Art for the ages', *Perspectives in Computing*, 5, (1985), pp. 4–13.
14. Maitre, H., Private communication.

Part III
DATABASES AND DATA MODELLING

8
A Selective Survey of Systems of Subject Classification

Colum Hourihane

Introduction

It is only within the last twenty years that there has been an attempt to facilitate access to images through indexing the subject content. Standard 'fields' such as artist, date, medium and school provide a much less difficult approach to the problem of classification than does iconography. However, with the amassing of further information, the increase in the available material, the increasing interest in iconography and the harnessing of the computer for rapid indexing, there has been a greater demand to develop an approach whereby content or subject matter forms the basis of classification.

For a number of reasons, there has developed not one but a variety of iconographical classification systems. As Thomas Ohlgren (1980) has pointed out in a pioneering article, there appears to have been a lack of cooperation between the various institutions and individuals involved in the development of these systems. This is particularly true in America where major research has been undertaken in this field. Museums, photo archives and other image collections have operated as autonomous bodies with a resultant focus on satisfying only their own requirements and needs. France, and to a lesser extent Canada, operate a national or near-national approach to subject classification. The major French institutions which classify images on an iconographical basis are obliged to use the Garnier system. This is enforced through the Ministry of Culture, Canada, in an attempt to keep the number of options available low and to encourage the adoption of a standard approach. The Ministry has developed a thesaurus which is meant to provide a framework for future developments within that country. These systems, and others, are discussed individually later in this paper.

With the exception of the Garnier System and a system called Iconclass, which were developed independently of any project, all systems of iconographical classification have arisen from the particular needs of individual bodies. The various approaches that have developed have come about in relation to the particular requirements and needs of the institutions involved. Different institutions deal with different material and so require different systems to handle their images. The iconography of a large collection of abstract or surrealist images differs considerably from that of medieval manuscript illuminations. Independent projects have felt little need to develop large-scale systems which could incorporate material other than that in their own collection. Most systems have in fact been created and developed as the actual process of classification was going forward. The systems expanded to their present state as the need arose.

The purposes of classification may also differ between institutions. Apart from a difference in subject matter, the classifier may display individual preferences. Classifiers of folk art are likely to use a more ethnographic approach than classifiers of a Renaissance subject. Whereas most published systems allow for expansion beyond their immediate focus, and actively encourage such use and adaption, it is clear that such additions may all too often be done haphazardly. Most of the systems are used solely by their founding bodies. There have been few attempts to apply any of the systems to projects other than those for which they were developed.

Some classifiers have in fact chosen to disregard both the available systems and the problem of creating their own in favour of applying bibliographic subject headings such as the *Sears List of Subject Headings* to visual images. The difference between a visual image and a written text, however, poses considerable problems. This method has not been found sufficiently accurate for most purposes.

There are different approaches to iconographic indexing, employing a variety of systems using natural language, numerical notation, codes or a combination of all three.

Systems that employ natural language may either use a controlled vocabulary or free language indexing. The former is by far the more popular approach and reduces significantly the risk of error which is

SYSTEMS OF SUBJECT CLASSIFICATION

	FORMAT	CODED	PRIMARY	SECONDARY	TERTIARY ETC.	EQUAL
GARNIER	Thes.		Found in class. Not exp.	Found in class. Not exp.	Tert. — Not exp. Others — exp.	
GLASS	Thes.					Alphab. Listed
ICONCLASS	Thes.	Numerical notation	Not exp.	Not exp.	Exp.	
IKONOTEEK	Thes.	Numerical notation	Not exp.	Not exp.		
LIBRARY OF CONGRESS	Subject Headings					Randomly listed
PRINCETON INDEX	Subject Headings					
PUBLIC ARCHIVES CANADA	Thes.		Found in class. Not exp.	Found in class. Not exp.	Exp.	
SMITHSONIAN	Thes.		Not exp.	Exp.	Exp.	
YALE	Thes.		Exp.	Specifics	Tert. — Not exp. Others — exp.	

Thes. — Thesaurus format employed
Found in Class. — Found in the system as a guideline but not expressed in the classification
Exp. — Expressed in the classification

possible in free language indexing. Controlled vocabulary indexing may use either key words or subject headings. The controlled terms are usually structured either in a thesaurus format or on a hierarchical basis. The thesaurus format is much the more widely used. It provides a framework whereby word lists can be incorporated and expanded. Whether or not a thesaurus is employed, guidelines are usually given for the meaning of controlled words.

Although the numerical approach to subject classification is ideally suited to computer usage, it is rarely employed in a pure form. ICONCLASS and Ikonoteek (both described below), for example, use an alpha-numerical decimal approach.

A limited amount of synonym-definition, or word-merging, has taken place within individual systems. (For example, the term 'pedlar' may be equated with 'vendor', 'seller', and so forth.) But this process has not taken place between systems, with the inevitable and highly unfortunate result that basic terms can have different meanings in different systems. This lack of a universally adopted, comprehensive thesaurus of controlled terms is highlighted when, for example, we compare the way in which a simple landscape is classified under the Yale and the Smithsonian systems.

In the Smithsonian system, foreign landscapes — i.e., non-American ones — are coded Landscape–Foreign–⟨Country⟩ or Cityscape–⟨Country⟩–⟨City⟩. In the Yale system such an image would be classified under the term 'exotic' — i.e., Landscape-Exotic–⟨Country⟩. The different factors governing the use of the words 'exotic' or 'foreign' need not be discussed here, but they illustrate the subjective differences existing between the approaches employed. This lack of a comprehensive, standard vocabulary was the motivating force behind the project undertaken by the Art & Architecture Thesaurus. This developing thesaurus, it is hoped, will function as a guide and cross-reference to other objects which may be relevant. Authority lists from established sources are compiled and analysed with a view to standardization. To date approximately 35,000 terms of architectural interest have been arranged into sixteen hierarchies. Of those, four hierarchies covering 12,000 items are of strictly architectural interest.

A similar but more specific thesaurus is being developed by the Picture Division of the Public Archives of Canada for application in 150 federal, provincial and municipal museums throughout Canada. Its function is similar to that of the Art & Architecture Thesaurus.

Most systems classify an individual image into a broad overall primary category such as Landscape, Still Life, Abstract, etc. These may vary in number from one system to another between five and approximately forty. The primary categories in each system are always fixed in number, and the list is not capable of expansion by the user. Some systems such as the Garnier system and Iconclass have a structured format within each primary category. This attempts to subdivide all that is representable in the world. The secondary division — i.e., the first subdivision of the primary category — is usually generic. In a number of systems, this secondary division is capable of expansion. The tertiary division is capable of expansion as the need arises in nearly every system. This is usually the division in which the specifics of the image are defined. People, places, etc., are all listed within this division.

Not all systems code their information in this way. In some instances proper information is relegated to a further subdivision and the generic information is further expanded. On the other hand, some systems do not divide the information into primary, secondary, and tertiary categories but give equal emphasis to all the elements within the image, which are usually listed alphabetically.

ICONCLASS

This system is the most widely used of all included in this survey. It was developed by Professor Henri Van der Waal of the University of Leiden shortly after World War II, 1948–50. After his death the project was carried on by a team of art historians based at the University of Leiden headed by Leendert Couprie. The system was developed independently of any project and is readily available in published form to anyone interested in using it.[5] It is an alpha-numerical decimal system in which every phenomenon within an image is given a code. Such a structure makes it ideally suitable for computer use. As a published system, ICONCLASS is divided into nine primary divisions. These are: (1) Supernatural, God, Religion; (2) Nature; (3) Human Beings, Man in General; (4) Society, Civilization, Culture; (5) Abstract Ideas and Concepts; (6) History; (7) Bible; (8) Non-classical Myths, Tales, & Legends; (9) Classical Mythology & Religion.

The notational code applied to each subject consist of a combination of Arabic numbers and capital letters. The primary divisions (numbered as above) are divided into secondary subdivisions (numbered) which are in turn further subdivided into tertiary divisions indicated by capital letters. This tertiary division can be further subdivided, and so on. Each combination of figures and letters is called a notation. That part of the notation which follows the capital letter is called the 'queue'. Each subdivision implies a differentiation of the foregoing one. The decimal construction of the system means that it can be extended.

Some of the notations, it was felt, were not specific enough to satisfy requirements; certain notations shared common characteristics within specific categories. To avoid losing such specifics and to save space, 'keys' were invented. These are again done in a decimal format and consist of a plus sign placed in front of a single figure and enclosed within a bracket after the notation. Combined notations are shown where a particular relationship is indicated between two or more phenomena. This is indicated by means of a colon and is similar to the usage of the Garnier System. The use of proper names is recommended by means of the term '(with name)'.

Example:

2. NATURE >>>>> 21 The four elements
22 Natural phenomena
23 Time
24 The heavens
25 Earth >>>>>> (A) Maps, Atlases. . .
(H) Landscapes >>>>> 25H1 (Landscapes)
>>>>> 25H11 Mountains

As I have said, ICONCLASS is widely employed. It is used at the University of Leiden where approximately 25,000 images have been classified and at the Decimal Index of the Art of the Low Countries, the Bildarchiv Photo Marburg, the Prague Documentation Centre, the Free University of Amsterdam, the Fogg Art Museum at Harvard University, the Witt Library Computer Index at the Courtauld Institute, London, the Provenance Index at the Getty Center, Santa Monica, and the Kunst Indeks Project, Denmark. It is also hoped to use it at the Instituto per il Catalogo e la Documentatione in Rome.

The system goes beyond the purely art historical domain. The classifications were devised from real objects in the real world and not from visual representations. The system as a classifier of images has been criticized because art historians have claimed that it should have been devised from the represented sources and not from what may be represented in reality. This procedure and format indicate the ambitiousness and comprehensive aims of the system. The accompanying bibliographic volumes are not geared to individual objects but to subjects and themes. A three-volume index to the system, arranged alphabetically, was published in 1985 and includes substantial changes to the original seven-volume work published at various dates between 1974 and 1981. One of the major advantages of the system is its flexibility and elasticity. The structure permits additions.

Yale Center for British Art

The project, started in 1976 at the Yale Center for British Art, Yale University, New Haven, is a computerized index of British Art within the period 1500–1915. Photographic reproductions of watercolours, drawings, oil paintings, prints and sculpture are classified on subject matter in a system devised specifically for the project. Classification is on a three-level basis. Subject matter is first classified into an overall primary division, such as Landscape, Still Life, etc. The second level is a list of the specific information within the image, generally found in a tertiary position in other systems. This secondary level in the Yale system is called the Proper Subject. There is no hierarchical arrangement within this division, unlike the levels above and below it; the terms are arranged randomly. Proper Subjects are listed in an inverted manner, similar to the practice found in other projects, so that the most important word is first. There is no limit on the number of terms for each image.

The third level has been called the Generic Subject. This level employs a thesaurus format. There are thirty-seven major generic terms and hundreds of subsets. Each subset is more specific and modifies its predecessor — e.g., Landscape; Water; River. Approximately 80,000 photographs have so far been classified using this system.

The Garnier system

This system, officially called Thesaurus Iconographique, Systeme Descriptif de Representations, was devised by Françoise Garnier and published by the French Ministry of Culture in 1984. It was started in 1976 without reference to any particular project and claims to be a universally applicable system. It is a controlled-word system which is capable of limited expansion. Subject matter is divided firstly into twenty-three primary divisions. There is a subdivision within this primary category into subjects drawn from the real world and those derived from literary sources. The former are called 'Themes', of which there are fifteen, and the latter are 'Subjects', numbering eight. These divisions loosely correspond with the 'Proper' and 'Generic' levels of the Yale Centre for British Art system. A similar division exists in the structure of ICONCLASS. 'Themes' include such general categories as Nature, Agriculture, Society & Social Life, The Body & Material Life, etc., while 'Subjects' include Geographical Subjects, Historical Persons, Imaginary Persons, and Biblical Subjects. These general headings do not appear on the classification entry, but act as a guideline for the classifier and user. There are four further subdivisions of these general headings, none of which are capable of expansion except for the last. Each of the divisions modifies its predecessor in thesaurus format.

For example, the primary 'Theme' Arms & Military Life is divided into secondary divisions of Military Life, Military Architecture, Military Camps, Arms, and so on. 'Arms' is then further divided on the tertiary level into Defensive Arms, Offensive Arms, Machines of War, etc. 'Offensive Arms' is subdivided again into Biological War, Chemical War, etc.

Example:

ARMS & >>>>>>>> Military Life
MILITARY LIFE Military Architecture
Military Camps
Arms >>>>>> Defensive Arms
War machines
Offensive arms >>>>>> Biological arms
Chemical arms
Explosive arms >>>
>>> Bomb
Grenade
(etc.)

The controlled words are not arranged in alphabetical order. The system also takes into account the general characteristics of the image and a limited amount of stylistic information such as location of an image in a picture, the nature of the image in relation to others, the dominance of a particular technique such as relief, colour, perspective, etc.

This is the only system to include any element of style in the classification; all of the other systems have chosen to disregard the problem of interpretation, which is left as the researcher's task. The system has been applied throughout all the major French museums and is not restricted in its application to material of any one kind. There is no limit on the number of entries for any image.

Glass system

This system is officially entitled a Subject Index for the Visual Arts. It was published in 1969 and was developed in relation to the Prints Department at the Victoria and Albert Museum, London. The two-volume work consists of a combination of subject headings and a thesaurus of format terms. Terms in the thesaurus are expanded to a secondary and tertiary level, and all the words are included in the classification. When classifying a representation of a doctor, for example, the entry would read: 'TRADE & OCCUPATIONS Doctor' (Primary, Secondary). Similarly, for an interesting representation of a collar the entry would be 'COSTUME; Civil; Collar' (Primary, Secondary, Tertiary). Equal importance is given to all subjects within an image and the codes are listed alphabetically. It is a general system which allows for considerable expansion and additions. The second volume consists of cross references only, and acts as a guide to related subjects for particular terms. This system does not appear to have been widely used outside the Victoria and Albert Museum, and within that institution the information has not been computerized.

National Museum of American Art and the Smithsonian

This system was developed in 1973 for the Slide and Photographic Archive in the National Museum of American Art in Washington, D.C., and has been applied to four other projects under the aegis of that institution. These are the Peter A. Juley & Son Collection, the pre-1877 Art Exhibition Catalogue Index, the Smithsonian Art Index and the Inventory of American Painting. These projects differ widely, and the application of a single system to such diverse material was to ensure compatibility and standardization. It is a controlled-vocabulary system using words from an established authority list. There is a thesaurus format employed. The system uses three levels of classification. The first of these is a broad primary division with forty-one established terms which are not capable of expansion. The secondary division lists the specific details within the image such as the name of people and places. A tertiary level expands the secondary further and is generic in quality. All terms are alphabetically arranged. A maximum limit of eighteen terms per image has been imposed. This allows a possible six terms in each of the levels. The secondary and tertiary levels can be expanded as the need arises. Approximately 500,000 images have so far been catalogued. Unlike other systems this one was specifically developed with computerization of the information in mind. Despite the success of this system, the projects are contemplating a change to ICONCLASS.

Library of Congress Subject Headings

A system has been developed in the Prints and Photographic Division of the Library of Congress based on and developed from the Library of Congress Subject Headings. This is a system of bibliographic classification which it was felt could be adapted and modified to the visual as distinct from the written image. As the name of the system implies, it is based on controlled subject headings. The system consists of 3,500 controlled subject headings which are arranged alphabetically. Each image has a maximum list of four subject headings.

Ikonoteek

This system was developed in Lund in 1962, and has been used and extended at the University of Uppsala since 1973. The system has been applied to a photographic collection dealing mainly with ethnology and cultural history. The system, which was developed by Professor Anna Brigitta Rooth, is similar to ICONCLASS but has a less universal application. It is an alpha-numerical system where every phenomenon within an image is given a code from a systematic code catalogue. This catalogue is not capable of expansion. In the primary classification, each subject is firstly given a letter of the alphabet (excluding W and Z) which corresponds to a specific division — e.g., J designates the division Crafts, Trades and Industries. The secondary classification consists of a figure. Within the division J the figure 620 designates a representation of a stoneworker, 245 a cooper, and so forth. The primary letter is then combined with the secondary figure to form the coded entry for each subject. There is no limit on the number of codes applicable to each image. This system has, to date, been used to classify approximately 40,000 photographs of everyday life and folklore at Uppsala.

Princeton Index of Christian Art

The Index of Christian Art was begun in 1917 by Professor Charles Rufus Morey, and was first planned as a listing of subjects and objects of early Christian art up until 700 AD. The time span has since been extended to 1400 AD. Whereas the system of classification was obviously not initially devised with a view to computerization, plans are presently underway to transfer the information, currently stored on index cards, to a computer. The collection consists of over 200,000 photographs. A thesaurus format is employed which grew from the subjects encountered while indexing. There are five primary categories which do not appear on the index but which act as a guideline for the indexer and user. These are Figures, Scenes, Objects, Nature and Miscellaneous. These are further subdivided, and the secondary division is again divided. The secondary and tertiary divisions are the only ones which appear on the index card. Whereas the language used is controlled, the secondary and tertiary divisions are capable of expansion as the need arises. Such extensions, however, are done only under strict supervision.

Apart from the main index card files, which are arranged alphabetically and include all the subject headings of the index and many cross references, there is also a subject file. This includes lists of persons, scenes, objects, etc. A fuller and more complete description is given on the subject card of the details of each image.

Summary

The history of subject classification systems within the last twenty years can be divided into two phases. The first of these corresponds with the initial developments in the field. A considerable number of these were undertaken in the United States of America. Various factors led to a great number of systems being developed independently, many of which were applied only to the project for which they were developed. Slight differences in approach and terminology prevented any unification. The need for a single thesaurus was recognized after this initial phase of development had subsided. Little attention has been focused on the formats employed. This is in contrast to the terminology and scope of the various systems, which have proved to be the most problematic areas.

Developments which, it is hoped, will lead to a more unified approach have tended to occupy the major research in this area within the last five years. This second phase of unifying the various systems or at least of unifying the terms employed corresponds with the publications of several large-scale schemes which were developed independently of any projects but are now in the process of being tested. These universally applicable approaches reflect the European solution to the problems of the independently developed classification systems which were developed mainly in the United States. Whereas American systems were rarely applied to European projects, several European systems have now been adopted in America. There has been a recent decrease in system development and a greater concentration on the merging and unification of those already existing. Such an approach can only lead to a more orderly and standardized method of classification in the future.

Notes

Couprie, Leendert, 'Iconclass, a device for the iconographical analysis of art objects', *Museum*, 30, (1978), 194–8.

Couprie, Leendert, 'Iconclass, an iconographical classification system', *Art Libraries Journal*, 8/2, (1983), 32–49.

Fink, Eleanor, 'Subject access to the photographic reproductions of American paintings at the National Collection of Fine Arts', in *Data Bases in the Humanities and Social Sciences*, ed. by J. Raben and G. Marks, Amsterdam, North-Holland Publishing Co., 1980, 229–32.

Garnier, Françoise, *Thesaurus Iconographique, Système Descriptif des Représentations*, Paris, le Leopard d'Or, 1984.

Glass, Elizabeth, *A Subject Index for the Visual Arts*, London, HMSO, 1969.

Molholt, Pat, 'The Art & Architecture Thesaurus: a project report', *Visual Resources*, vol. 1, no. 2/3, (Winter 1981), 193–9.

Ohlgren, Thomas, 'Subject indexing of visual resources: a survey', *Visual Resources*, vol. 1, no. 1, (Spring 1980), 67–73.

Ohlgren, Thomas, 'Image analysis and indexing in North America: a survey', *Art Libraries Journal*, vol. 7, no. 2 (Summer 1982).

Sobinski-Smith, M., 'The Yale Center for British Art: the photographic archive and iconographic access', *Visual Resources*, vol. 1, no. 2/3, (Winter 1981), 173–87.

9

The Catalogue as a Database: The Indexing of Information in Visual Archives

John Sunderland

Introduction

This paper deals somewhat discursively with some of the problems and questions which arise in computer indexes and catalogues of works of art. However, in the endnotes readers will find may references to much more precise information dealing with the areas touched upon.

I do not intend to describe in any detail the Witt Computer Index, with which I am closely involved, but as my own experience has been primarily with the Witt, I shall start from this point and it is therefore necessary to provide a sketchy picture of the nature and purpose of the Witt Index and its structure and organization.[1]

The initial aim which led to the development of the Witt Library Computer Index was the desire to build up a subject index. This arose from the simple fact that the photographs and illustrations in the Witt Library (now more than 1.5 million) are arranged on the shelves within national sections by artist. There are only limited and incomplete ways of searching for subject matter and these are almost entirely portrait indexes. Seriours consideration of a computerized subject index took place in about 1970 at the time of the establishment of IRGMA (The Information Retrieval Group of the Museums Association). Later, in about 1980, the British Library Research and Development Department provided some support for the project. But it was the foundation of the J. Paul Getty Trust and its interest in the Witt Library plans which led to the all important funding for the scheme.

The Witt Computer Index forms part of AHIP (The Art History Information Program of the Getty Trust), which aims to accumulate, co-ordinate and make available art historical information.

The original idea for the index was to produce a very simple and short record; that is to say to have catalogue entries for each painting, drawing or engraving illustrated in the Witt containing the most basic kinds of information, such as NAME OF ARTIST, SUBJECT OR TITLE, MEDIUM AND SIZE, and LOCATION. The idea was, of course, to achieve speed and the quickest possible completion of the project. In terms of the 1.5 million illustrations in the Witt this would still have meant, even with a staff of, say, ten, a timescale to completion of about twenty years or more. It is difficult to have realistic thoughts about such lengths of time for a project, although there are many art historical works which have taken longer, for example the Thieme-Becker dictionary or the cataloguing of the holdings of some museums and galleries. With our present computer record, which is much longer and more complex than the original plan, we are of course faced with similar if not greater problems of completion time, although this has not been multiplied to the extent that one might think, largely because the software is designed to facilitate quick data-entry.

One can only emphasize that it takes time to create a large database and especially if the archive or collection has its information in a form which needs considerable change in order to be entered into a computer. The work is also like a continual attack on a backlog. In the case of the majority of bibliographic databases or library catalogues data entry is usually a process dealing with current material and is not retrospective. But in the case of a museum collection or an archive the problem is that of recording a vast amount of existing facts, figures and records. Recording information of this kind by data-entry into a computer system may be seen by a computer programmer as 'conversion', something to be done ideally automatically, provided the right program and techniques could be devised to effect it. But there are no automatic techniques at present capable of reading into a computer disparate and variegated textual material, some handwritten, some typed, some printed, and editing and re-arranging, checking and verifying that material at the same time. For the art historian, librarian or archivist this is the central core of the work, requiring qualified staff and involving financial costs for staff time which will almost certainly outstrip those for hardware and software.

The nature of the information

This general and in practical terms important point gives rise to a number of significant issues which relate to the nature of the material which is to be recorded and how the recording is to be done. One of the most crucial questions is, 'How accurate is the information?' As art historians we deal with information of all different kinds, but at the moment let us examine two sorts. First, simple facts of a physical kind, such as the dimensions of a painting. Second, questions of attribution as to the artist. The dimensions of a painting are fairly straightforward if the picture is available to be measured and in the case of a museum catalogue database this should be straightforward. But in the case of a photographic archive the dimensions of the painting are likely to be taken from a catalogue or a book, or in other words from a bibliographic source. If more than one source is available it is, maybe surprisingly, quite likely for the sources to differ even in such an apparently simple matter. In the more complex case of attribution, which is dependent on so many factors, on the sifting of evidence of all kinds, on individual perception and response, it is sometimes difficult to make a clearcut decision as to the artist and it may well be necessary to provide more than one name. Even with apparently simple descriptive catalogues it is difficult to model for the computer the degree of accuracy and thus the validity of the material to be recorded.

It is often assumed that the information stored in and retrieved from a computer is, by virtue of the computer itself, accurate and authoritative. People talk about something being 'on computer' as if it is thereby given some enhanced quality and validity it would otherwise not have. This is of course nonsense and no more correct than assuming that information found on the printed page is more authoritative than handwritten or typed information. But although it is true that information on or in computers is no more or less valid than other kinds of information it is important to recognize that because computer information is likely to be used for statistical analysis the question of the accuracy of information is likely to be of some significance. To choose a hackneyed example: if all the paintings in the Witt Library in the Corot files were listed in a catalogue the anecdote, 'There are four thousand paintings by Corot, eight thousand of which are in America' would take on a new relevance. To overcome this problem of accuracy and statistics with regard to information two things are necessary: users of the computer database must accept that information in the computer is not more or less accurate than information in a book or in any other source; and those producing databases have to find a way of presenting information in a form which as honestly as possible models the nature of the material.

The presentation of information

To put the theoretical and practical problems of accuracy in art historical information into a more realistic context, the different approaches used by the Marburg Foto Bildarchiv[2] and the Witt Library to create art historical databases, will be discussed.

The two collections have striking similarities. Both are large photographic archives which cover a wide range of Western art. The photographs are in both cases associated with descriptive text. Both archives have been built up to cater for serious academic study and to aid research. There are also differences as Marburg has large holdings of architectural and sculptural illustrative material, but the similarities in the computer projects are still close because the Marburg database deals only with paintings. Marburg started to compile its database before the Witt and the Witt has certainly learnt a great deal from Marburg, but differences in practice have emerged which are caused by factors other than financial constraints or other external factors and these differences shed some light both on the nature of the information being dealt with and on the differing approaches of Marburg and the Witt to their data.

Marburg decided, after a great deal of thought, to limit the number of fields or categories in their catalogue to a small number of essential kinds of information. At the same time it was decided to spend a good deal of time and effort in verifying and checking the information to be entered against the literature, especially scholarly catalogues, as most of the paintings to be recorded are in public or private collections. Only after this preparatory work has been done is the information recorded. The photograph is catalogued *as if* it is the original not just a representation of it and at the same time the information is presented as absolutely valid with no suggestion that it may be subject to any degree of doubt. This approach has great advantages because in terms of statistics it is always going to present firm data and the actual database stands as the product of Marburg, however much it may rely on the support of published scholarship, for the final judgements about the validity of any piece of information are made by the staff of the project at Marburg, although some degree of sourcing is being introduced as in some cases this is not a matter of principle but of practical concerns involving the method of data entry. The Marburg has already produced over 60,000 records and both the photographs and the information are generated on microfiches, the text microfiches being a series of indexes to the pictures.[3]

The question of the photograph being treated *as if* it is the original is a crucial one both in theory and in practice for a photographic archive. Such an archive has the quality of a surrogate; its contents stand for something else, the original works of art. But these photographs or reproductions are also objects in their own right. It may be that there will be many reproductions, possibly made at quite different times, showing the same work of art. It is possible, and it may be desirable, to catalogue the photograph within the archive as an object as well as to catalogue the photograph as if it was the original that it reproduces.

Something of the same distinction may be made with regard to the information which makes up the catalogue or database. This can be recorded as an authoritative statement of fact, or it may be decided that information needs to be supported by references and sources. This leads to the idea that it is possible to envisage not only differing opinions but also different ideas as to factual or apparently factual information.

The Witt approach, unlike that of Marburg, has been to aim to enter information so that it is, to a large extent, fully sourced. This will enable the user to say, in effect, 'How do you know that?', or 'Who said that?' and to get an answer, usually in the form of a literary reference. The Witt has also tried to treat the reproduction both as the original and as an item to be catalogued. The approach has required the creation of complex software and a record with a complicated structure. The end result is a compromise between the absolutist and the relativist idea. The record starts with a series of cataloguing statements which relate directly to the work of art in an unconditional way. This 'first page' of the record includes the subject indexing. After this the record becomes involved with indexing the photograph or illustration together with its mount; then the information held on the mount, whether added by library staff or taken from published sources, is entered with referencing to the relevant sources. But all this information is related and linked to the 'first page' or object record. The aim is to both catalogue the work of art itself and to record its representation and description in the form of reproduction and textual information in the Witt Library.

This difference with Marburg again reflects the different nature of the collections as well as a different approach. Marburg has relatively short text associated with its photographs in the archive, providing very basic information such as size and medium, location, title and name of artist. But this information is more consistently applied throughout the archive than that in the Witt. In the Witt the information varies from very full catalogue entries derived from possibly a number of sale and exhibition catalogues to nothing more than the name of the artist. Also this information, often cut from published text, has on the whole not been subjected to any control or critical judgement from library staff. Therefore its value and accuracy may be questionable. In addition, some of the information is old and could well be out of date, both with regard to accuracy and with regard to current scholarship in terms of attribution. It is not necessary here to go into the value, from a historical point of view, of information of this kind. But it did become apparent that it was advisable, in indexing this information, to source it, rather than presenting it in the database without any qualification. Sourcing the material not only has the advantage of being correct from a scholarly point of view; it also has practical advantages from the point of data-entry because it obviates the need for elaborate checking of information before it is entered. Provided the cataloguing information is entered accurately with the correct references, data-entry can be done much more quickly than if material has first to be checked in reference books and catalogues external to the archive itself. In order to avoid a chaos of sourced information which might lead to quite misleading statistical output, for example finding that one painting was indexed as by three different artists, thus resulting in being counted as three different paintings, it is necessary to have a record which is carefully structured and which has clear links and relationships. All information about one painting will have to be clearly linked to a single record for the purpose of logic and retrieval. This leads on to another crucial question in a catalogue database, that of authority files and authority control.

Authority files

All projects which have dealt with large amounts of information about works of art and artists, whether biographical, bibliographical or of whatever kind, have come early on to require some kind of authority control. This is not a controversial issue except in so far as different projects will build their authorities in different ways and with different fields. In fact what happens is that mini-dictionaries or lexicons are created, covering proper names, both personal and geographical, and names of institutions or indeed any other kind of category which is liable to occur regularly within the database. The advantages are very considerable, both from the point of view of the content of the database, which is quite external to the computer aspect, and from the point of view of the software, for this can enable authority files to be created and structured and to be linked to all appropriate sections of the records. This can mean that in the process of data entry a change within say a name or date within an authority file can be globally changed throughout the database, provided it is all on-line, which is a most convenient aspect. The great advantage, of course, is that basic names and places can be standardized so that ambiguity is avoided. But at the same time the creation of authority files, say one for the name and brief biography of an artist, can in itself build up to a useful dictionary and may even be worth printing and publishing as a useful reference work in itself. At the same time it would be possible to merge and even harmonize the authority files of different projects. This is something on which the Getty Trust AHIP is now actively involved in working.[4] The production of such authority files has already occurred in many cases. The Marburg text microfiches provide this sort of information as well as many other fields. The Museum of American Art in the Smithsonian, Washington, D.C., has provided from its computer project a list of American artists. The Yale Center for British Art has also produced useful indexes of British Art in American collections. Many of these indexes and lists have not been published in the conventional sense but they are available to colleagues, serious students and so forth. The point is that the mini-dictionaries which authority files can become are useful in their own right and can be detached from their central function as structural members of the database.

Subject indexing

Subject indexing has been one of the major concerns of the Witt Index. By 'subject' I mean the representation apparent in the visual image; not a type or class of object as, for example, 'stained glass' or 'armour', which is the sense in which 'subject' is often used in library classification systems.[5] In about 1982 the Witt looked carefully into the various available kinds of subject indexing which were being used. There were then, as there are now, three basic kinds of system to choose from, taking into consideration that the information was to be entered onto a computer, though it should be pointed out that the computer element in this situation may be overemphasized. It is also worth pointing out that the three systems mentioned here are not necessarily distinct from one another as separate species, nor is it necessarily very important which 'system' is chosen; the important thing is the application and intelligence with which the system is applied together with the number of records which are entered. A subject index becomes more useful according to its size.

The three systems, and here we are only concerned with paintings and drawings in Western Art, were ICONCLASS, a Structured Thesaurus, and a 'full text' description with indexed terms. Although these appear to be quite different, they are in fact very similar in the sense that basically they are all descriptions of subject matter using words. They do differ in structure, modes of presentation and the body of information which they initially make available. ICONCLASS is both a system and its content. It is an alphanumeric coded arrangement with a very strong and precise heirarchical emphasis having usually about seven or eight levels. I shall not discuss it in any detail as it is published and there is literature available.[6] As the ICONCLASS notations read from left to right it is easy for a straightforward computer character search program to truncate to the left, thus allowing for a search of the notation using any level of the subject description, from the broadest to the narrowest and most precise definition. For example, a notation as follows: 71 U 42 73 means *Judith beheading Holofernes*. A search could cite simply 71 (which means all scenes from the Old Testament) or it could specify the complete notation with all its descriptive levels, simply by using the notation as a free text field and using truncation and the wildcard in retrieval. ICONCLASS also provides content which is very wide and far ranging, from detailed descriptions of existing narrative and iconography in important texts such as the Bible and Classical Mythology to a coverage of concepts of all kinds, i.e. Love, Fear, Violence, etc., and to Common Objects which have no conceptual or iconographic meaning, i.e. tables and chairs. ICONCLASS, which is the system which the Witt project chose, as it had earlier been chosen by Marburg, has received a great deal of careful scrutiny by the art historical community in recent years, and it has become accepted as one of the most valuable systems for the subject indexing of Western Art if undertaken on a large scale and with a large number of works to index. Some training or learning is required with the system, but, once the principle ideas are understood, what may initially look like the problem of deciphering the Rosetta stone becomes simply an interesting discipline.

ICONCLASS does not look like a structured Thesaurus, but in fact it is. The usual seven or eight digits of the notation are actually seven or eight levels which can be represented by words, as indeed they are in the published index and in the system itself which gives the word description next to the codes. The advantage of ICONCLASS is that as the words are represented by alphanumeric characters there is very little problem of terminology, standardization of terms or linguistic differences. This problem of standardizing vocabulary is one of the main concerns of a Thesaurus and accounts for the amount of space which it is necessary to give to the cross-referencing aspects or the 'related terms'. Nonetheless the attractions of the Thesaurus, or more properly in this context the Hierarchically Structured Thesaurus, usually at three levels, is considerable and many projects have used one, such as the Yale Center for British Art computer database[7] and the Smithsonian Museum of American Art in Washington, D.C.[8] Unlike ICONCLASS, which is both a system and also the content, a Thesaurus, until compiled, is only like a blank page with divisions. It requires a specialized vocabulary indicating relationships between 'broader' and 'narrower' terms. But all the content, all the words, can be filled in by the compiler. This has the great advantage of allowing the maximum amount of freedom to the descriptive terms, so that they can most satisfactorily cover the subject matter of the collection.[9] So the Thesaurus of the Canadian Heritage Project[10] in dealing with visual records of Canada's history requires quite a different set of terms and words from the Yale Center's British Art database. The creation of the terms within a Thesaurus, however, can involve a great deal of work over very basic matters of description and standardization. These problems have been addressed in particular by the AAT (The Art and Architecture Thesaurus), although it has dealt mainly with architectural terminology.[11] A somewhat similar system which I have not given a separate category here is that of 'keywords'. The terms are carefully controlled and chosen, as in a Thesaurus, but they do not have any hierarchical connection and do not relate to one another in 'broader' and 'narrower' contexts. Although the vocabulary must be controlled, the system is looser and less structured.

The third category is that of 'full text' or 'free text' or where this text is conditioned by indexed words. This is a system, or lack of system, which has been advocated by some computer experts on the grounds that the massive advances that have taken place in the size of computer storage capability together with the increases in processing and calculating speeds make any kind of search on characters much easier than before at the same time as the amount of text stored can grow considerably. This means that individual words and terms within long descriptive passages can be much more quickly retrieved. Programs such as STATUS are designed for this sort of application. Therefore it can be argued that if a great deal of detail and subtle definition is required for the description of a subject then free text is the best method. The indexed terms can act as some form of controlling aspects in frequently recurring or important terms. This kind of approach is often advocated by those who argue either that the subject they are dealing with does not conform to any pattern that can be imposed or that subject matter in general cannot be regularized and has to be described without recourse to any inhibiting or falsifying system. This view has largely been followed by the Catalogue of Italian Art which has been built up since the early 1970s, mainly dealing with painting of the early Renaissance in Siena and Rimini.[12] This has concentrated on very detailed descriptions of paintings using a largely free text method. Such free text has to be controlled, of course, not so much in its detailed words as in the particular approach and understanding of the indexer. The freer the description, it may be argued, the more rigorously controlled must be attitude of the person who does the data entry, for his or her knowledge of the iconography of the subject must be not only informed but also compatible with that of fellow workers, as large projects are almost certainly, by their very nature, carried out by a team. It is also necessary, in any complex catalogue record, for the subject index to be separated from other cataloguing fields in order to prevent a search, say, for a 'bath' in a picture of a bathroom from also finding 'Lord Bath' who may have been an owner of paintings and the town of the same name.

Since the early 1980s other systems of subject indexing have appeared. Possibly the best known of these is the Garnier system which is being used in many French computer projects.[13] It has many similarities with ICONCLASS. The available 'systems' have many apparent differences and many very basic similarities. ICONCLASS, with its short notations of a few characters has a great advantage in that it can be entered into a computer and can take up very little space, whereas a long free text passage will take up much more. It should be pointed out, however, that the most important consideration is the perception and knowledge and judgement of the indexer. Whatever system may be used it is what the indexer can see in the painting and what the indexer considers to be of interest and importance which is of the greatest significance. Although the subject of a painting can often be copied from its title there are likely to be many other aspects of the work which may be of interest. Here we are involved with the question of the potential user of the database. It is a subject which can never be satisfactorily covered, for one never knows what may or may not be of interest. For example, the subject of *Ulysses Deriding Polyphemus* can easily be indexed as a subject from Classical Mythology and Homer's *Odyssey*, but it also includes, at least in Turner's painting, a ship. But the ship is not an early nineteenth century ship, but Turner's idea of what an ancient Greek ship was like. Might such a depiction be of interest to a naval historian? The subject indexer can therefore be aware that the audience or users of the subject index can be various and not by any means limited to art historians. Indeed art historians may be interested in many aspects of subject which are not in traditional terms 'art historical'. But if the indexer takes the view that almost everything may be of interest he or she may take so much time in indexing a single composition that the work goes ahead extremely slowly and little of use can result. There is, in fact, a continual balance which has to be struck between the inherent interest of subject matter with the enormous variety of approaches that can be taken to it and the need to press ahead and produce useful indexes within a reasonable time.[14]

I have discussed the nature of information to a certain extent in this paper. In particular I have made the distinction between information which is sourced, as in a conventional footnote, and information which is given as inherently accurate or authoritative, without need for support. Information about subject matter falls into the second category except where a title or text within the archive may be followed. The identification and description of a subject is a judgement largely made by the indexer or by the indexing team. Therefore, although apparently authoritative, it can have a subjective quality even when a quite tight system is being used. In the case of ICONCLASS it has been found that different projects use the system in somewhat different ways. In the Getty AHIP Projects a study group has been set up to co-ordinate practice in consultation with Leendert Couprie's Leiden University Department which has developed and published the system originally devised by Henri van de Waal. ICONCLASS is, as previously mentioned, being applied in Marburg's Index, one of the original users, in the Witt Project, in the Getty AHIP Provenance Index and in the Photographic Archives in the Fogg Art Museum for some religious iconography.[15] It has become more firmly established in the last few years in its application in visual archives dealing with painting in the Western tradition. The monitoring of the way the system is applied and the development of some of its aspects has brought about useful international cooperation which may lead to the acceptance of ICONCLASS as a standard, at least for certain kinds of collections dealing with European Art.

The end product

Those in the process of creating large databases hope that at some stage they will be complete, or at least that they will reach a point where they can be made available to users. Databases are likely, of course, to be in a continual process of updating as this is one of the major advantages of a computer database over printed material which cannot be changed. But how is the material in the computer bank, which has been so carefully built up, to be presented to its audience?

There are a number of databases in the visual arts which are being used and there are two in particular which are known to me which show quite different user formats. The Marburg Index has regularly provided microfiches of both image and text catalogues which are gradually building up printed indexes. Their advantage is that they are thus already available for use whilst the project is going on to subscribers to the Index and to those who have access to the sets of microfiches. This 'hard copy' has to be updated by supplements and like all hard copy becomes out of date. It is, however, extremely valuable to have the material available. The Yale Center for British Art database is quite different in that it is available at Yale on-line, whilst printouts can also be generated, either to show the results of specific searches or as more complete lists and catalogues, for example of the 14,000 works of British Art in North American collections recorded at Yale. But more imaginative ways of using the database are also being tried, such as downloading the results of searches onto the personal computers of users, thus allowing them not only to study information but also to correct and add to the information before sending it back to the mainframe, obviously with the necessary agreements and permission.[16]

In other cases it is likely that databases, when available, will be mounted on public utilities such as DIALOG. RILA (Répertoire international de la littérature de l'art), one of the major art historical bibliographies, is available on DIALOG, whilst catalogues of the

British Library, for example, are available on BLAISE. One important if rather basic aspect of these large databanks is that they charge for use. These charges are not inconsiderable for the individual scholar who has been used to carrying out research in archives and libraries usually without payment. Catalogue databases will also become available in the same way and charges for use will be made. It is certainly becoming apparent to librarians and to university administrators that the costs involved for individual scholars in using databases will probably have to subsidized by institutional budgets, if this is not already the case.

Notes

1. For further information see: John Sunderland, 'The Witt Library Getty Project' *Art Libraries Journal*, 7, Summer 1983, pp. 27–31; John Sunderland and Catherine Gordon, 'The Witt Computer Index', *Visual Resources*, IV, no. 2, 1987, pp. 141–51.
2. Lutz Heusinger, 'Marburger Index' in *Papers: Automatic Processing of Art History Data and Documents*, Scuola Normale Superiore, Pisa and J. Paul Getty Trust, Los Angeles, I, 1984, pp. 43–62.
3. K.G. Saur, München, *Marburger Index: Inventory of Art in Germany*, English Translation, 1st edition, 1984.
4. The *Vocabulary Co-ordination Group* of the Art History Information Program of the Getty Trust.
5. A good example of a subject index which covers both meanings of the term is *A Subject Index for the Visual Arts*, compiled by Elizabeth Glass for the Victoria and Albert Museum, Department of Prints and Drawings and Department of Paintings, London, HMSO, 1969.
6. The Iconclass System exists in published form: Henri van de Waal, *Iconclass: an iconographic classification system*, North Holland Publishing Company, Amsterdam: Koninklijke Nederlandse Akademie van Wetenschappen. The *System* itself is in 7 volumes, published 1974–81; the *Bibliography* is in 7 volumes, published 1973–83 (indexing published literature according to Iconclass); and the *Alphabetical Index* is in 3 volumes, published in 1985 (enabling one to use the system without knowing the notations, although it should be pointed out that a proper working knowledge of Iconclass requires an understanding of its structure). There is a fair amount of literature on Iconclass, but a good introduction can be obtained from: Leendert Couprie, 'Iconclass: An Iconographic Classification System', *Art Libraries Journal*, 8, Summer 1983, pp. 32–49; Claire Richter Sherman, 'Iconclass: A Historical Perspective', *Visual Resources*, IV, 1988, pp. 237–46.
7. Yale Center for British Art, *Subject Authority Used by the Photographic Archive*,

New Haven, 1979; Mary Jane Sobinski-Smith, 'The Yale Center for British Art: The Photographic Archive and iconographic access', *Visual Resources*, I, no. 2/3, Fall 1980/Winter 1981, pp. 173–87; Anne-Marie Logan, 'Online Subject Access in the Photographic Archives at the Yale Center for British Art', in *Information Interaction; Proceedings of the American Society for Information Science*, Edited by Anthony E. Petrarca, Celianna I. Taylor and Robert S. Kohn, Knowledge Industry Publications, White Plains, N.Y., 1982, pp. 169–72.

8. Eleanor Fink, 'Subject Access to the Photographic Reproductions of American Paintings at the National Collection of Fine Arts', in *Data Bases in the Humanities and Social Sciences*, Edited by Joseph Raben and Gregory Marks, Amsterdam: North-Holland Publishing Company, 1980, pp. 229–32.
9. A good example of the compilation of terms suitable to the collection is the Glass system referred to in footnote 5, although the Victoria and Albert Museum has such wide ranging coverage that the subject terms are capable of application in many other contexts.
10. Douglas Schoenherr, 'Standards Developed by the Picture Division of the Public Archives of Canada for the Description of Works of Art', in *Computerized Inventory Standards for Works of Art*, Compiled by Raymond Vezina, Editions Fides, Montreal, 1981, pp. 233–60.
11. Toni Petersen, 'Computer-aided indexing in the arts: the case for a thesaurus of art terms', *Art Libraries Journal*, 6, Autumn 1981, pp. 6–11.
12. Fabio Bisogni, 'Notes on The "Catalogue of Italian Art": including iconographical analysis realized with the use of the computer', *Museum*, XXX, 1978, pp. 199–204.
13. François Garnier, *Thesaurus Iconographique: système descriptif des représentations*, Ministère de la Culture, Paris, 1984.
14. For a clear analysis of subject indexing systems making useful distinctions see: Lenore Sarasan, 'Visual Content Access: An Approach to the Automatic Retrieval of Visual Information', in *Papers: Automatic Processing of Art History Data and Documents*, Scuola Normale Superiore, Pisa and J. Paul Getty Trust, Los Angeles, I, 1984, pp. 389–406.
15. Helene E. Roberts, *Iconographical Index to Old Testament Subjects represented in Photographs & Slides of Paintings in the Visual Collections, Fine Arts Library, Harvard University*, Garland Reference Library of the Humanities. Vol. 729, Garland, N.Y., 1987.
16. Interesting ideas about the ways a database can be made available can be found in: Anne-Marie Logan, 'The Costs of Building and Maintaining an Art History Database', *Visual Resources*, IV, no. 1, Spring 1987, pp. 71–82.

10

The British Government Art Collection Computer System: The User's View

Mary Beal

> 'It must be remembered that there is nothing more difficult to plan, more doubtful of success, nor more dangerous to manage than the creation of a new system, for the initiator has the enmity of all who would profit by the preservation of the old institution and merely lukewarm defenders in those who gain by the new one.'
>
> Niccolo Machiavelli (1469–1527)

I first became involved in the planning for the installation of a computer system for the British Government Art Collection in 1979. This paper summarizes what the department has learnt about computers since then.

The first, now antique, British Government Art Collection microcomputer system was installed in 1982 to keep track of the approximately 16,000 works of art in the collection which are located in about 700 British government buildings at home and abroad. As the locations of these items change frequently, the main problem is keeping track of their movements throughout the world. It is essential, therefore, to be able to amend and retrieve data from the computer instantly.

The day-to-day management of the Collection, including the purchase of new acquisitions, is handled by a small staff. On the curatorial side, this comprises the Curator, the Assistant Curator and three Curator G's (a civil service grade equivalent to an administrative officer), and on the administrative side a Higher Executive Officer, an Executive Officer and two Administrative Officers. In 1978, when the present Curator, Dr Wendy Baron, and Assistant Curator, myself, were appointed, we found that the manual records of the Collection were inaccurate, incomplete and internally inconsistent. An improved system of record keeping was essential.

Options

In order to improve the records four options were considered, of which three were rejected: a new manual system; or a terminal connection to a remote mainframe in either (a) batch, or (b) interactive mode. Only the fourth option, a micro-computer system, could meet our requirements to any degree of satisfaction.

Acquisition of the system: procedure

A carefully worded and fully reasoned report explained why a micro-computer system was needed to provide a single, accurate and immediately accessible record of the Collection, which would also produce straightforward catalogue entries on each work of art.

The report was written in October 1979, and in January 1981 it was at last accepted by the then parent department, the Department of Education and Science, and an appropriate consultancy was selected to write the software and advise on the acquisition of the hardware. The software took almost a year to write, and the system was finally installed in January 1982.

Designing the system: mutual co-operation

Throughout the whole of 1981, the Curator, the Assistant Curator and the Higher Executive Officer from the Government Art Collection (GAC), the consultancy and the Management Services Division were in constant communication. All took part in lengthy discussions, sometimes lasting for days, on how to design a system which was both feasible, from the consultancy's point of view, and which satisfied all the requirements of the GAC. The importance of making an exhaustive study of the way in which *all* one's staff work, and the purpose of *each* member's work at this stage, cannot be emphasized strongly enough. It is imperative that all those involved in designing the system have understood down to the last detail how the department runs and the consequent priorities needed. It is absolutely crucial not to overlook or gloss over any fact or potential difficulty at this stage. Every point *must* be thrashed out in full by both sides, since misunderstandings can and do frequently occur as a result of mutual confusion over the other side's day-to-day vocabulary, jargon and working methods.

Data input

Each work of art in the Collection is allocated a Master Record which contains the essential information on the object required for daily management. This information is collated from various manual sources onto a data input sheet, usually by the Curator G's and/or the administrative staff, and the sheet is then passed to the Curator and the Assistant Curator for checking and valuation. The information on the datasheet is then typed into the computer usually by the Curator G's or by the administrative staff, a straightforward process since the datasheet is a replica of the Master Record fields which appear on the VDU screen.

Data input is a long, tiring and very time-consuming process, which depends entirely on the dedication of each member of staff to this end. About 12,000 records have been entered in nearly seven years and it is estimated that it will take about another two years before all 16,000 records are computerized. To avoid the problems of 'garbage in, garbage out', the data input process must be strictly supervised at each stage to maintain accuracy and consistency. Staff have had to dovetail their work so that the process passes smoothly from one hand to the next like a conveyor belt. The importance of co-ordinating and integrating the staff's work successfully is paramount.

Change-over from manual to computerized system

Since all the records cannot be computerized overnight, we still have to keep up-to-date tedious and cumbersome manual records for all those items which have not yet been computerized. The brunt of this complex record keeping is carried out by administrative officers, and those working in the department are admirably conscientious. However, training newly appointed administrative officers to master a hybrid computerized/manual system of record keeping is a complex and lengthy task, the importance of which should not be underestimated. The deadline for total computerization was considerably delayed as a result of a disturbingly large turnover of staff. Within twelve months a new higher executive officer, three new administrative officers and a new curator G had to be trained, a situation to be avoided if at all possible since not only did the computerization process slow down substantially, but record keeping errors occurred as a result of very understandable misunderstandings by everyone over the relationship of the manual system to the computer system.

Problems

Because none of us had had any first-hand experience in using a computer, we had no idea what to expect, and consequently we did not have an 'acceptance testing' period. We just started keying in data, and coped as best we could with each problem as it arose. Looking back, I do wish we had had such a period.

1. Hardware

There were many hardware problems, some more serious than others. The worst were early on, with the two VDU's, the printer and the CPU, much of which had to be replaced. One of the exchangeable discs became incomprehensibly and alarmingly corrupted, and also had to be replaced, as did one of the VDU's, after the cursor seized up regularly after about thirty minutes' use each day. The cause seemed to be overheating during hot summer weather; an electric fan was provided to control the temperature which solved that problem. We also experienced what everyone dreads: a headcrash.

A contract which guarantees a visit from the representative of the computer maintenance firm within twenty-four hours is therefore strongly recommended; it works out far cheaper than paying for every maintenance visit separately.

2. Software

To our immense delight and relief, we found that all the hard work the consultancy and the GAC had invested in designing the system paid off, and its enormous benefits over the manual system were soon apparent. However, some modifications were necessary.

a. Safeguards against losing computerized data

i. It was possible to get into serious trouble with the system by making a simple typing error in response to a question posed by the machine, making the inexperienced user feel as vulnerable as a learner driver in charge of a powerful car without a driving licence. For example, the whole inventory of one building was wiped out by mistake during an early back-up session, and the back-up routine underwent numerous modifications at our request to reduce the possibility of making such a mistake again. It is very important to establish the back-up procedure as a regular routine which every member of the department should be able to do without difficulty. No one member of the department should be labelled as the 'computer person', without whom all computer housekeeping grinds to a halt: everyone should be encouraged to take an active part in familiarizing themselves with the machine to the best of their ability. Even at the very basic level, this is good for office morale all round, and does not leave everyone in the lurch when the 'computer person' eventually moves on.

b. Space shortage

After the first year, however, by far the most serious problem encountered was space shortage; it is vitally important not to underestimate the amount of space required for the data. Treat with extreme caution any blithe and sanguine reassurances of computer firms over-anxious to sell their product that their system is large enough to meet your requirements. In our case we found that with only one quarter of the records on computer, the space for sorting the data was already exhausted. We found, for example, that the artists' file had only 16 per cent of space on it after 4,000 records had been inserted, because we had underestimated the number of pictures by anonymous artists, each of which had to be identified separately. To get round this space problem, an updated version of the housekeeping system was installed, which took up less space on the disc than the previous system. We also had to pay for a modification to the search routine which used less space for searching and sorting records than the original search routine had needed.

c. Training

The consultancy gave an admirable amount of thought to making the GAC tailor-written part of the system as user-friendly as possible, and the GAC staff learnt to use it with ease and speed.

The search and housekeeping parts of the system, however, proved far more problematic in the beginning, particularly as the two day training session took place during their installation when only the Curator was present as a result of a train strike. For almost five years our use of the system was dogged by the problems of having inadequate documentation and inadequate user manuals, which could only be described as user-opaque, for the search and housekeeping parts of the system.

The ability of staff to master computer concepts and logic can vary considerably. Some people have a natural flair and can master quite complicated search routines within a reasonably short period; others will only ever really feel at home with straightforward user-friendly instructions from a tailor-written menu.

Having invested the time and effort in training staff to a good standard, try to keep them for at least two years before they move on, and when they do leave, try to ensure a hand-over period to the new incumbent of several weeks.

Future

It is very important to:

a. Plan ahead, in particular for the acquisition of new software and hardware and for the transfer of data to the new equipment; and
b. To think through the problems and intricacies of handing over the system to new incumbents of the more senior posts in your department. There *must* be satisfactory documentation for the system for the new incumbents to study and master without undue difficulty, even if they do not possess great computer talents, and there must be a consistently knowledgeable support network. Knowledge of the idiosyncracies of any computer system must *not* rest in the heads of the few who set it up. If it does, subsequent users will soon be faced with the task of interpreting a system which is about as immediately reader-friendly as the Rosetta Stone.

The GAC's fears concerning the problems of passing on the knowledge of the system to new incumbents were amplified in October 1985 when the consultancy unexpectedly notified us that, following a review by their director, they could no longer 'continue to give ongoing support to systems developed and maintained by them following the expiration of any maintenance agreement'. They suggested two options: either ask the small systems group in the department to support directly the system, or establish an arrangement with another software house whereby they maintained and if necessary, enchanced the system. While the consultancy doubtless had its own good reasons for withdrawing its support, this news was about as welcome as a headcrash.

At that stage, the consultancy had still not fully documented the system in user-friendly manuals and it was difficult to imagine how a new software house would be able to pick up the reins. We therefore wrote back to them stressing that it was crucial that they advised us fully as to the software houses available, and likely maintenance charges. It was also crucial that, before transfer, the consultancy provided:

1. Comprehensive guidelines for the general housekeeping of the system.
2. Complete documentation on every aspect of the system.
3. A user-friendly search routine manual, so that we did not have to ask for outside tuition.
4. A source to whom we could turn if we needed special software to correct and modify as necessary software inadequacies and corruptions and new software for the time we needed to transfer our data onto new hardware.

Three months later the consultancy replied that:

1. The maintenance charges of another software house would be considerably higher than those charged by the consultancy (actually about five times the amount).
2. All the staff at the consultancy who had detailed knowledge of our system had moved on and that perhaps another software house could take on 'this extremely resource-consuming task' of providing documentation.
3. Another software house might be able to write the search routine manual and that it should be able to help us develop our system.

We did not find these replies reassuring, so we responded by asking who would bear the cost of providing the documentation, which presumably would be very high if carried out by another software house. We also asked whether it was indeed likely that another firm would agree to take on a 'tailor-made' system which had not been equipped with comprehensive documentation, and whether the consultancy could evade this responsibility of providing it.

Silence followed for a good number of weeks and then the consultancy gave way. They agreed to write a search routine manual and to provide housekeeping guidelines at our request and carry out an inspection of our documentation, which they eventually did. They finally withdrew support completely in April 1987.

In retrospect, we should have insisted that user-friendly documentation was supplied at the time the software was installed. Thinking that there will be time to 'pick up' documentation in retrospect is almost cloud-cuckoo land; staff from the consultancy move on, your own staff move on, other urgent demands and pressures not connected with the computer appear on the scene, and it is all too easy to find yourself in the situation which confronted us.

In some ways, this transfer of responsibility from the consultancy was a blessing in disguise, since this move forced the consultancy to write the documentation which it should have done in the first place.

Meanwhile the consultancy also warned us that maintenance charges for our system would soon escalate because the hardware and software were rapidly becoming antiquated.

Within weeks of this warning, the computer, no doubt aware of developments, started to play up, and hardened its policy of non-co-operation, such as by claiming that the same picture was in two buildings at the same time and so on. This was because the machine had finally run out of space. When the system was installed we were told that it would be able to hold 20,000 records, as we requested; in fact it could only hold about 10,500 records. At this late stage, we realized the value of having a *contract* with the consultancy in which the clauses were spelt out which we did not have.

Faced with no more space and by now antiquated hardware and software, with nobody prepared to take it on, we had no option but to grasp the nettle and dump the dinosaur.

With the aid of the Information Technology and Methods Branch of our present parent department, the Cabinet Office, who had already said that the staff there were in no position to support us in any way if we retained our old system, we have now transferred all our data to a new machine, to a new operating system and to new applications software, which are all compatible with the machines and systems at present running in the Cabinet Office. This is a multi-user/multi-tasking system, running under the Xenix operating system, supporting at present three terminals and a printer with a possibility of expansion to take in extra users.

In common with other more modern systems, this new system

should be far more flexible than our old one with search routines and facilities considerably less rigid and confined than those imposed on us in 1982. For the first time we shall also be in a position to write some of our own programs for our own specific uses.

In order to negotiate the possibility of translating our old system into a new one, the Information Technology and Methods Branch of the Cabinet Office had to understand our old system. A detailed dossier of how our system worked was required, which we had to write ourselves, a skull-exploding operation which took two of us a fortnight to write, but we did learn a lot about our system from it.

In order to install a computer system as painlessly as possible, therefore, I offer you the following summary of guidelines:

A. Acquisition of the system

1. Consider all the options. At this stage you may decide you do not need a computer after all.
2. Write a fully-reasoned report stating why you need a computer. (At this stage you may still decide you do not need a computer after all).

B. Design of the system

1. Study:
   a. The priorities of the department.
   b. The functions of all the staff.
2. Thrash out each point and confusion.
3. *Never* gloss over facts and potential difficulties.

C. Data input

1. Allow sufficient time for data input and then double (at least) the time estimated.
2. Dovetail staff work.
3. Supervise strictly each stage of input.

D. Change-over from the manual to the computer system

Allow sufficient time for training staff to manage two systems.

E. Trouble shooting

1. Hardware: Take out a twenty-four hour maintenance contract.
2. Software:
   a. Ensure safeguards against losing data.

   b. Back-up regularly.
   c. Involve *all* staff: not one 'computer person'.
3. Training:
   a. Have user-friendly manuals.
   b. Keep staff for at least two years.
   c. Plan staff hand-over period of several weeks.

F. The Future

Plan for:

a. Acquisition of new hardware and software.
b. More space for new data.
c. Hand-over to new senior staff.

G. Conclusions

Allow generous time for:

1. Initial planning of the system.
2. Learning to master the system yourself.
3. Training all staff to master the system.
4. Planning and budgeting for future enhancements and modifications.

Insist on:

1. Software and hardware contracts you can understand and which are comprehensive.
2. Documentation you can use yourself and which arrives when the system is installed.
3. A maintenance contract to cover all eventualities.
4. A consistent knowledgeable support network.

11

Computerize and be Damned! The Computerization of the National Gallery of Ireland

Ray Keaveney

The National Gallery of Ireland first contemplated the acquisition of a computer to assist with the cataloguing of the collection and the production of publications as far back as 1984. The initial brief, at that particular time, was in fact more orientated towards the library and the cataloguing of the book stock than towards the gallery proper and its collection. This approach was due primarily to the fact that the use of computers in libraries had by then become an accepted fact of life and systems had been developed to cater adequately for the needs of those working in such institutions.

At that time the gallery employed three fully qualified librarians who were all well acquainted with the application of the new technology to their line of work and had no difficulty seeing how such facilities could be used within the gallery. A survey was carried out to determine and define how various other departments might benefit from the introduction of computer technology and a written brief was prepared for a proposed system, outlining the basic requirements, the standard applications, and the performance parameters of the system required. From the beginning a multi-user system was envisaged as the most appropriate to our needs, providing staff access to information from a number of terminals located about the building. After a six-month period of investigation and negotiation, however, the project was dropped, primarily as a consequence of our not having sufficient funding available, as well as not being sufficiently confident that the systems reviewed could deliver the kind of service we required, despite their considerable complexity and cost.

Though this initial venture into the world of computers ended in failure, for the reasons just outlined, the process of investigation and negotiation proved both educational and beneficial. We learned a great deal about the nature of computers, how they operate, and the kinds of services they could or could not provide. We were considerably enlightened about the inadequacies of our initial approach, both technically and financially, and were, as a result, made more acutely aware of what was required if we were to pursue the objective again at some future date. Another crucial benefit of this 'failed' venture was the generation of limited, though useful, funds from central coffers to assist with the computerization of certain standard routines, as it was then government policy to introduce computerization to any department which could make a valid argument for its benefits.

All this hard-won experience was to prove invaluable when, some eighteen months later, we reconsidered the feasibility of computerizing the management of the collection. And yet in a very crucial way, we were no wiser about the course we should take. For though library computer systems continued to flourish, there were as yet no standards established for the automation of collection management. We surveyed the literature and found that in the United States a number of groups had been set up to study the problems presented by the computerization of museum records. We wrote to some of the individuals involved, but it was something of a disappointment to learn that no standards had been agreed and that basically it was up to each museum to determine what system to purchase and what formats to use for the compilation of its own records. This meant that we were more or less on our own with the task of designing a system without the benefit of working to agreed standards or procedures.

In retrospect, this apparent difficulty was no bad thing, though it did occasionally leave us not a little bewildered. The chief source of our bewilderment was the vast array of hardware and software which had been developed for the business community and from which we had to choose a particular combination which would most adequately serve our needs, without being entirely confident that such systems could successfully be adapted to the museum environment.

As with our initial project some eighteen months previously we again set about establishing the basic parameters of the system, this time being more definite and to a degree more ambitious in our outline brief, as well as more specific about key details. Being a large national institution, we needed a relatively powerful installation with the facility to allow staff to access, from a network of terminals dotted about the building, a central database capable of containing all the relevant information on every item in the collection. The database must be capable of holding not simply basic descriptive data on the paintings and drawings, such as the artist's names, titles of paintings and their location, etc., but also the full text of any *catalogue raisonné* entry from relevant publications and articles wherever this was deemed appropriate. More than this, it must be capable of retrieving all the relevant information on any particular item, regardless of the manner in which this information was entered.

In addition we wanted to be able, at some later date, to accommodate and manage as part of our system a powerful database on Irish art and artists. This would list entries from sales catalogues, exhibition catalogues and other sources, providing documented details on the lives of hundres — if not thousands — of native artists. The ideal system would also be capable of being adapted to catalogue the book stock in the Gallery library, a not inconsiderable task as we had some 30,000 volumes already on the shelves. In this instance, the ability to link with the OCLC network was considered desirable. Parallel to these sophisticated requirements was the more mundane though no less pressing desire to provide the secretarial and publications staff with much-needed word processing equipment. Finally, whatever system was chosen had to be fundamentally simple to operate, as we had no allocation of funds to establish a data processing department and no flexibility in staffing to allow for the appointment of even one person to operate the system.

When we had more or less established our requirements and set down performance parameters for the projected system, we set about searching for business concerns who we felt might be capable of providing the desired installation. The choice of supplier would be crucial in the success of the project and we were aware that we needed to be extremely careful in screening the applicants. We felt, and I believe justifiably so, that we could easily get involved with an unscrupulous supplier who would promise the earth and deliver a lot of impressive high tech equipment which, however, would not provide the kind of results we needed. More worryingly, there was also the possibility that a supplier might honestly tender for the contract and design a system which seemed adequate at the time but which would ultimately prove deficient. Given the substantial sums of money that would be involved, we also had to be confident that the company which supplied the system was financially sound — otherwise, though we might have acquired the right system, it could evaporate before our very eyes, a not uncommon fact of life in the cut-throat business of selling computers. These considerations also covered the critical area of support and backup of the system after its installation, something which we needed to be very careful about, given that there would be no trained computer operator on our staff. The cost of backup also needed to be considered, as the overheads of running any system can be quite substantial and need to be as carefully considered as the initial purchase price. The nature of the support also needed to be discussed, as there are varying interpretations as to what is included in such an agreement and what comes as extra. Finally, the cost of future development of the program to accommodate additional facilities needed to be studied, as this would be of relevance to the setting up of future databases.

After having studied the market and made enquiries as to which might be the most suitable concerns to do business with, we eventually settled on a choice of four main bidders for the contract. The first of these proposed a networked system running on IBM or Compaq equipment, with dBase III providing the database facility and Word Perfect as our word processor. Another company offered a multi-user setup running on Altos equipment more suited to multi-tasking operations than the MS-DOS employed on PC equipment. The third proposal was to employ a Northstar multi-user system, with Dataflex as the crucial database management program. A fourth proposal was to install a minicomputer and run a program called Basis, designed specifically to supply full text retrieval facilities in a fully fledged multi-user, multi-tasking minicomputer environment. Not surprisingly, the costs involved in purchasing a minicomputer system initially scared us away from considering this option and we set about first examining the PC-based proposals.

We soon learned two crucial facts, however: the PC option would not be as cheap as we had thought, nor would it easily deliver the kind of facilities we required. The full text retrieval requirement meant that the programs to be employed needed to be developed to the limits of their capabilities and event then, they would not have the power or flexibility we deemed necessary. For an eight-user system, the cost of the top two contenders ran somewhere between IR £20,000 and £30,000. Had we felt confident that such a system could deliver the goods, we would most probably have opted for one of these packages, which could then have been purchased over a number of years. Under the circumstances, however, we decided to take another look at the mini-based system and see how it performed and what it would cost.

We were first given a demonstration of Basis running on a Microvax, and were greatly impressed with its power and ease of use, and encouraged to investigate further. We discussed with the supplier the nature of the information we wished to store on the computer and provided them with a template of the layout of the projected database, listing the most important fields to be included in the records to be compiled on each item in the collection. This involved determining what categories of information we wished to establish on each picture: inventory number, artist, artist's dates, title, technique, dimensions, inscriptions, provenance, exhibitions, literature, location, valuation, restoration history, photographic reproductions, texts from *catalogue raisonné* entries and articles, previous attributions — and more. Together with determining the relevance of each field, we also needed to project how many characters each field would contain, as this would have some bearing on the nature of each field and whether it would be listed as a 'standard' or a 'long text' field.

When PC-based systems, this presented considerable problems, as many of the database programs could only hold a limited number of characters per field, although in some instances it was possible to get round this difficulty at least in part by stringing fields together. The same held true for complete records: again, there was often a standard limit on the size of each record which, if exceeded, meant that complex record-linking techniques had to be employed. Though dBase III, among other MS-DOS systems, was capable of handling a limited amount of free text in a special 'memo' or 'text' field, the size of the field was still limited and the text could not be searched. Another factor which we needed to keep in mind was the possibility that at some future date we might wish to alter the nature of individual fields and to modify the record structure.

Basic seemed capable of accommodating all our demands much more easily and with fewer complications than any of the PC-based programs. This is made immediately apparent when one considers that the standard field length in Basis is a massive 10,000 characters. Long text fields are achieved by linking together a number of standard units of 10,000. Another crucial advantage of Basis is the manner in which it actually stores the data. Each record is given a unique number — for the management of the collection, this number is normally the inventory number of the object referred to. The indexed terms are each provided with the address of the head file text by means of the unique number allocated. Another major benefit of the technique used to store the data is that the system only allocates sufficient storage to file the text actually supplied. No space is wasted storing room for non-existent data. This is very different from most MS-DOS based programs which automatically store all the character spaces allocated to a specific field regardless of the number of characters actually required. (For example, if you allocated sixty characters to the ARTISTS — NAME field, and an artist's name was George Armpit, then most programs would store the thirteen characters of the name together with the remaining unused forty-seven spaces, whether you liked it or not.) This approach also poses problems when the information turns out to contain more characters than you initially envisaged.

Where Basis really shone, however, was in the ease with which data could be entered or updated, and, even more impressively and crucially, the power to index and retrieve virtually every word in the database, regardless of its context or of how it was entered. Entering data is by means of standard templates, which look for all the world like a routine questionnaire or form, with the title of the data field listed to the left and the blank for the data to the right. The ability to receive text generated using certain word-processing packages is also available, greatly easing the imputting of long text fields. Retrieving information is by means of a relatively simply query syntax which approximates spoken English, though it is more brief and economic. The standard query takes the form: ⟨find X = Y⟩ — for example, ⟨find artist = Reynolds⟩. Nothing could be simpler. The system supports Boolean logic searches and also comprehensive range searchers covering numerical data and dates, allowing you to seek integers of equal value, lesser value, greater value, equal and lesser values, and equal and greater values.

To run the program it was initially suggested that we purchase a Microvax computer. The cost of such an option would have proved too high, however, and would have put the system beyond our reach. We explained that we could not afford any package which cost more than the PC-based systems already reviewed and that if we were to proceed with the project and bring it to a successful conclusion, then some mechanism would have to be found to achieve this, or else we would have to drop the project altogether and wait again until some new, more affordable offering became available. Though this did not look too hopeful, as the proposed package would have cost more than double the funds allocated, we pursued the matter and eventually achieved our goal by opting for a second-hand Vax 11/730 minicomputer. This machine operates on the standard VMS operating system of the Vax family of minicomputers which are manufactured by the Digital Equipment Corporation (DEC). The machine comes with a 121 megabyte hard disk to provide storage, and has eight terminal ports provided as standard, though it is possible to connect up more than double this number. The terminals may be either dumb VI100 consoles or intelligent DECmate units, though other terminals with enhanced features may also be used. An advantage of choosing the Vax computer is the VMS operating system, which is the standard operating environment for the complete range of Vax machines, from the smallest to the largest. This feature will allow us, at a future date, to replace the 11/730 with any machine in the Vax range without any need to reprocess or translate the data already compiled. For terminals we negotiated the free presentation of five VT100 dumb consoles from another government department which at the time was upgrading its own Vax equipment. To provide the much-needed word processing facilities we managed to obtain three DECmate III machines through sponsorship and one further unit was purchased second-hand. When we installed the system in 1986, we wired it up to accommodate access from twenty-four locations around the building, allowing terminals to be unhooked from one location and moved to another as needs changed.

After this brief summary of the process of acquisition of the system, I believe it would be of use here to provide a few examples of some of its most useful features. It already stores the complete descriptive data on all 4,000 engravings in our collection. As mentioned earlier, one of the most impressive aspects of Basis is its ability to retrieve any word or combination of words stored anywhere on the system. For instance, if we take a simple entry for the title of an engraving, it can be demonstrated that any term in the entry can be retrieved and displayed, regardless of the manner in which it was entered.

> 'Title: Barry Yelverton, 1736–1805.
> Chief Baron of the Exchequer, later 1st
> Viscount Avonmore, against his home,
> Fortfield House, Terenure, Co. Dublin.'

The information in this particular entry contains approximately 150 characters. Though it could easily contain 10,000, or indeed more, it only takes up the storage space necessary for the characters actually used. Every word in the entry is indexed if the field is established as an indexed field. It may not be beneficial to index every field, and so one has the option to set up a field as 'indexed' or 'non-indexed'. Non-indexed fields may later be converted to indexed status if so desired. The prime factor controlling this choice is the amount of storage available, as all terms in an indexed field must be stored in the index though some may be there already, of course, in which case only the new address takes up additional storage space.

Retrieval of any relevant term may be achieved through the use of a relatively simple query syntax, with more complex search strategies available through the use of Boolean operators — any, or, and not, etc. A thesaurus facility is also available, and further vocabularly control facilities are being developed. A sample search might go as follows, each one providing a positive response:

find title = yelverton
find title = barry
find title = yelverton and title = barry
find title = barry and title = yelverton
find title = viscount
find title = viscount and title = yelverton
find title = yelverton and not title = duke
find title = yelverton and title = barry and title = viscount
find title = fortfield
find title = 1736

Multiple fields may be searched simultaneously to obtain the relevant records:

find artist = robinson and title = yelverton and technique
= mezzotint

When the user has identified the records which are relevant to his search he may request the data to be displayed in any sequence he wishes:

display artist, title, provenance for 1, 3, 6

This will instruct the system to display on screen the artist field, the title field, and the provenance field for the first record, the third record and the sixth record.

A very useful facility offered by the program is the instruction used to call up the display of what are known as mapped fields. This is very useful in a database which has a great number of fields used to record differing categories of data. The facility allows the user to call up a predetermined list of fields without the need to list all the fields every time a request is made. Thus, should the registrar normally require only the following information: inventory number, artist's name, title, dimensions, location, and valuation, then a mapped field named ⟨reg⟩ could be generated which would display the information in these fields, and only these, with the instruction

display reg for x, x, x, x

Search strategies which regularly seek information on the same fields may also be abbreviated through the generation of profiles.

A feature which can prove very useful when searching a large database and save a great deal of time is the facility to restrict a specific search to a limited group of relevant documents, rather than having to search the complete database every time a query is entered. For example, if one is researching views of London, and one is only interested in paintings which have this as their subject, then, depending on how the database is set up, one can restrict all searches to pictures which have London as their subject. This strategy is also useful in that it avoids the recall of spurious or irrelevant records. In other words, if one asks:

find title = st mary's

using this strategy, only a St. Mary's located in London will be retrieved. To activate this facility one simply issues the following instructions:

find subject = London
set universe on

All subsequent searches will be limited to records with London in the subject field. With engravings, you could easily limit your search to plates printed by a particular publisher, regardless of the artist's name:

find publisher = Junket
set universe on

All subsequent searches will be restricted to plated published by Junket. Thus, if you proceeded to ask

find artist = bounder

only engravings published by Junket and designed by Bounder would be retrieved.

Another standard facility is provided by the instruction ⟨list⟩ which instructs the program to list all the searches executed in any session, with the option of storing the documents retrieved for access at some future time, or indeed for immediate access so that one can review the material retrieved.

Apart from full range of search and display instructions to cover almost every conceivable requirement, the program also provides a comprehensive range of management facilities which allow the systems manager to strictly monitor and control access to data, including the ability to chart access from fee-paying users who are charged according to the time spent using the system or the number of relevant documents retrieved.

12

Computer-Aided Cataloguing in Moray District, Scotland

Ian Morrison

The background

Microcomputers are now capable of providing considerable assistance with many museum documentation problems. Until recently the quantity and complexity of museum records could only be dealt with on a main-frame and this led to problems of incompatibility between museums' computer systems. Main-frame applications also tended to be the reserve of computer specialists. Database management systems, for example dBase II, had limitations which deterred many potential users while the Museum Documentation Association's (MDA) own system, GOS, required considerable knowledge of programming to implement. Over the last year or so the price of 'micros' has tumbled and specifications have increased. Powerful low price software and large capacity hard disks have brought the new technology within the reach of many small museums. In Moray District the decision was taken to computerise museum records in September 1986. By the end of October a Tandon PCA-40 (IBM AT compatible with 40 megabyte hard disk) had been purchased along with dBase III PLUS software, a Canon A-50 printer and a tape streamer. The latter provides a very necessary facility for backing-up the entire contents of the hard disk on a regular basis. Records can be destroyed by user errors or corrupted by power failures but the back-up allows speedy restoration of the data.

Since 1979 the museum collections had been recorded on MDA

cards and it was estimated that there were about 12,000 records of around 20,000 objects. Indexing was a major problem involving much staff time with results of limited usefulness. There were index references to the donor, associated people and SHIC classification (Social History and Industrial Classification) but no ready means of accessing storage and other collections management information. In a service with seven small museums scattered over an area of 600 square miles it was virtually impossible to identify any individual object's current location. No practical manual system was available.

The solution

The first task was to set up a database structure in dBase to accommodate the essential elements of our records. The result is shown in Fig. 1. Although based on a structure developed by the North East of Scotland Museums Service in dBase II, it has been modified to our own needs. dBase is particularly suited to small museums as it can cope with tens of thousands of records in a single file yet is flexible enough to accommodate MDA standards.

Fields can be up to 254 characters long and of five types — character, numeric, date, logical or memo. Entries can be filtered to ensure that they comply with users' needs or that they contain a limited range of characters. A bell rings when a field is filled or a mistake is made. Records can be carried though to the next blank 'form' so that data which remains the same throughout a group of records does not need to be retyped. Various other choices can be made and incorporated in a data entry program (Fig. 2).

At the beginning it was estimated that it would take about one year to transfer records but in fact it was completed in less than five months, in conjunction with many other curatorial tasks. In all about 320 man-hours were involved for entering 7,477 records of 22,612 objects. It was decided not to catalogue collections such as herbaria in detail at this stage, hence the average of over three objects per record. The database occupies over 5 megabytes of disk space, with indexes, etc., adding about the same again. Two copies of the hard disk are kept on cartridge tape, one updated daily if work is in progress, the other updated weekly. The latter tape acts as a security copy and is stored in a fire safe.

dBase III PLUS incorporates a programming language approximating to English. Programs have been writtten in this, for example, to update storage information rapidly and in bulk. There is also an

Number of data records: 8154

Date of last update: 27/10/1987

Field	Field Name	Type	Width
1	MDACODE	Character	5
2	ACCESSNO	Character	20
3	GENERCLASS	Character	1
4	SIMPLENAME	Character	30
5	FULLNAME	Character	100
6	QUANTITY	Numeric	5
7	PRODCLASS	Character	10
8	PRODNAME	Character	20
9	PRODLOCDAT	Character	50
10	PRODDATE	Date	8
11	USECLASS	Character	10
12	USENAME	Character	30
13	USELOCDATE	Character	50
14	TYPE	Character	1
15	NUMBER	Character	4
16	USEDATE	Date	8
17	DONNAMEADD	Character	30
18	ACQUISMETH	Character	1
19	ACQUISDATE	Date	8
20	PRICE	Numeric	8
21	VALUEDATE	Character	17
22	CONDITION	Character	8
23	MATERIAL	Character	30
24	PERMSTDATE	Character	20
25	TEMPLOCADA	Character	20
26	DIMENSIONS	Character	15
27	TRANSCRIPT	Character	100
28	NEGATIVENO	Character	10
29	LABNO	Character	5
30	ALTNO	Character	18
31	RECDATE	Character	15
32	NOTES	Memo	
Total			668

Figure 1. Objects Database File — C:objects.dbf.

```
SET HEADING OFF
SET SAFETY OFF
* The following command adjusts the year in dates to four digits
SET CENTURY ON
SET BELL ON
* The following command allows the previous record to be
   carried forward.
SET CARRY ON
DO WHILE .T.
  CLEAR
    * The following command identifies the database to be USEd
  USE OBJECTS
    * and these are the indexes to be updated automatically
  SET INDEX TO IITEM, INAME, ICLASS, IDONOR, PERMSTOR,
  TEMPLOC, USENAME
  @ 10,0
    * The following command opens a memory variable called
        "choice" to store the next response.
  STORE '  ' TO CHOICE
  ACCEPT 'DO YOU WANT TO ENTER ANOTHER RECORD (y/n)' TO
  CHOICE
  IF CHOICE = 'n'
ENDDO
  ENDIF
CLEAR
SET BELL OFF
SET CARRY OFF
RETURN
    * The program now returns to the "calling" program
```

Figure 2. Program used for adding new records.

'applications generator' which writes a program around a few key items of information. This was used to develop a set of programs to create a geological locality database linked to the main object-based database. Conservation records and detailed catalogues of collections such as herbaria, documents and the works of Peter Anson (800 water-colours and drawings) will be added as further databases with slightly differing structures but linked to the main database with common fields. In dBase III PLUS this allows 'view' files to be created combin-ing information from the various sources.

The results

Already many possibilities are opening up. As anticipated, the most frequent use of the system is to change information on the location of objects as they move around the District. This means that audit checks will be simple and printed shelf lists can be compiled or changed, as appropriate, very quickly. The two fields 'permstdate' and 'templocada' have corresponding indexes 'permstor' and 'temploc' which are among the seven indexes automatically updated whenever records are edited. In dBase a shelf list, such as that shown in Fig. 3, is produced simply by creating a 'report' form through the 'Assistant' menus then defining search conditions (for example, a specific store location) through the 'Retrieve' menu. If the operations have been carried out correctly, a printed list soon appears in the format defined during the first stage. Lists can also be produced showing items which have no recorded location. These proved very useful to check the quality of the

STORE: TY.02.12

DATE	Accession No.	Simple Name	No.
6.1.1987	1977–2a	photograph	1
6.1.1987	1977–2b	photograph	2
6.1.1987	1977–8	drawing	1
6.1.1987	1978–245	shield	1
6.1.1987	1978–270	print	1
6.1.1987	1978–274	painting	1
6.1.1987	1978–275	photograph	1
6.1.1987	1978–315	print	1
6.1.1987	1978–316	print	1
6.1.1987	1978–318	drawing	1
6.1.1987	1978–322au	photograph	1
6.1.1987	1979–220	print	1
6.1.1987	1982–155	print	1
6.1.1987	1983–5	print	1
6.1.1987	1985–118m	photograph	1
6.1.1987	1985–118bm	photograph	1
6.1.1987	1985–118bn	photograph	1
6.1.1987	1979–5ad	print	

Figure 3. List of items on one shelf in the museum store.

initial data entry. The same technique was used to check other aspects of the records, for example consistency in the use of simple names or localities. Rather than scanning through a long list on the monitor, it is usually more efficient to produce a printed list arranged in a particular order. Inconsistencies appear as misplaced items and it is easier on the eyes to read a print-out.

Similar techniques are used to answer 'one-off' enquiries, such as whether or not we have any items given by a particular person. A program has been constructed to provide an 'Editing Menu' (Fig. 4) listing the seven fields whose indexes are automatically updated. These fields were chosen as the ones likely to be used most frequently to access the database.

In the case of a donor query, the appropriate arrangement would be selected by pressing the 'A' key which selects the 'idonor' index automatically arranging the database in alphabetical order of donor's name (recorded in the usual MDA form of surname, Christian names, title). The user is then prompted to enter the name required. In our system the full name does not need to be given but what is typed must be entered exactly. For example, searching for an item given by 'Smith, John Edward, Sir', the name 'Smith' alone could be given or 'Smith,J' but not 'Smith, J' or 'Smith,J.'. The screen now shows a resume of the first item in the database which corresponds to what has been typed and asks if this is the correct item. If the user responds by typing 'y' (for 'yes') the full record comes up on the screen for editing

---

WHICH ITEM DO YOU WISH TO USE TO LOCATE RECORD

1. Accession Number
2. Simple Name
3. Production Classification (SHIC/IGS)
4. Donor's Name
5. Permanent Store
6. Temporary Location
7. User/Collector's Name
8. Exit to Main Menu

ENTER THE NUMBER REQUIRED

Figure 4. Editing menu.

or just scanning. If 'n' (for 'no') is entered the next item in the database is produced in the same way, and so on.

Even if a field is not indexed it can be searched by constructing an index through the 'Assistant' menus then accessing it in the same way. For example, searching for works by a particular artist ('producer' in our database structure) would be done by making a 'prodname' index then using the 'Retrieve' menu to search the ordered database. This would be quicker than searching through the entire database ordered in some other way, and the new index can be used over and over again, though it will not be updated automatically when records are added or edited.

Auxiliary programs

A more flexible means of searching for information is to 'export' a part of the database to Framework II. For example, to find a figure by a sculptor with the first name Shakespeare, the database could be 'filtered' into a Framework format for 'simplename = "figure" '. This would produce a new database of figures. The powerful text-searching facilities of Framework can then be used to find the word 'Shakespeare' in the database. Figures of William Shakespeare would appear, if we had any, as well as the item we are looking for, a figure by Shakespeare Wood. It is not practical to put the whole database into Framework format as the latter can only cope efficiently with a maximum size of around 200 kilobytes, even with 'expanded memory' in operation. In the case quoted above it took eleven minutes to load the filtered database into Framework, resulting in 65 records. It then took just three seconds to find the word 'Shakespeare'. No doubt the whole operation could be speeded up with a more powerful computer but such speeds illustrate just how useful such a system can be as compared with a manual catalogue.

Framework II has limited database handling capacities but is very good for producing spreadsheets and for word processing, being easier to use than WordStar for the latter purpose. This article was written using Framework. There is a spelling checker built in, which can also be used with databases, though the same provisos regarding size apply. All in all the most exciting prospect of the dBase/Framework system is being able to relate objects together in ways not previously considered viable.

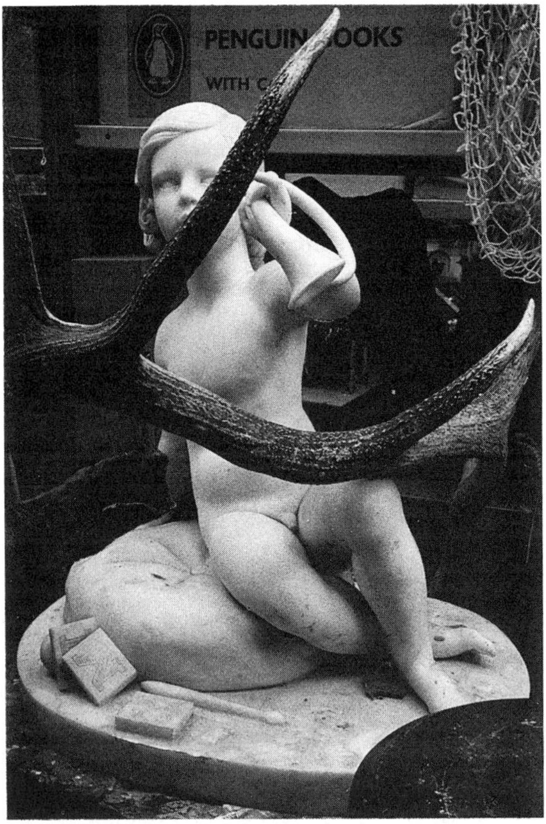

Figure 5. Sculpture by Shakespeare Wood, Rome 1839, in Moray District museum store, 1985. Photo credit: H. Miles.

MODES

At first it was intended to commence full cataloguing for new acquisitions using the MDA's Museum Object Data Entry System (MODES) when this became available (May, 1987). The first version of the software was purchased and some of the possibilities tested but it soon became clear that it will require much more curatorial input to produce an efficient structure and a system that works as well as the potentially more limited dBase III PLUS. It is an attempt to produce a data entry system for microcomputers fully compatible with the MDA cards. In theory it should help the establishment of uniform standards of museum documentation, though the MDA make it plain that it is not intended as a complete data management system in its own right, but as a 'front-end' for other systems. Is so, ease of use of the entire package will have to match that of well-established competitors such as dBase III PLUS.

Working with MODES involves a large amount of decision making on the part of the curator or 'system manager'. Fields have to be chosen from the wide range available to fit the data. It is not easy to find your way quickly to a screen data entry form even if one exists and constructing one can take quite a long time. The manual has been improved recently but still takes some effort to wade through.

Perhaps the most worrying feature of MODES as far as this user is concerned is the amount of space taken up by each record and the time it takes to enter even basic 'inventory' records.

On a trial run a brief inventory-style record of a recently acquired dead rabbit (which was going to be stuffed), took 4 minutes 35 seconds to enter (by carrying forward an existing record and altering it). It occupied 1,342 bytes of space on the hard disk. Exactly the same information entered in the same way on dBase III PLUS took 2 minutes 5 seconds and occupied 678 bytes. In both cases indexing is excluded, though the usual seven dBase indexes were automatically updated as the record was saved.

At these rates, which may not be typical, 50,000 records would take 3819 hours to enter on MODES, and would occupy 67 megabytes of disk space. In dBase III PLUS the same information could be entered in 1,736 hours and occupy 34 megabytes.

Another problem which was noticed was that deleted records appear to remain within MODES but are not accessible, thus using up disk space with no discernible benefit. In dBase, after records have been deleted and 'packed' the space they took up is available immediately.

Within minutes of installing MODES for the first time I had our computer 'locked-up' and this has happened many times since, simply by pressing the wrong key at the wrong time! This may be due to the fact that so many parts of the system, such as validation, are not yet implemented. In a year of constant use a similar event has happened only once in dBase and that was probably due to a mains power surge. Mains voltages are by no means reliable and surge protection devices are absolutely necessary for computer systems.

MODES has to be manipulated to work well with disk directories, such as are widely used on micros with hard disks. I overcame a problem of this nature by setting up a batch file in DOS (the operating system of IBM-PCs and compatibles) to enable the 'display' command to work. Perhaps this drawback will be eliminated in future releases.

It is easy to be critical of a new package which is intended to be developed in the light of experience but there are worrying features, particularly relating to the time taken to enter data and the space that this takes up on the disk. So far I can see no advantages in MODES over dBase III PLUS except that it is specifically designed with the intention of improving museum documentation standards and for that alone the MDA must be congratulated. However we shall not be using it for anything other than experimental purposes until it can be shown to be superior to dBase in those areas which are important to us.

Although computers are good at tasks such as database management it has to be emphasized that the user must have a clear idea of what is needed to get the best results. Woolly thinking produces very woolly results, no matter how clever the software. Computers are tools, albeit very logical ones, but they can play an impressively useful role in museums, removing much of the tedious work and allowing us to use our infinitely more flexible brains for the creative side of our work.

13

The British Architectural Library Biography Project

Jonathan Franklin

British Architectural Biography 1834–1914 is the title of a project to create a database of British architects active between 1834 and 1914, using as core material the sources held in the British Architectural Library at the Royal Institute of British Architects, London (RIBA). The database is therefore organized by names of architects, and is not designed to store images, although it does include references to images, namely portraits, architectural drawings, etc.

One theme that has emerged from this collection of papers is that one does not undertake computerization lightly, or just for the sake of it. *British Architectural Biography 1834–1914* was designed to take account of the external needs of the British Architectural Library's 'public' on the one hand, consisting in part of architectural historians, researchers, conservationists and others, and the internal needs of the Library on the other.

As anyone who has worked in the field of architectural history will be aware, the lack of a biographical reference source for British architects of the Victorian period, to follow on where the monumental work of Howard Colvin's *Biographical dictionary of British architects 1600–1840*[1] leaves off, has long been a handicap. The gap in the literature has become still more obvious with the publication in 1985 of A.S. Gray's *Edwardian architecture*,[2] with biographical entries for the years 1901–10. Other initiatives in this direction have, at least for the time being, succumbed to other pressures.

The British Architectural Library has unique and outstanding collections of material for the history of architecture. Not surprisingly, these are especially strong for the period after the RIBA's foundation in 1834. For biographical purposes, the Nomination papers of architects elected to membership of the RIBA, dating from 1834, are particularly significant, since they contain details of the candidate's education and training, and lists of buildings for which he was responsible. The Nomination papers presented three problems, or challenges.

Firstly, the physical condition of the older Nomination papers has deteriorated with age and heavy use. Secondly, access to the information contained in the Nomination papers is not easy: not only are they located in the British Architectural Library and nowhere else, but tracing the Nomination papers of a member, and even establishing whether an architect was a member in the first place, involves a cumbersome search through annual Kalendars. Thirdly, as they stand, the Nomination papers can only be searched by name of architect; the possibilities for manipulating their information content in other ways, for example to look up a building and discover the architect rather than vice versa, remain as yet untapped.

At the same time, the project had to be integrated with other computer developments in the British Architectural Library. The Library uses STATUS software on the RIBA's PRIME computer. There is an integrated database containing catalogue records for books and periodicals indexing records, and a number of satellite databases, all of which send short-form records to the Integrated database. These satellite databases contain records for drawings, photographs, manuscripts and early imprints. The biographical database involved in the project has been designed as a further satellite database, which also sends short-form records to the Integrated database; these short-form records function as names authority file records for cataloguing and indexing operations in the Library. The books-catalogue and periodicals-indexing parts of the Integrated database are already available on-line through the international computer host DIALOG.

There are three aspects to be considered in relation the structure of the database records. Firstly, the format in which the information is entered. Secondly, the manipulation of the information content which is seen as desirable once the information has been entered in the database. Thirdly, the documentation of the sources for the information which has been entered in the database.

The structure of the database records has been designed to some extent on the model of the Nomination papers, but with additions.

These additions permit firstly the inclusion of other fields in the individual records, for example bibliographical information and space for a short essay; and secondly the creation of records for practices, firms and organizations.

The manipulation of the data which will be possible within the database is based upon the capabilities of a STATUS system. Searching is fundamentally free-text: in other words, any word in any part of the record can be searched and retrieved apart from 'common words' such as 'and', 'in', etc. Individual records are divided into named sections, and it is possible to search for records in which the search term occurs only in one or more specified named sections: for example, searching for the name 'Donaldson' at Main Entry only avoids retrieving all the records in which Donaldson occurs as patron, proposer or partner rather than as the biographical subject of the record.

Named sections are one feature of the database; keyed fields are another. Keyed fields accord strings of characters a value instead of treating them simply as strings of characters. For example, the database includes keyed fields for the start-date and end-date of the architect. These dates are the same as dates of birth and death, but can be manipulated in accordance with their numerical value. Thus it is possible to search, using these keyed fields, for all architects born after 1815, or dying before 1908. Similarly architects can be sorted so that the records are in chronological order by date of birth or death. Alphabetical as well as numerical values can be manipulated by keyed fields: thus the database has a sort field which allows records to be sorted alphabetically by architect's name.

Searches using named sections and keyed fields can be combined in various ways either to retrieve a particular record or set of records, or in order to analyse the overall content of the database. The question of information retrieval raises the very important issue of the terminology used in the database. Although there can be alternative spellings of personal names, geographical names and subjects are more of a problem: if the county of Warwick is entered as Warwickshire, Warwicks, and Warks in different records, retrieval will be adversely affected. Terminology does not need to be strictly controlled in all parts of the database, and the flexibility to suggest new terms is always essential, but this is an aspect of database development which needs particular premeditation. Fortunately, lists of standard terms such as *Architectural keywords*[3] produced by the British Architectural Library are either available or, as in the case of the Art & Architecture Thesaurus which has been selected as the source of standard descriptors for the project, under development.

The documentation of sources for the information contained in a database of this kind is essential in order to prevent it becoming a jumble of unsubstantiated fragments of information. In a rigidly structured record this can present difficulties which do not arise in free text. In the case of an architect, perhaps the nucleus of biographical information in which the documentation of sources is most vital is the list of buildings which he designed. The project will create records in which the buildings are cross-referenced by numbers to the list of bibliographical references also contained in the record. Each record also contains a repeating field at the end which allows the authors of subsequent modifications to the record to inscribe their initials and the date on which the modification was made. However, without further cross-referencing, which would be undesirably cumbersome, it is not possible to indicate who modified what.

The entry of information on the database is not yet underway except on a small scale. It is envisaged that the information content of the RIBA Nomination papers and other sources in the British Architectural Library will be entered in three chronological phases: 1834–1869; 1870–1899; 1900–1914. The contents of the database will be available within the British Architectural Library while the project is in progress. As the phases of the project are completed, it is hoped that they can be made available internationally through DIALOG, the database host through which parts of the British Architectural Library's Integrated database are already available. The possibility of conventional paper publication will also be considered in due course. The eventual total number of records contained in the database in the course of the project should be about 6,500. However, the design of the database is such that the chronological and geographical limits could be extended at a future date.

Notes

1. Colvin, Howard, *A biographical dictionary of British architects 1600–1840*, London: John Murray, 1978.
2. Gray, A. Stuart, *Edwardian architecture: a biographical dictionary*, London: Duckworth, 1985.
3. *Architectural keywords*, London: RIBA Publications for the British Architectural Library, 1982.

Part IV
APPLICATIONS

14
Environmental Monitoring: A Case for a Computerized System

Mary Macqueen

In 1985 the Mary Rose Trust in Portsmouth installed the first phase of a two phase system linked to a small computer, for monitoring temperature, humidity and light levels in the showcases and gallery of the exhibition hall. This paper discusses the aims of the project and the results achieved within the first year.

Why monitor?

The first question to be asked is why monitor at all? Why use a computerized system? What are the advantages of a computer system over a manual system? It is quite normal for museums to have some form of manual monitoring within their buildings; possibly one or two thermohygrometers, placed centrally in the room or gallery. This type of system has been found to be inadequate, especially if the gallery or showcase (as one will increasingly find), is air-conditioned. Manual systems are very time consuming. If there are many areas which need monitoring, and if each time the charts need changing, several showcases have to be opened, then charts cannot be changed when the public are in the galleries. Another disadvantage is that light readings are spot readings and are not integrated.

I had previously done a small amount of work on environmental monitoring at the Horniman Museum in South East London. I monitored fifty showcases in two of the permanent galleries and approximately twenty showcases in the temporary exhibition gallery which was air-conditioned. With air-conditioning systems there are often fluctuations within a band of control and these need to be monitored.

When I arrived at the Mary Rose Trust in July 1984, the Museum was just about to be opened by Prince Charles. A museum to house the collections of artifacts from the Mary Rose Trust had been planned from quite an early date in the project's history but the decision to use an historic building within the naval dockyard had been taken in 1982. The building chosen, No. 5 Boathouse, a large open wooden building with a single skin, was very difficult to control environmentally.

Showcase air-conditioning down the centre of the building with the plant at one end was chosen by the architects and designers as a suitable answer. The original idea was that the non-air-conditioned showcases along the side of the building would not be used for the archaeological artifacts, but during the work on the gallery shortage of exhibition space became a problem and one or two showcases which were not fully air-conditioned were also used for artifacts.

A further difficulty in the control of the environment within the building was that the building sat over water, and as a result humidities could become very high. There was also to be a glass fronted tank for the polyethelene glycol (PEG) treatment of some of the larger objects so that the public could see exactly what was going on.

The showcases were designed to be airtight as possible and vapour proof. The air-conditioned system is essentially a closed system with 80 per cent of air recirculating and 20 per cent make-up of ambient air. The showcases themselves were to have mixed materials within them, organic and inorganic. A conflict exists because organic materials require a higher relative humidity (RH) than inorganic materials. Metals, especially those from a marine environment where the salt levels have been high, require a very low RH. The showcase air-conditioning could only be set at a compromise level between the two opposing conditions which would do the least damage to both types of materials. This situation is very common within museums. The control settings were to be 18°C with a relative humidity of 53 per cent.

The equipment was designed to perform within the ranges of +– 5 per cent RH and +– 2° C temp. The acceptable band of conditions would therefore be:

temp. 16°C to 20°C and RH 48 per cent to 58 per cent.

Alarm settings would be outside the ranges:

temp. 14°C to 22°C and RH 46 per cent to 60 per cent.

Very large objects, such as the bronze guns and some of the iron guns, are on open display in the ambient atmosphere of the building.

There were, therefore, a number of differing environments within the building:

1. The ambient environment, with large guns on open display.
2. Partially-controlled showcases, with mixed displays.
3. Fully air-conditioned showcases, with mixed displays.

It was not possible to use thermohygrometers in many of the showcases. As a museum's task is to preserve the collection, so a good environment must play a very important part in that aim. Poor environment and inadequate monitoring of the environment leads to many problems which the conservator at the bench may face but which cannot always be put right at that point. If textile has faded its colour cannot be restored; if wood has warped this cannot be corrected. Corrosion of metal is difficult to check if the artifacts contain large amounts of chloride and the relative humidity is high.

How can adequate control be achieved without monitoring? The monitoring must always be done in close proximity to the artifact being monitored. Unless monitoring is very thorough it is impossible to know what is going on, nor can adequate control measures be effected. Improvements can nearly always be made if the exact facts are known.

My experience of air-conditioning plants is that when they fail, the risk of sudden and damaging changes in environment is great. This led me to believe in an independent computerized monitoring system separate from the plant controls for supervision of the environment. In discussion with representatives of firms who were tendering for the contract it was often quite difficult to get across the point of the importance of independent monitoring.

The aims for the systems were therefore to monitor temperature and relative humidity conditions night and day, without being subject to electricity cuts or other power failure problems.

The aims of the system for monitoring light were twofold:

1. Short-term, to gain specific information on a particular showcase before light-sensitive material is placed in it.
2. The long-term aim of continuous monitoring is to keep a check on the total light levels over the years. A policy of movement of objects from display to storage is envisaged.

   50 lux for 1 hour = 50 lux hrs

   50 lux for 10 hours = 500 lux hrs

50 lux for 70 hours (one week) = 3,500 lux hrs

50 lux for 30 days (one month) = 15,000 lux hrs

15,000 lux for 12 months = 180,000 lux hrs

Objects exposed to changing RH require constant observation. In 1984 the monitoring used by the Mary Rose Trust was a Kane and May portable electronic sensor at the two vents of the air-conditioning system. The showcases themselves did not have thermohygrometers or any other form of permanent showcase monitoring, and the air-conditioning plant had no form of fail-safe, so the objects were not being watched carefully enough, and there was the always-present risk of plant breakdown. Also one did not know exactly what was happening within the showcases. Some surface drying of the wood appeared to be occurring and this aesthetically was displeasing and could also have been damaging to the structure of the wood.

While I was studying the systems available, their costs and assessing what was necessary, a technician was appointed to carry out a more thorough manual monitoring programme.

The brief for the computerized environmental monitoring of the Mary Rose Museum and air-conditioned showcases

1. The twenty air-conditoned showcases were each to be monitored with a dual sensor, for both relative humidity and temperature. Some of these showcases were also to have light meters, where textiles and other very sensitive material had been placed. Eventually four light meters were required.
2. All four of the uncontrolled cases were to be monitored.
3. The ambient air was to be monitored. Specific areas included the site of the bronze guns near the entrance of the museum and the iron guns in the south-west area of the building.
4. A fail-safe system for the automatic shutting down of the plant in the event of a serious mechanical failure was needed with an over-ride switch to be fitted into the equipment so that the air-conditioning system could be started manually if required, for example, for testing after servicing, etc.

The system had to be flexible enough to cope with additional sensors from other buildings linked to the same dedicated computer system.

This was important as the museum stores were to be moved to a new location in the naval dockyard.

The qualities required in an appropriate system were:

1. A reliable, accurate, small dual sensor suitable for the showcase. It needed to be flexible, able to be mounted at the top or bottom of the showcase, taking into account the design of the showcase and aesthetics.
2. The central microprocessing equipment with memory (front end processor) to scan the sensors in turn continuously, ideally every few minutes. Changes could then be seen very readily.
3. The system to store on disk and to print out at intervals (and if necessary, changed), a reading for the temperature, the relative humidity, and a spot reading as well as an integrated reading for the light levels. Each showcase to be listed in order with the time, place and date.

With the aid of the computer the information could then studied and analysed. The printout interval must be capable of being altered, with the program of the computer being designed for this aspect. At this early stage a computer program could not be written, and this fact was stressed in the initial brief and an existing or modified program was required to come with the package. The type of information being studied was quite common and there existed programs already written which, with limited modifications, were suitable for the system.

4. While scanning, it would detect faults within predetermined and pre-programmed limits and print these out with time and date. An audible alarm or flashing light would be incorporated into the system so that the staff on duty were warned of a fault. They would then follow clearly defined procedures for informing the conservation and curatorial staff.
5. A separate fail-safe system would be needed. This facility to shut the air-conditioning plant down in the event of a failure is also essential but the plant cannot be shut down on every minor alarm or if only one showcase goes above the limit, therefore there had to be alarm limits.
6. Each sensor to respond to excessively high or low temperature within defined limits.
7. Each sensor to respond to excessively high or low RH within defined limits.

8. The equipment to work twenty-four hours a day. Back-up power was required in the event of a power failure to ensure that no data could be lost.
9. Each sensor to be capable of independent alarm settings. As discussed earlier, different areas of the building required different conditions, and monitoring had to be able to deal with those variations within an exhibition hall. These variations would also be required if the system were to be used for a museum with many different galleries all perhaps needing slightly different conditions.
10. A sensor to activate the fail-safe would be placed within the supply duct close to the sensor controlling the air-conditioning plant. When this sensor reached certain set limits the plant would cut out. It may be preferable to hold poor conditions, perhaps overnight, and then return them very slowly to normal, than allow conditions to continue deteriorating without control. If a computerized monitoring system were to be used for showcases without air-conditioning then a fail-safe is not so necessary.
11. The final item of the brief was that to facilitate interpretation and analysis, the system should not be simply a data logger, but should be computer-linkable, and the information stored. It is recommended that records be planned to last for ten years or longer. Graphs of conditions on a weekly, monthly, quarterly and annual basis could be drawn and used as the basis for improvements to conditions, and for planning the rotation of objects between display and store. The amount of information provided by this system would be substantial and the computer would be essential.

The equipment

As there is a proliferation of potentially suitable equipment on the market, quotations from nine tenders were acquired:

1. Kane and May Measuring Instruments

Twenty-five Kane and May sensors linked to a data logger with a computer interface from Control and Readout Limited £12,288

2. Wessex Power Technology

Twenty-four sensors, 4 × 16 channel 32 K memory Grant Squirrel microprocessor with Vaisala or Kane and May sensors. The Grant Squirrel is used by the National Trust, but for the purpose of the Mary

Rose Trust's proposed system it was too small, with not enough flexibility £14,353

3. Stirling University Microprocessor
Twenty-four sensors Sterling unit. This unit was under development and although it looked very promising it was rather limited in capacity and therefore not suitable £12,650

4. Trend Control System Ltd
Thirty channel system £25,990

5. Ancom Limited
Recommended by Stirling University. Thirty-two channel system with Apple IIe microcomputer, with their own sensors £14,197

6. Rosemount Engineering Co. Ltd
Five hundred channel data logger using either Vaisala or Lee and Dickens sensors. £17,037

7. Testoterm Limited
Sanyo microcomputer with Testoterm sensors, twenty-five channels £26,748

8. Vaisala (UK) Ltd
Twenty-five sensors but capable of expansion, with a Torch CF500 computer £14,143

9. Lee and Dickens Ltd
A 200 channel data logging but no computer interface, using their own sensors. £9,000

Before the final choice was made all the companies short-listed — Ancom, Rosemount, Vaisala and Lee and Dickens — were invited to the museum to demonstrate their equipment.

The system chosen, given the needs of the Mary Rose Trust at the time, and which appeared to fulfil many, though not quite all, the conditions required was Vaisala (UK) Ltd of Cambridge. The quality of the sensors was good, and the main advantage was that the firm agreed to modify the sensor slightly to provide one which was more acceptable to museum showcases where the sensor is not the first item one wishes a visitor's eye to rest upon.

The quotation included:

	£
One fail-safe and sensor 122Y	575
25 HMP 111Y sensors (modified) @ £172 each	4375
One front end processor with program	2550
One Epson printer	398
One NEC 8201 personal computer (P 1)	395
One Torch CF500 computer (including software)	3950
Installation costs	1900
Total costs	£4143.00

Implementation

Due to a number of factors it was decided that the project could not be implemented in one year and therefore it was necessary to have two phases. The first phases of the project included:

The fail-safe probe and relay HMP122Y.
Ten dual sensors (humidity and temperature), HMP111Y.
The front end processor (where the analog signal from the sensors is converted to digital form, and where some of the processing is done).
Four integrated light sensors.
The personal computer NEC 8201A.
The Epson RX80 printer
The humidity calibration kit.

This equipment cost approximately £8,883.

The first ten RH and temperature sensors and the four light sensors were installed with no major problems but it was important to keep cable lengths short and very well insulated to protect against noise on the lines.

Initially I worked with the following alarm limits for all air-conditioned showcases which had mixed collections of wood, leather and other organic materials, and also metals:

RH	A low limit of 46 per cent RH and a high limit of 58 per cent.
Temp.	A low limit of 15°C and a high limit of 22°C.

For the fail-safe supply duct system:

RH	A low of 45 per cent RH and a high of 61 per cent.
Temp.	A low of 15°C and a high of 23°C.

For the ambient (information only):

RH	A low of 40 per cent RH and a high of 65 per cent.
Temp.	A low of 12°C and a high of 25°C.

These limits had to be modified several times as experience was gained, and it was realized that under certain circumstances the air-conditioning plant could not give quite such tight control as one had expected.

The data are presented in the following forms:

Museum Name	*Date*	*Time*	*Scan*
Mary Rose Trust list	1985 6 3	23.02	16

Location	*C*	*RH*	*Lux Lux Hours*
1. Longbows			
2. Textiles			
3. Bronze guns			
4. Rigging			
5. A/C return duct			
6. Barber surgeons			
7. Swivel guns			
8. Carpenters			
9. Domestic			
10. Music and pastimes			
11. Galley			
12. Religion			
13. A/C supply duct			

This currently is what is being monitored. The light meter gives two readings. A spot reading is taken at the same time as the scan interval and this is added to the total lux hours to give an integrated reading at the end of each year. This will have to be reset to zero but the total for a year will give a much better indication of exactly how the daily variation mounts up.

Conclusion

During the running-in phase we did experience a number of minor problems and for about a week we were without the monitoring information, but whenever the need arose Vaisala would come and repair the system or sort out the fault, and the service they gave was very good. I left the Mary Rose Trust in November 1986 and up to that point the Trust had been quite satisfied with the system.

From my experience a computerized environmental monitoring system is time-saving for the conservator in the long run. I feel that although initially it does require capital expenditure it is the type of system which can be built up over the years, if the original design is satisfactory and there are enough channels for the information which will eventually be required. The amount of memory which the computer will need to store a full year's information is quite considerable and this also has to be taken into account. Further work is certainly necessary

The Mary Rose Trust found that the showcases were not as airtight as they should have been. Analysis of data over an extended period of time indicated this conclusively. Work was then done on the showcases to correct the problem.

Phase two was never completed. Monitoring is still being done with information stored on paper from the printer, without being further analysed by the computer.

15

Using a Portable Computer in Art Historical Research

Leslie Carlyle

Introduction

This paper is based on experience gained in using a portable computer while researching for a PhD thesis.[1] A brief overview of the types of portable computers currently available is given, with some comments on issues regarding the use of a portable and on the software package used.

The topic of the PhD research proposal is 'A Critical Analysis of British Handbooks, Manuals, and Treatises on Oil Painting Published in the Nineteenth Century'. The nature of the research lends itself well to the use of a computerized file system, since it involves the collection of recipes, instructions and advice on how to paint in oils. The database created by entering information from the texts on computer will be used to develop the thesis; the thesis will involve an assessment of the technical contents of the texts, comparing them and identifying their sources of information, and determining whether the advice and recommendations were an accurate reflection of contemporary practices in oil painting.

It is anticipated that the database will stand alone as a resource in itself, and will eventually be available through an international

1. This paper was researched and written in 1987. Technical developments in computers change rapidly, therefore allowance must be made for any out-of-date or superseded information.

database called the Conservation Information Network. Since the research database consists of direct quotes from the sources, other conservators, conservation scientists and art historians will be able to conduct individual searches through the information.

Restrictions with the search capacity of the current software package can be overcome once the material has been loaded into a mainframe computer available through the Canadian Heritage Information Network, which is an organization working with the Conservation Information Network.

Application of the system in the research

In order to collect information on nineteenth century oil painting techniques and materials from the various sources, it was necessary to devise a versatile filing system. I wanted to organize the information so that searches could be made not only in a broad category, for example varnish recipes, but on a narrower basis as well, such as all the varnish recipes containing a given material.

From my perspective as a paintings conservator, I approached the data-collection in much the same format that condition reports are made: by layers possibly present in an oil painting. This automatically gave the broad categories needed: Varnish, Pigment, Medium, Ground, Support. Two more categories were added: Varnish-Modifiers, and Medium-Modifiers.

These headings effectively covered the information I was finding in the texts on the materials the artist was being advised (or not advised) to use. Each file in my software package has a limit of ten pages, with a virtually unlimited number of fields per page. The first page of every file is identical, and contains all the bibliographic fields, the second page contains summary fields, such as a field entitled 'Materials' where the ingredients of a recipe are simply listed. This allows all the varnish recipes containing, for example, 'egg white' to be called up quickly by searching in a limited field, rather than through extensive text.

A number of other categories soon proved necessary, in order to record the authors' viewpoints on subjects such as the education of the artist, the anticipation of change in colours and materials with time, or what problems may arise with various technical faults. Again broad categories were devised, but it was necessary to subdivide them further. Hence under the category of 'Method' are sections on

'Application techniques', 'Isolation Layers', 'Education of the Artist', and 'Appearance of the Painting'.

A separate file system was designed for pigments in response to the greater uniformity of information available in the texts — this allowed files with significantly more summary fields. In all the files, throughout the data base, every summary field has an accompanying text field where the original quote supporting the 'summary' may be entered. In the files on pigments for example, there is a field entitled 'Adulterants' where the materials are simply listed, then immediately below this is a field entitled 'Adulterant Notes' where the actual quote referring to the above adulterant materials is entered. The page number of the source being consulted is entered for reference.

Aside from simply collecting a large amount of information on the materials themselves, the database is being used as a template of sorts — to compare the different sources with one another, and the different editions of the same sources. In order to provide myself with an initial point of comparison, I have entered information comprehensively from Field's *Chromatography*,[1] a book which was first published in 1835 and subsequently went through 'enlarged and improved' editions throughout the century: by the author in 1841, then by two other editors, in 1869 and again in 1885. By annotating the original version with information from the other editions I am able to chart the changes in materials, and in outlook, as the book is transformed from 1835 to 1869. Fortunately, this manual was recognized both in the nineteenth century and in the early twentieth century as a significant sourcebook for artists. The 1869 and 1885 editions are published by Winsor and Newton, and the editors of these editions were both Winsor and Newton research chemists.

Once the information from a restricted number of 'key' books has been entered, the other sources can be treated in relation to this core of information, so that only variations in methods and materials need be actually entered. Since there were a tremendous number of books on how to paint in oil published throughout the century, I have adopted the wildly optimistic view that most of them were copied from a fairly small group. For a description of the hardware and the software package used see the Appendix.

Using a portable computer

The primary advantage of using a portable computer, whether simply for note-taking, or for the creation of a database, is the possibility of using it directly with the original sources. This eliminates the need to write notes in longhand, and then type them into a computer later — a step I was most anxious to eliminate in my own work, since the majority of the sources I consult are only available in non-lending libraries.

There are a number of ways to introduce 'portability' in library research with a computer:

1. By using a note-taking device such as the Cambridge Z88: the contents are then down-loaded into a micro-computer.
2. By using a more powerful computer with some ability to carry out word processing and file management.
3. By using a portable computer with a hard disk.

The first option to consider is the use of a small note-taking computer. Although these are the most inexpensive form of portable computer available, for anything other than limited word processing, there has to be another computer around somewhere to receive the notes being made.

Until recently, the process of getting the two systems to communicate was not particularly straightforward, but now, with the Z88 this problem has been overcome and I understand that data can be transferred to IBM PC compatible computers quite simply.

The second route is to use one of the less expensive portables which rely on single or dual floppy disks. The only drawback with this equipment is the lack of a hard disk. This will primarily affect people working with a database since it will be slower to use. The information from the disks will have to be loaded onto the machine each time, and it takes substantially longer to access the information from diskettes (or floppy disks) than it does from a hard disk.

However, with a good understanding of any of the file management programs, it should be quite possible to separate out the tasks of creating a database and of searching it. Once information has been entered on diskettes using a portable, it could then be loaded onto a more powerful machine with a hard disk, for the purposes of carrying out searches and creating reports.

At the moment one practical problem is the necessity of having additional equipment to be able to use $3\frac{1}{2}$ inch disks standard in most portables with a desk top which uses $5\frac{1}{4}$ inch floppies. (The differences between the two diskettes are briefly discussed under general considerations in purchasing which follows). Since the industry standard will be changing over to the $3\frac{1}{2}$ inch disks, this will be less of a problem in the future.

For powerful word processing, including extensive note-taking, and the limited use of file-management and database software, the single and dual floppy portables would be very useful. If you are arriving at one directly via an electric typewriter, the inconvenience of doing without a hard disk will seem minor in comparison.

The third category of portable computers are those which come equipped with a hard disk. They have one major disadvantage: at the time of writing, there was a significant difference in the cost of these machines compared with the portables previously mentioned.

However, the necessity of having a portable computer with a hard disk containing all the information becomes apparent when comparisons are being made between editions of the same book at different locations.

None of the editions of one of my major sources, Field's *Chromatography*, are available on loan from the few libraries which have one or more of them; and none of the libraries contain a complete set of all of the editions. The British Library is missing the author's enlarged 1841 edition which formed the basis for the later revisions. Without a hard disk containing all my files, the comparison between these books would have taken much longer — in fact, probably longer than if I had recorded the information conventionally on index cards.

General considerations for purchasing

There are many portable computers now available — the largest choice is in the dual floppy units. The best way to compare them is by reading the reviews in the computer magazines, and when possible by attending computer exhibitions such as the annual Which Computer Show. The major issues to consider are:

Memory capacity (RAM)
Presence or absence of hard disk
Speed (type of processor)
Screen type — Liquid Crystal display (LCD), LCD super-twist, LCD backlit, gas plasma
Manufacturer's reputation
Power supply (if battery operation is an issue)

Expandability and communications
Weight (anything over fifteen pounds will be difficult)
Cost

Generally the major portables are all IBM PC compatible. The $3\frac{1}{2}$ inch floppies are the portable standard, although there are a number of machines, for example the Compac, and the Flyer, which offer the option of using $5\frac{1}{4}$ inch floppies. The $3\frac{1}{2}$ inch disks are sturdier than the $5\frac{1}{4}$ and they hold twice as much information. Most computer stores and software outlets can provide software on the $3\frac{1}{2}$ inch disks now.

Issues particular to using a portable

There are three: library facilities, insurance, and international travel.

Other issues which affect any computer owner but are worth discussing in relation to a portable include: power supply, maintenance, warranty, and possible disk corruption from magnetic fields.

Library facilities

Libraries in London, such as the British Library, the Royal Academy library, and the libraries at the Courtauld Institute and the Tate Gallery have dealt with portables so far on an individual basis, and have been immediately and generously accommodating. However, once the use of portables increases, hitherto unforeseen problems could arise.

The major problem is noise. It is primarily associated with the use of the keyboard. There is also noise involved when the computer's disk heads are operating, and my machine's tiny cooling fan makes a constant perceptible hum. As you would expect, the nuisance factor of the noise produced depends a great deal on the amount of background noise already present. For example, in the British Library reading rooms, it would be very disruptive for readers sitting in the immediate vicinity of someone with a portable. In other locations where the general noise level is higher it would not necessarily present a problem.

The British Library provides a typing room to isolate readers with typewriters. Desk space has been allocated for approximately twenty people, each place having an individual power supply (originally intended for electric typewriters).

Another consideration is the security of the portable if you want to take a temporary break — they are generally bulky, fairly heavy, require time to pack up, and are not the kind of thing you want to spill coffee and soup on. It is possible to rent a lockable storage cabinet in the British Library typing room which will accommodate a portable computer. However, there is a waiting list. The staff are not in a position to accept responsibility for temporary storage of computers during lunch breaks, and the coat-check in the British Library will not store any articles for persons leaving the building.

Generally there is a spirit of comradeship in the typing room and other readers will watch equipment left for a short period. I have been told that the use of portable computers has been anticipated in the plans for the new British Library.

Insurance

Insurance proved to be a problem since a normal household contents package will not allow such an expensive 'floater' to be added on, and finding a company that would insure a valuable piece of equipment which is taken out of the home regularly was difficult. Ultimately an insurance package specifically for the computer and the printer was drawn up by Guardian Royal Exchange Assurance.

International travel

Thanks to an article by Ian Fraser,[2] I am now aware that taking a portable computer out of the country, however temporarily, involves paperwork and significant expense. The London Chamber of Commerce requires an expensive carnet: this will be good for up to a year. And the Department of Trade requires an export licence which is free but one is required for each occasion. Both involve acquiring and completing forms, and having those forms processed.

Enquiries were made with the British Overseas Trade officer to see if it would be possible to receive an academic exemption. No such thing actually exists, but there may be a way to leave a deposit of some percentage of the duty on the equipment with the customs people in the country being visited. Ian Fraser goes into considerably more detail and his article is well worth reading.

Power supply

On one occasion while working in the British Library typing room I experienced a sudden unaccountable loss of information which I suspect resulted from a power supply problem. Since the room has many power outlets I thought other people plugging in with various equipment may have caused a disruption. I purchased a 'spike protector plug' for around £9 which I installed in place of the regular three pronged plug that came with the machine. Since then I have not had any further problems.

The spike protector only accounts for power surges, not power interruptions which could be equally if not more disastrous. It is possible to buy power protection units which ensure a continuous supply over minor surges and interruptions. However, these units are not particularly portable, and are generally expensive.

Computer maintenance packages

Since one is moving about with the portable it is naturally subject to greater wear and tear than a stationary desktop unit, therefore it does make sense to take out some form of maintenance package once the initial manufacturers warranty period has expired. Unfortunately these 'packages' appear to be geared to the commercial user and are extremely expensive. The October 1987 edition of the *Which Computer* magazine featured an article on the various maintenance companies with a comparison of what they offer and what they charge. The conclusion was that the maintenance companies contracts are heavily weighted in their favour.

Warranties

Manufacturers' warranties may not be as portable as the computer. Since no one in the business of selling computers wants anyone to take advantage of lower purchase costs from one country to another they were eager to convince me that the warranty will not be honoured if the unit is taken out of the country where it was purchased. Before I left Canada I was unable to get a consistent answer regarding warranty protection for a new machine from the various computer manufacturers.

Regarding the purchase of 'ex-demonstrators' in Britain: although the manufacturer's warranty may be about to expire on the unit you purchase, the British 'Sale of Goods Act' stipulates that a vendor must provide the buyer with goods 'fit for use' up to one year after the purchase date. Although the individual dealer may not respond well to being reminded of the Sale of Goods Act, it was, in my case, effective, and when problems arose the warranty period for my machine was finally determined to be one full year from the date I purchased it rather than from the time it was purchased from the manufacturer by the company who sold it to me.

Disk corruption from magnetic fields

The disk manufacturers say the diskettes should be kept at least 50 cm (20 inches) away from any magnetic material. The problem with a portable computer, is knowing the whereabouts of possible sources in a huge variety of locations. I have not had any experiences with disk corruption so far; however as a precaution I generally carry the backup disks for the day in a separate case to the computer hoping that both carrying bags will not be exposed together.

Software

The software package — 'Q & A' — was chosen on the basis that it was, at the time, the most user-friendly file-management software package available anywhere, and I believe that is still the case. It is produced by Symantecs Corporation in California.

It has one really irritating problem for use in Britain: it is set up for American standards. This affects the size of paper used in the printer, and the spell check uses American (not Canadian or British) spelling. Finding out how to readjust the program to British standard paper size has not been immediately obvious. The solution for that problem was to buy $9\frac{1}{2}$ by 11 inch paper.

I hold Q & A responsible for making my transition from computer illiterate to my current semi-literate status almost entirely painless, and definitely enjoyable. The Q & A package features on-line help that is so comprehensive one can almost do without the manual, especially in the initial stages. In addition, if at any time the data is in danger of being altered or erased the software has a built-in warning and requires approving the action before proceeding. It also uses flashing messages to tell you if it is saving, working on, or searching files, so that you are not left wondering whether it is actually doing anything or if it is hung up somewhere.

Another feature of Q & A is its use of artificial intelligence in the form of 'the intelligent assistant', a selection on the menu which allows you to create reports and carry out searches by asking for the information in full English sentences: such as 'list all the authors alphabetically for the books published between 1800 and 1835'. I have not explored this option very extensively yet. Once a data file has been 'introduced' to the intelligent assistant section of the software, it actually slows down routine backups onto the diskettes. As a result, I have only tried it on a few sections of my database. Q & A also has a 'report' function which will carry out more conventional searches and so far it has been completely adequate for my current needs.

After being exposed to the luxury of software hand-holding throughout the learning experience I was highly unprepared to tackle MS-DOS. Leaving Q & A for DOS was like stepping out into a void — most unsettling experience when I had heard about reformatting the hard disk by mistake and could imagine other equally disastrous commands which will be done without warning.

Fortunately I found a source of external DOS hand-holding in the form of the University College London Computer Centre's advisory office. I have been helped out on a number of occasions and I thoroughly appreciate being able to go there. Here is another advantage of having a portable since you can take your computer to the source of help rather than trying to solve problems over the phone. The same applies regarding the ease of picking up and delivering the machine for maintenance.

Conclusion

Despite the current cost and weight, the availability of portable computers today is remarkable when you compare one to its equivalent desk-top computer and realize that they both run the same software packages and basically have the same capabilities. Still, I do look forward to the time when powerful portables will weigh less than a pound and cost the same as a pocket calculator, or even to the point where, with every new magazine subscription, you get a free portable with a 500 megabyte hard disk.

Appendix

Hardware

A Toshiba T3100 Personal Computer with a 10 megabyte hard disk, and Gas Plasma Display.
640 KB memory.
Weight: 15 pounds.

Power source: switchable 230/115 VAC.
'Spike Protector Plug' installed.
An Epson LX-86 Dot Matrix Printer.

Software

'Q & A' File Management and Word Processing Program.
Requires a minimum of 512 KB. memory — optimally 640 KB.

Notes

1. Field, George, *Chromatography; or, A Treatise on Colours and Pigments, and of their Powers in Painting &c.*, London, Charles Tilt, 1835.
2. Fraser, Ian, 'Your PC needs an export licence', *IBM PC User Group Newsletter*, vol. 4, no. 11 (1987).

16

Computers and Manuscript Illumination

Michael Michael

Many introductions to using computers in the arts concentrate on 'do-it-yourself' programming and quite advanced descriptions of the processes to which a computer may be put without introducing the reader to the philosophical implications of using a computer. This may, of course, be taken as read by the author, but arts users are often alienated by such assumptions. Many need a context in which to put new technology before they can understand the possibilities which are opened up by using a computer, even for quite basic tasks. In this short piece I shall be writing as an art historian with a particular interest in medieval manuscripts and their illustrations.

Many of the uses to which I put the computer may seem banal to the initiated but, at the same time, attractive and unattainable to the uninitiated. To the uninitiated, who may not have used a computer at all, and even to those who are familiar with word-processors, my first point will be to suggest that using a computer may not necessarily add to your initial knowledge of a subject. The fact that you have used a computer program to help you will not make your philosophical argument any better, although it can, perhaps more often than not, give a certain lustre to a dull thesis. My second and third points will deal with the type of information contained in medieval illuminated manuscripts, whether textual, iconographical or codicological and how a computer might help with the problems a medievalist might have with this information. To the initiated, who may have already stopped reading, my fourth point will be to suggest that many people from the arts have the ability to understand quite complicated instructions and quite complicated tasks, but can only do so if basic concepts about programming and using computers are explained in a practical way.

This final point about practicality and training is an important one: both those who teach and those who wish to learn computing should be aware of it. No amount of literature on computing can be a substitute for hands-on training and a sure grasp of the philosophical context in which a computer is used.

The phrase which most often comes to mind when talking about computers is: 'Know what you want before you start'. This is not a deliberate attempt to discourage users, although it is a phrase often used by computer experts in just this way. It is an invitation for clear thinking. Often knowing what you want means identifying the means by which information can be recorded and interpreted in a clear way. The form in which written notes are taken from an original source will almost certainly influence our view of the object or document. Systematic archaeological examination of documents or objects or even buildings can be achieved through the use of mnemonic labels for reference. This is a method well known to historians who have often utilized shoe-boxes for storing endless record cards with cross-referenced information. This type of recording lends itself most readily to a computer-based data recording system. It ensures that the same points of reference have been checked on each object or document so that a pseudo-scientific result will ensue. It also leads to the recording of negative data which can be of great importance. For instance, in panel painting recording whether or not a picture has its original frame and the date of the current frame, may lead to interesting observations on the quantity of surviving original frames and the periods when most pictures were re-framed. This information may be only marginally relevant to the research of the recorder, but may be of great interest to others and may lead them on to new ideas. In using this type of method it soon becomes clear that the questions put to the computer are as important as the material itself. However, it does not always follow that the fuller the records stored on the computer the more interesting the questions that can be put. For it is often the case that the choice of which things are to be recorded is governed by the questions which are to be asked. Basically, it is essential to know what you want before you start. Nevertheless, through familiarizing yourself with this type of problem it becomes easier and easier to identify the areas where a computer can help with interpreting information and, thus, the questions begin to ask themselves before you start recording. It is certainly the case that the computer will not be able to answer any questions unless all the answers have already been fed into the computer. It follows that if the person who records the material puts it on the computer, they will have already seen everything on the database. With large quantities of information, of course, the human brain cannot keep an over-view of all the records at once. However, the human brain can formulate an idea which might lead to an interesting question being posed 'because the information is on the computer'. This leads to the inexorable conclusion that through using computers eventually better questions and answers will be produced. Nevertheless, the computer will only be aware of as many answers as have been put into it in the first place.

In the field of manuscripts, and particularly illuminated manuscripts, the history of their study can be used to illustrate the development of modern systematized ways of recording information which (with a little encouragement) can be seen as naturally leading to the use of computers. A similar analogy, which will perhaps be recognized by those interested in early printing and illustrated printed books, can be made for the invention of the printing press. The organization of book production into more and more systematic ways of production (almost a factory type of mass production) occurred before the mass production of printed books through the invention of the printing press. Similarly the systematic description of manuscripts in catalogues and the analysis of this information through the use of card indexes and other 'primitive' means of cross-referencing occurred long before the invention of the 'database'. In many ways a database can be viewed as a larger and more convenient form of such an index.

Early descriptions of manuscripts tend to give basic information, text and author and perhaps size being the main elements. Later the distinction between parchment and paper becomes important, later still the number of folios (although this is sometimes given in medieval indexes). More detailed descriptions of size come in the early nineteenth century together with some indication of whether or not a text is illuminated. By the late nineteenth century an accepted norm for describing a manuscript is hammered out by M.R. James[1] although his earlier attempts at cataloguing are still inconsistent. The basic elements are: text, author, material, size, number of illustrations, the folios on which illustrations occur, basic observations on Calendars and Litanies in Liturgical books and the Sanctorale in Breviaries and Missals etc. For the art historian of the nineteenth century only the information about the illustrations was of particular interest and this is still the case in some circles where manuscripts are discarded and their illustration with a fragment of text on the reverse only survives for sale as an 'art object'. Palaeographers, on the other hand, were becoming more and more interested in the relationship between text, image and decoration in illuminated manuscripts. This type of inter-disciplinary view of the book has led to the creation of the term codicology. Codicology is the study of the book as a whole: pictures, binding, sewing, ruling, minor ornament, scribes. Each of these subjects has a literature of its own, but each is dependant on knowledge of the others. To the art historian, the study of manuscript illumination in the Middle Ages is also the study of painting in the Middle Ages, but the localization of painting styles, the roots and dating of particular iconographies, lies in the study of the book. The type of information offered by books with pictures is not unique but the amount of information and the inter-disciplinary nature of the information is. This makes the task of the art historian much more difficult than it would appear at first sight. Some knowledge of literature, textual analysis, cultural history (which is in many ways art history), economics, demography etc. is required before the real significance of any piece of illumination can be understood.

The most heavily illuminated books of the Middle Ages during the Gothic period were books of hours, psalters, Bibles, missals and even breviaries. In the earlier period, gospels, sacramentaries and evangeliaries, were more popular. For the art historian the book of hours is interesting not only for the illustrations included, but for the type and order of the textual material and the minor differences of text between books. For it was certainly the case that a book made for a particular area would be provided with a text that had the signature of a 'local use'. Thus the use of Sarum says 'Quando natus' at one point while that of Paris says 'beata es Maria'; the rest of this part of the text being identical. Such textual differences were brilliantly classified by Leroquais in his survey of liturgical manuscripts in French public libraries in the nineteenth century,[2] although James also provided an interesting introduction in his catalogue of the Fitzwilliam Museum Collection.[3] There are, however, pitfalls in finding local uses. Firstly, no short cuts can be made. Texts are long and may vary at different points. No 'sample of information' can suffice (as has been suggested by one historian, erroneously)[4] unless great care is taken in finding the points at which the text ceases to be standard and becomes variable.

In one sense this type of detective work emulates the original text compiler's work in creating the text. There is a certain amount of mystery still shrouding this type of textual analysis, but to those who practise it the problems are clear: no understanding of the meaning of the text is required to analyse text in this way. In many ways this is an ideal application for the 'dumb' computer. The computer will be able to sort which elements are similar and which are unique, which are always variable, which are sometimes similar etc. To the computer the mysteries of the meaning of the text, which are still obscure even to the modern reader, are not relevant. The words might as well be figures. Where a database becomes useful in this case is in dealing with quantities of information which would otherwise become unmanageable. The text of the Book of Hours is not the only one which might lend itself to such analysis. Calendars, which preface most books of hours, psalters and missals, and are included in breviaries, have similarly variable texts and so do litanies. Calendars list the particularly important feast days for an area and litanies the saints associated with a particular form of observance, which might coincidentally be of a particular area.

The information from litanies is the most difficult to analyse as the Litany takes the form of separate parts, each of which might vary. The principle parts are the orders of saints who are invoked to intercede for mankind: apostles, martyrs, confessors and virgins. These lists vary in length and content. The proliferation of these lists means that a coherent analysis of them without the aid of a computer is very difficult. Each needs to be compared with the others in its group to see by how much it varies from its neighbour. However, the variability of the texts means that initial sorting must be done by hand, to avoid disasters. Once this has been done simple joining programs can print combinations of text to illustrate the validity of various juxtapositions and simple numbering programs can be used to indicate the incidence of saints. Great problems arise when these lists are required to be printed. Indeed, the formatting of information after it has been processed by the computer can be as important for understanding the results as the information itself.

A database can also be used to store information about the sizes of text and the types of text which have a particular size. This type of sorting can genuinely be claimed to be the most fruitful in terms of opening up new lines of connection between manuscripts. Certain truths are always apparent: canon law books are large, statutes of England small. These things are known to specialists in the field; what these statements gain through the use of computerization, is the assurance of exactitude. I can, therefore, justly claim that in early fourteenth-century England it is statistically the case that statutes of England are almost always of a particular size. However, there are a number of exceptions which only further knowledge of the individual books will explain. Information which can help cross-fertilize knowledge can also be included: type of text, where it was written, who illuminated it at what time. Once on a database, the information can be printed in different orders of priority. In some cases the order in which this information is printed can offer new insights into old material.

However, it would be unwise to assume that a page from a book of a particular size, with no text and a picture, came from a statutes of England, for it is not always possible to reverse the significance of the information. Indeed, this is another key point in understanding how this information may be used. It is no use, for instance, feeding in the entire text of 200 prayerbooks with pictures and asking the computer to group all those with 'Ave Maria' together. The types of information which are put in the database must be selected carefully and the questions asked must have been already answered in a smaller sample, manually, before the computer is asked to do the same thing. The descriptions of the miniatures and the initials in a manuscript can also be recorded in a similar way, but once the information has been processed, the computer will not be able to print it without a complex chart building program being applied to the database. If the person creating the database has not produced a hand drawn examplar from which to work, building charts from the database may prove frustrating and the exercise almost useless.

Almost all the tasks I have been talking about are done on a computer which has enough power and is designed to have so-called 'shell commands' available to the ordinary user. Basic commands, understandable by the ordinary user of a word processor, can, by the judicious use and understanding of some basic computer grammar, be used to execute quite complex tasks. Searching through a database for particular words, or even through a text such as this for recurring themes can be achieved by the simplest of commands. All the information analysed may be recorded using a Famulus database, but even without using Famulus it is possible to record information in separate files within a computer and ask a computer to look at the information contained in those files at the same time. Many programmers feel that this is in some ways cheating, but to the individual user this is often the quickest and most economical use of the computer. Analysis of 800 books of hours, for instance, would be more economically done with a Famulus database and programs. Analysis of ten books of hours may be done very successfully by transferring information already recorded perhaps on record cards on to a computer and then using 'shell commands' alone. Identifying the point at which a project becomes one which requires a real program is a skill which must be learned by both those interested in teaching computing in the arts and those using it. For the undergraduate, for instance, it should not be necessary for a full database to be used, but by learning the principal of storing information on the computer in files which can be read simultaneously, more complicated tasks can be learned much more easily. Until the use of a computer, if only for basic word processing, becomes as natural as writing or recording on record cards, there will still be those who will ignore the possibilities of using a computer, because of the basically Luddite view that there is nothing a computer has to offer in the form of interpretation. If it becomes more widely known that computers are only capable of doing exactly what you tell them to do, and that anyone can use them to record information, then a real revolution in the accuracy of observation of the relics of history may occur. For it is certainly the case that the answers may always have been with us, but it is in finding out what the questions are that we have always had difficulty.

Acknowledgements

I should like to thank all those in the Computer Unit at Westfield College, University of London, for their invaluable help over the past few years, in particular François Compton-Roberts, Jay Harrison and Brian Place for their encouragement.

Notes

1. James, M.R., *A Descriptive Catalogue of the Manuscripts in the Fitzwilliam Museum*, Cambridge 1895.
2. Leroquais, Abbé V., *Les Livres d'Heures Manuscripts de la Bibliothèque Nationale*, Paris, 1927 etc.
3. See note 1 above, in particular his introduction 'Points to be observed in the cataloguing of manuscripts, particularly Books of Hours'.
4. Madan, F., 'Hours of the Virgin Mary (Tests for localisation)', *Bodleian Quarterly Record*, 3, no. 26, 1920, pp. 40–4, Leroquais, see note 2 above, vol. I, p. xxxvi, points out both the usefulness of Medan's general approach and its unreliability in many cases, caused by too small a sample of tests being taken.

Contributors

Mary Beal, Assistant Curator, The British Government Art Collection, London

Leslie Carlyle, Research Student, Courtauld Institute of Art, University of London (on education leave from the Canadian Conservation Institute)

Jonathan Franklin, British Architectural Library, Royal Institute of British Architects, London

Anthony Hamber, Department of History of Art, Birkbeck College, University of London

Julie Hausman, Curator of Visual Materials, School of Art and Art History, University of Iowa, U.S.A.

Lutz Heusinger, Director of Foto Archiv, Marburg, West Germany

Colum Hourihane, Witt Library Computer Index, Courtauld Institute, University of London

Wim Jansen, Educational Technologist at the Open University of the Netherlands

Lisa M. Kamisher, Consultant, formerly Aga Khan Program for Islamic Architecture

Ray Keaveney, Assistant Director, National Gallery of Ireland

Mary Macqueen, Private Conservator

Michael Michael, Christie's Fine Arts Course, London

Ian Morrison, District Curator, Moray District Council, Scotland

David Saunders, Scientific Department, The National Gallery, London

John Sunderland, Witt Librarian, Courtauld Institute of Art, University of London

William Vaughan, Professor of the History of Art, Birkbeck College, University of London

Index

Note: Page references in *italics* indicate illustrations and diagrams.